Reflecting on America

Reflecting on America

Anthropological Views of U.S. Culture

Clare L. Boulanger, Editor

Mesa State College

Boston • New York • San Francisco
Mexico City • Montreal • Toronto • London • Madrid • Munich • Paris
Hong Kong • Singapore • Tokyo • Cape Town • Sydney

Acquisitions Editor: Dave Repetto
Editorial Assistant: Jack Cashman
Marketing Manager: Laura Lee Manley
Production Supervisor: Roberta Sherman
Editorial-Production and Electronic Composition Services: TexTech, Inc.
Composition Buyer: Linda Cox
Manufacturing Buyer: Debbie Rossi
Cover Administrator: Joel Gendron

For related titles and support materials, visit our online catalog at www.ablongman.com.

Between the time website information is gathered and then published, it is not unusual for some sites to have closed. Also, the transcription of URLs can result in typographical errors. The publisher would appreciate notification where these errors occur so that they may be corrected in subsequent editions.

Library of Congress Cataloging-in-Publication Data

Reflecting on America : anthropological views on U.S. culture / [edited by] Clare L. Boulanger.
        p.   cm.
    Includes bibliographical references.
    ISBN-13: 978-0-205-48143-9   ISBN-10: 0-205-48143-4
        1. Anthropology—United States—History.   2. Anthropology—United States—Philosophy.
    3. Ethnology—United States—Philosophy.   4. United States—Civilization—1945–
    5. United States—Ethnic relations.   I. Boulanger, Clare L.
    GN17.3.U6R44   2008
    306.0973—dc22   2007024568

Printed in the United States of America

10 9 8 7 6 5 4 3   11 10

Contents

Acknowledgments

In some ways this anthology was long in the making, harking back to my 1977 "Comparative Cultures" class taught by Phil DeVita at the State University of New York at Plattsburgh. Things started to get serious after two American culture sessions sponsored by the Federation of Small Anthropology Programs (FOSAP) were presented at the annual American Anthropological Association meeting in 2003 and 2004. Following each session, we would discuss the possibility of producing an anthology, but when the first year's efforts came to nothing, I decided to pursue this project the second year. Of the contributors to this volume, FOSAP members Bob Myers (Alfred University) and Paul Grebinger (Rochester Institute of Technology) deserve a special measure of gratitude, although I thank all of the contributors not only for answering my out-of-the-blue call for papers but also for following through on their commitment. Even so, the anthology might have foundered were it not for my professor and friend Richard Robbins, also at SUNY-Plattsburgh, on whose advice Allyn & Bacon accepted the project. I'd like to thank Dave Repetto, Jack Cashman, and Roberta Sherman, at Allyn & Bacon as well as Mike Shally-Jensen and Dennis Troutman at TexTech Inc., who have seen this project through to its conclusion patiently and efficiently, handling my many inquiries along the way. I would like to thank the following reviewers for their suggestions, which were instrumental in fashioning the final product: Mike Alvard, Texas A&M University; Jessica Amato, Napa Valley College; Diane Ballinger, University of North Texas-Denton; Vaughn Bryant, Texas A&M University; David Jurji, Bellevue Community College; and Raghuraman S. Trichur, California State University-Sacramento.

Thanks also to my Mesa State colleague, Barry Michrina, who helped review page proofs.

This is perhaps dangerous to confess, but this project has been a joy from start to finish. I take full responsibility if readers do not, even in some small way, share in that joy.

C. L. B.

Reflecting on America

The Land and Its People

Introduction: We Have Met the Nacirema, and They Are Us(ans)

Clare L. Boulanger
Mesa State College

> *Nacirema culture is characterized by a highly developed market economy which has evolved in a rich natural habitat. While much of the people's time is devoted to economic pursuits, a large part of the fruits of these labors and a considerable portion of the day are spent in ritual activity. The focus of this activity is the human body, the appearance and health of which loom as a dominant concern in the ethos of the people. While such a concern is certainly not unusual, its ceremonial aspects and associated philosophy are unique. (Miner 1956: 503)*

What appears above is a passage from Horace Miner's famous article, "Body Ritual among the Nacirema," which has introduced thousands of American anthropology students to the evidently startling idea that they, no less than the Ju/'hoansi or the Yanomami, may have a culture. Despite the fact that the article is seriously dated, I can attest that at least within the first few paragraphs students can still be tricked into believing they are reading about an exotic people halfway around the globe. There remains that "a-ha" moment when the American reader grasps that he is seeing himself in the mirror of anthropology.

But as quickly as this vision appears, it may soon fade. It could be that the Miner article is too clever for its own good, rather like an advertisement that is so entertaining no one remembers the product being sold. Most students are mildly amused; some are irritated at themselves for not having caught the joke earlier. Ethnographies written in the style Miner lampoons are now rare, and for all that, the illusion of bounded societies has been thoroughly exposed, not least because such anthropological mainstay peoples as the Nuer are now refugees in cities throughout the United States (see Shandy 2000) and the Trobrianders are constituents within Papua New Guinea, itself a sovereign nation made up of the "tribes" that anthropologists studied as societies in and of themselves. With the encouragement of their postmodern professors, students may be likelier nowadays to extend discussions of Miner into an inquiry on whether the concept of culture itself is outmoded in our transnational world, thus conveniently skirting the issue of American culture to take up an allegedly more sophisticated topic.

In my opinion there is a problem here, but it is not with the concept of culture, which is a perfectly reasonable way of framing why it is that, for instance, Malaysians sacrifice their sleep to watch the World Cup soccer matches (when the Malaysian team has never qualified, no less) while most Americans remain bored by soccer despite numerous attempts to sell the sport in the United States over the years. The problem is what culture has become outside of anthropology. Within anthropology, the term "culture" was intended to encapsulate how humans not only construct their realities but come to believe in them wholeheartedly, despite their contradictions and slipshod logics. But once the concept of culture was coaxed out of the anthropological domain, it was reduced to something like "custom." Economic and political systems were cast as phenomena different from culture, which was often derided as a trivial add-on. This is not only wrong, but suspect. It is my view that anthropologists must reclaim and reinvigorate the concept of culture if we are to have any impact within the social sciences and beyond. We can start by applying it where it has not heretofore been welcome—the United States.

Thus, this anthology will not skirt the issue of American culture. While acknowledging that culture is of necessity a complex phenomenon that is neither self-enclosed nor static, the articles in this volume dare to make heuristic generalizations to help the world understand Americans and to help Americans know themselves. Americans often object to such generalizations—"we are all individuals," they protest, seemingly unaware that the statement itself is a generalization. They are also unaware that their readiness to farm out the concept of culture to other settings while denying it a place in the U.S. mainstream constitutes an important component of the American system of social control. Americans can fully and sincerely invest in the conviction theirs is the best country in the world when other societies, including minority enclaves within the United States itself, are rendered incomparable—and perhaps, almost irresistibly, inferior (see Abu-Lughod 1991)—via the application of culture as a segregating device.

An alternative view holds that there is no one culture in the United States, but many— so many, in fact, that an anthropological inquiry into "American culture" is at best naively reductionist, at worst willfully racist. The anthropologist who dares to venture past this gatekeeper quickly finds, however, that the diversity Americans allegedly appreciate can be readily sorted into good diversity and bad diversity. Good diversity includes those distinctions that can be teased out of a cultural system and shared in that superficial-yet-mandatory manner Moffatt (1989: 43–45) has described as "friend*ly*," such as ethnic cuisine, certain items of dress, and the odd foreign catchphrase or two (spoken with an American accent). Bad diversity comprises any challenge to American convictions regarding the rightness of capitalism, democracy, and/or the universality of God, and whole languages wherein subversion might be concealed. Kottak (1990: 101–105) sees these attitudes regarding diversity renewed whenever the Thanksgiving myth is told, or retold in the form, for instance, of *Star Trek*. The crews of the various starships *Enterprise* have included a tremendous number of diverse beings not only from various parts of Earth but from other planets yet it is hard not to notice that there is something of a "bottom line" with respect to the degree of diversity allowed. All crew members speak English and subscribe to the worthiness of the ship's mission of exploration. They may contribute their ethnic "gifts" to the table for the good of all, but must otherwise confine their differences, beyond those features they cannot control, to their quarters.

So Americans, whether they cite individualism or ethnic diversity as the reason, remain resistant to the notion that the United States has a culture. To overcome this resistance, this volume stresses neither of these attributes of American life, and the reader in search of concerted work on such subjects is encouraged to look elsewhere. Books on individualism abound across the disciplines, and the subject of American ethnic diversity (as well as other forms of diversity, such as gender and sexuality) has been treated so effectively by anthropologists that it is one of the few areas where the anthropological voice is occasionally heard outside of the academy. With respect to the concept of an overarching U.S. culture, however, anthropologists have not been so lucky as to obtain widespread publicity, though it is not for want of trying. The Miner article appeared after decades of ethnographic work had already been carried out (see di Leonardo 1998: 25–29). Such influential anthropologists as Franz Boas (1928) and Margaret Mead (1943) considered the study of U.S. culture to be not only worthwhile but imperative. Miner was the first to deploy the exoticizing label of "Nacirema," but other authors took up the term (e.g., Savishinsky 1998) or at least the sensibility behind its use. In the mid-1970s two anthologies were published, *The Nacirema* (Spradley and Rynkiewich 1975) and *The American Dimension* (Arens and Montague 1976). Though the articles in these volumes were of sufficient quality to interest scholars, they could also appeal to undergraduate students, and indeed, the books were required reading for my introductory course in cultural anthropology at the State University of New York at Plattsburgh. It was my intention, in drawing together this anthology, to emulate these two predecessors, although in the end I refrained from calling this book *American Dementia,* my pet name for the project.

The title *Reflecting on America* draws on the potent, if somewhat shopworn, image of ethnology (i.e., comparative ethnography) as a means of illuminating not only the culture under scrutiny but the culture of the scrutinizer—meant to be one and the same with respect to this anthology. Anthropological titles have often played off the conviction that ethnographic study provides us with a different, and illuminating, way of seeing. We gaze at others through the "anthropological lens," as Peacock (1986) would put it, and we look back at ourselves via Kluckhohn's "mirror for man" (1949) or Kottak's updated "mirror for humanity" (1996). Foreign observers act as "distant mirrors" in the DeVita and Armstrong anthology thus entitled (1993). But in fact, all of these ways of seeing imply distance, whether created by a lens or reflected by a mirror, and distance has been an essential component of the anthropological research process from the time it was first designed. The anthropologist is not only participant but observer, stepping back from his or her work to gain perspective. This mandate exploits a personality trait that is often portrayed as a prerequisite for taking on anthropology as an avocation—some semblance of alienation from one's own culture. To be alienated from one's culture does not necessarily equate to being alienated from society (though some anthropologists, alas, fall into this misanthropic category), but it does entail a capacity, sometimes if not always born of personal and/or social trauma, to analyze one's culture as though it were an object that could be removed from oneself. However this sense of detachment originates, it is further cultivated in anthropology via comparativism. The "observer" within participant observation does not stand in an objective place, but one which is formed by the intersection of myriad lifeways of which the anthropologist has either personal knowledge or knowledge through ethnography. Hence anthropologists cannot see American culture as a phenomenon in and of itself; what they see is passed through the prism of Kelabit culture, Brazilian culture, the culture of the U.S. military, the culture of African American drug users, or the culture of wherever and/or with whom they do their work. Even if they do not draw overt comparisons, comparison alters their view.

The readings included in this volume follow through on the promise of comparison by drawing on field experience, both within and outside of the United States, and applying it toward a portrait of "the American" that emerges from the patterned minutiae of everyday life. The anthology opens with my own tribute to Horace Miner. In the section entitled Myth and Ritual, Matthew Amster, whose overseas fieldwork has both upheld and challenged the notion of "society" in the case of the Kelabit people of the Bornean borderlands, turns his practiced ethnographic gaze on the Civil War reenactors who gather in Gettysburg, PA. Having participated, as an anthropologist, in reenacting, he knows personally the thrill of "Civil War moments" that transport Americans into the imagined past as effectively as any ritual meant to honor the ancestors. Barry Michrina, known as "M. Yrrab" in an article that draws on the tradition of Nacirema and similar inversions, participates in the lives of his coal-mining informants in a different fashion: he is commissioned to write the "people's history" of the region. In doing so, he notes that Americans are no less prone than peoples the world over to selective memory and a calculated, if not always entirely conscious, approach to rendering history in a way that both enhances the present fortunes of some Americans and erases the legacy of others. In her article on metakinesis, Tanya Luhrmann documents how Americans, mesmerized by modern media that facilitate trance, achieve with God the type of intense personal relationship that is absent from their daily lives. There could hardly be a better illustration of the Durkheimian principle that through religion, society—though, ironically, in this instance, a loose aggregate of individuals adrift—essentially worships itself. My piece, on a Usan (i.e., American) legend recurring in the plot lines of that mythic cycle we call *Star Trek,* follows, and the section closes with Kottak's observations on how national ethos, in this case that of the United States contrasted with that of Brazil, plays in the Olympic arena.

Anthropologists are perhaps more painfully aware than most social scientists of how difficult it is to contain different facets of culture in discrete categories, and, indeed, the readings included in the section entitled Economy, Society, Power will hardly abandon the subjects of myth and ritual. Even within this amorphous enclosure there is a shading from articles that have a more economic cast, to articles where the mutual construction of economy and society becomes even more evident, to articles that illustrate starkly that any such construction is thoroughly suffused with power. In the lead article, Richard Wilk marvels at the fact that Americans pay so little attention to their habits of material and social use. As if in response to Wilk's call for more research in this area, Paul Grebinger uses the "simple notion" of a button to illustrate how changes in U.S. culture transformed the manufacturing process. John Burton, who wrote for *The American Dimension,* contributes a piece here on American attitudes toward wilderness, nowadays something to be collected and slapped onto the illustrious résumés of ambitious youth. In her classic article on "kin-work," Micaela di Leonardo reminds us there is a good deal of vital productive activity that eludes our awareness because it is shunted into a domestic space and belittled as a womanly concern.

Following on the now-conjoined themes of gender and economy, Catherine Lutz demonstrates how a military installation transforms its environs, not only economically but through the generation of ominous ideologies on gender and race that pit the industrious "soldier" against the lax, effeminate "civilian." Through his research, Paul Durrenberger pointedly raises the issue of class in the United States, advising those who would dismiss its presence to pay less attention to what Americans say about class, and more to what they do. Class is recognized as an especially destructive force in the piece by Philippe Bourgois, who draws on his extensive fieldwork in one of the most down-and-out neighborhoods in New York City to pound home the point that the violence directed toward self and other in the inner city is essentially the visible manifestation of the structural violence exercised against the poor. The implication is that the true "underground economy," in terms of its insidious and entirely purposeful effects, may in fact be the economy most Americans think of as thoroughly legitimate and transparent. Richard Robbins would hardly disagree with this view in his hard-hitting piece on such seemingly benign cultural icons as Barbie and Mickey Mouse. His cautionary observation that children being transformed into consumers are actually children being consumed resonates forcefully with the theme of structural violence.

The final section, Language and Thought, opens with two articles by Robert Myers. In the first article, Myers, like Michrina, features the familiar-rendered-exotic appellation of the Nacirema, but clearly the article would not be "nuf" without this device. The second article is an exhaustive, "rapid-fire" review of the gun metaphor in American English, sure to prompt some reflection on the part of the reader as to the applicability of the Sapir–Whorf hypothesis—just how much does language shape perception? Liza Cerroni-Long, from her unique vantage point as a woman from Italy who has studied in Japan and now lives and works in the United States, feels ideally placed to observe that Americans indeed have a culture, despite their vehement denials. And if Americans are in denial of American culture overall, they are certainly unaware of the glaring contradictions within their culture, though Mark Cohen, in the final article of the collection, does his best to bring these to the fore.

The idea for this collection germinated following the "Beyond the exotic Other" session at the 103rd Annual Meeting of the American Anthropological Association in 2004 and grew in a reticulated fashion from that moment. Individuals from the initial group of contributors recommended additional contributors, and eventually a full volume came together. Given this less-than-methodical means of assembly, the anthology varies in approach and tone from article to article. There is something of a common thread, however, in that the overall effect is not mild-mannered. While these are scholarly pieces, well grounded in field research and well worked in terms of analysis, they are also, frequently, passionate, in ways that may startle and even put off some readers. Anthropologists seem to go out of their way to disturb that natural tendency people have to see their own cultures as normal. Indeed, such ethnocentrism is ordinarily harmless, but the United States has commanded sufficient power in this world to impose its version of normalcy on other societies. We Americans assume that what we convey is good, but how do we judge what is good? Are our standards universally worthwhile, or are they derived primarily from the vested interests of those who most benefit from them? Alexis de Tocqueville once wrote of Americans, far earlier than one might expect: "The majority lives in the perpetual utterance of self-applause; and there are certain truths which the Americans can only learn from strangers or from experience" (1835: 265). In this anthology, we do not need to add to the self-applause that continues to emanate from any number of quarters. But anthropologists may be sufficiently strange and sufficiently experienced to make "certain truths" heard above the din.

Acknowledgments

This introduction was shaped by editorial commentary from Matthew Amster, Liza Cerroni-Long, Tanya Luhrmann, and Robert Myers.

References

Abu-Lughod, Lila. 1991. Writing against culture. In Richard G. Fox, ed., *Recapturing anthropology: working the present*. Santa Fe: School of American Research, 137–162.

Arens, William, and Susan P. Montague, eds. 1976. *The American dimension: cultural myths and social realities*. Port Washington, NY: Alfred Publishing.

Boas, Franz. 1928. *Anthropology and modern life*. New York: Morton.

DeVita, Philip R., and James D. Armstrong, eds. 1993. *Distant mirrors: America as a foreign culture*, 1st edition. Belmont, CA: Wadsworth/Thomson Learning.

di Leonardo, Micaela. 1998. *Exotics at home: anthropologies, others, American modernity*. Chicago: University of Chicago Press.

Kluckhohn, Clyde. 1949. *Mirror for man*. New York: McGraw-Hill.

Kottak, Conrad Philip. 1990. *Prime-time society: an anthropological analysis of television and culture*. Belmont: Wadsworth.

———. 1996. *Mirror for humanity: a concise introduction to cultural anthropology*. New York: McGraw-Hill.

Mead, Margaret. 1943. *And keep your powder dry*. New York: Morton.

Miner, Horace. 1956. Body ritual among the Nacirema. *American Anthropologist* 58, 3: 503–507.

Moffatt, Michael. 1989. *Coming of age in New Jersey: college and American culture*. New Brunswick: Rutgers University Press.

Peacock, James L. 1986. *The anthropological lens: harsh light, soft focus*, 1st edition. Cambridge: Cambridge University Press.

Savishinsky, Joel. 1998. The Nacirema and the *tsiruot*. *International Journal of intercultural relations* 22, 3: 369–374.

Shandy, Dianna J. 2000. Nuer in the United States. *General anthropology* (bulletin of the General Anthropology Division) 7, 1: 1, 7–9.

Spradley, James P., and Michael A. Rynkiewich, eds. 1975. *The Nacirema: readings on American culture*. Boston: Little, Brown, & Co.

Tocqueville, Alexis de. 1835. *Democracy in America*. Translated by Henry Reeve. Volume 1. London: Saunders and Otley.

1

Usans: "The Real People" Confront Globalization

Clare L. Boulanger

Mesa State College

> *The frog that lives under a coconut shell thinks that the shell is the sky.*
>
> — Malay proverb

Like other peoples that anthropologists have studied, Usans are wrestling with the question of how to maintain cultural identity in a world where territorial boundaries are becoming increasingly permeable to capital, labor, and the media. Usans reside within a huge swath of territory that cuts across the North American continent and then some, as outlying lands were colonized as well. As the last phrase indicates, Usans arrived as invaders, and the conquest of their present-day territory was world-renowned for the ruthlessness with which native peoples were dispatched. Formerly, anthropologists referred to Usans as the Nacirema, but it should be mentioned that, as is so often the case in the anthropological literature, neither of these terms is what Usans use to refer to themselves. Many anthropologists initially eschewed the indigenous term ("American"), fearing it might cause resentment among peoples to the north and south who could legitimately lay claim to it as well, but neighboring peoples, by and large, seem willing to cede their rights to the term, not least because they do not want to be equated with Usans. "Usan" is arguably the least controversial among the three terms and hence will be used throughout this essay, with apologies to those who might prefer otherwise. At the very least we all can rest assured that none of the terms mentioned above is derived from the derogatory opinions of Usan enemies.

Oddly enough, however, it is also true that none of the terms means what such terms so often mean in the local language: "The Real People," or "The Only People." This is especially strange in light of the fact that the Usan ethos certainly tends toward exceptionalism. Given their central location on the continent, Usans have absorbed countless foreigners into their population over the centuries (via intermarriage and migration), but it is strongly expected that these newcomers will quickly divest themselves of their origins and take on an exclusively Usan identity. The regularizing device par excellence is a corpus of ideologies known as "The Dream." The Dream is not a religious concept per se—there is no necessary reference to the primary deity most Usans worship—but rather, a program of "right behavior" which, if scrupulously followed, is said to guarantee the dedicated practitioner supreme happiness and security, with a measure of that security deriving from the existential satisfaction of knowing that one is fully a member of "The Real People." It should be noted that some Usans, such as those whose ancestors were subject to forced migration and those who were themselves forced migrants, are not always given a good-faith opportunity to pursue the Dream, and hence cannot be entirely sure that they are as "real" as other Usans.

Usans are hardly untouched by globalization; on the contrary, they have been instrumental in shaping the trend. But the Dream intensifies ethnocentrism, which skews Usans' impression of their impact on the world, and obscures any impact the world may have on Usan society. There is no indication at this time that Usan ethnocentrism will lessen; indeed, in response to recent violent events that virtually demand some attention be paid to world affairs, it has, almost pathologically, deepened.

One reason Usan ethnocentrism today verges on obsession is that it is adaptive. Ethnocentrism justifies a prerogative that Usans have claimed for quite some time—a disproportionate share of the world's resources. While other societies have long known of this situation and have begun to voice objections more openly, most Usans remain untroubled, and even unaware. Within the protective shell of their ethnocentrism, they are sheltered from the complaints of outsiders. On those few occasions when they are exposed to such complaints, they may hear them as merely envious or petty. They are generally firm in their conviction that Usan society, given its exemplary qualities, is only receiving its just due.

Usans apply this "just due" to a favorite cultural pastime—that of accumulation. Usans value accumulation for its own sake—indeed, they celebrate it in lavish rituals called "game shows"—and this sets their society apart from others anthropologists have studied. In non-state societies, individuals may have the leeway to accrue goods, but they are also enjoined by their fellows to be generous with their wealth. If the New Guinean "big man," for example, hoards his pigs rather than redistributing them, their numbers are of no consequence—his people will not only strip him of his rank but actively vilify him; in some traditions he may even be killed. In contrast, the Usan "big man" (and he *is* usually a man, though "big women" are not unknown) may or may not be generous with his wealth. If he adopts the first course of action, he may inspire a reaction akin to awe, but he is not reduced to a "rubbish man" if he chooses the second. Ordinary Usans may natter about him behind their hands but cannot levy overt accusations of stinginess to any worthwhile effect, since Usan society largely supports the "big man" and his quest for accumulation.

It should be pointed out, however, that Usa is a state society, and state societies frequently feature a different attitude toward the individual prerogative to pursue wealth. Even so, in many state societies there is an ambivalence about such ambitions, which sees expression in practical terms by governments imposing redistributive mechanisms on the wealthy and in ideological terms by spiritual proscriptions against greed and selfishness. Both institutions, in fact, exist in Usan society as well, but are severely undercut by the dazzling lure of accumulation. Wealthy Usans must set aside a portion of what they accumulate for the government, but this portion is not excessive and can even be reduced by a variety of legal and quasi-legal means. Because ordinary Usans are themselves liable to government tax and are often less than convinced that the ends toward which this is applied benefit society as a whole, they do not always begrudge the efforts of the Usan "big man" to escape the burden. As for ideology, sacred writings revered by most Usans do in fact inveigh against accumulation. The most exalted of Usan holy men, regarded as the embodiment of divinity, is reputed to have said that it was easier for a camel to pass through the eye of a needle than it was for a rich man to enter Heaven (an idyllic place where the virtuous dead reside). For years, Usans have wrestled with this statement, seeking an interpretation that could bring virtue and accumulation into harmony, but their efforts have borne little fruit, and what there is of it has tasted vaguely of hypocrisy. In desperation, some Usans, at the time of this writing, have unearthed an obscure passage from an earlier text in which one Jabez successfully petitions God to increase his wealth, and in this Usan "big men" and their supporters have found validation and spiritual solace.

While Usans prize accumulation for its own sake, this does not mean that the "big man" is merely a means through which it is accomplished. His ability to accumulate is believed to follow from additional culturally valued attributes, notably his desire to achieve and his capacity for "hard work," a mystical quality whose characteristics are elusive, though they would *not* seem to include the strenuous manual labor to which the expression literally refers. In short, the career of the "big man" is the Dream made visible, and thus ordinary Usans can rest assured that it is attainable. They are always haunted, however, by the fear that they may not have applied sufficient quantities of desire and "hard work" toward the realization of their goals, and it is these alleged faults in themselves, rather than the economic and political structure of the cultural system in which they are embedded, that they tend to blame for failure.

So, via ethnocentrism, Usans manage to preserve a key cultural value in these globalizing times, and this in itself is standard and even admirable human behavior. However, in this instance, as in many similar instances around the world, we must pose an age-old anthropological question: What happens when the vigorous pursuit of a cultural practice in one society actually constitutes a detriment for others? Are we called upon to act when culture generates oppression, both within and between societies? For most anthropologists, it is likely still debatable as to whether the Usan case has become extreme, let alone in need of redress, but while we argue, we should not be surprised if figures we consider to be far less rational seek to rectify global inequities in far less rational ways.

Acknowledgments

Paul Durrenberger contributed some of the observations made in this article.

Myth and Ritual

2

A Pilgrimage to the Past: Civil War Reenactors at Gettysburg

Matthew H. Amster
Gettysburg College

This article centers on the question: Why do some Americans take up the hobby of Civil War reenacting? In Matthew Amster's ethnographic work among the Kelabit, a small indigenous group living in the Malaysian–Indonesian borderlands on the island of Borneo, he developed an interest in the connection between ritual and identity. When he moved to Gettysburg, Pennsylvania, in 2002, Dr. Amster soon became curious about the crowds that come to the area to participate in period reenactments, and eventually decided to join a reenacting group himself. Viewing this first-hand experience through an anthropological lens, Amster came to see commonalities between reenacting and the many powerful rituals that anthropologists regularly examine in their work.

Matthew H. Amster teaches cultural anthropology in the Department of Sociology and Anthropology at Gettysburg College. He has published numerous articles on sociocultural change among the Kelabit, exploring such diverse topics as religious pilgrimage, religious conversion, gossip and social networks, and, most recently, the implications of cross-border movement along the international frontier. This is Dr. Amster's first article on reenacting.

It was nine o'clock on a hot Friday morning in early July, 2005, when I pulled my car into the parking lot at the Gettysburg National Military Park to meet a group of Civil War reenactors. When I had first contacted the group, back in April of that year, I had explained that I was an anthropologist wanting to do research on reenactors and that I was interested in joining them on their visit to Gettysburg that summer. The group's leader invited me for the Fourth of July weekend, when there would be a Living History demonstration, and allowed me, along with one of my students, to make use of his loaner uniforms, generally reserved for potential new recruits. As the reenactors assembled into their regiments, my student and

I made a quick change out of our shorts, T-shirts, and sandals into our new clothes for the weekend: heavy wool pants and coats, misshapen leather boots, leather sacks, and an array of Civil War–era military gear, including our bedrolls. We were also handed heavy replica Springfield rifles and—before we had time to absorb what was happening—were nineteenth-century infantrymen lined up for some basic training and drills. Soon we were heading out in military formation, our normal lives transformed with the flip of some giant imaginary switch.

It was then that I had my first flicker of a surreal moment. For just an instant—as a haze rose around us from the gravel under our feet, the group moving along the trail in unison, only the sound of our gear clanging and a sea of blue uniforms with rifles pointed skyward—I momentarily grasped just a tiny bit of what it might have felt like to be one of these men in the 1860s, marching in the hot sun with a heavy rifle under someone else's orders. Even though I'd only been doing this for a very short time, something visceral occurred that gave me a taste of what makes reenacting appealing. I began to think about the difficult life of the infantrymen who wore these hot wool uniforms, carried all this gear, and walked in these uncomfortable shoes, not just for "fun" on a weekend, but for months or years far from home, experiencing death and disease and hardships I could never begin to imagine. As time went on and I got to know reenactors better, I learned how such uncanny moments—described as "period rush," "going into the bubble," "time travel," or "Civil War moments"—are a significant part of what keeps them coming back year after year.

The author (left) and anthropology student Mike Leader at a Living History encampment, Gettysburg National Military Park, July 2005. (Photo by Wendy B. Halperin)

Who Are Civil War Reenactors?

When I moved to Gettysburg to teach anthropology, one of the first bits of advice I was given was to leave the town in the summer. People warned me that nearly two million visitors descend on the small town each year, many of them in the summer months, transforming the otherwise relative tranquility into a historical fantasyland. In Gettysburg, one often encounters people walking the streets in period dress, including women leading bands of tourists on "Ghost Tours" and Civil War reenactors who stroll the streets dressed as if it were still 1863. At first glance, the hobby seems quaint and, at times, fanatical, particularly the element within the reenacting community that talks about lost souls roaming the battlefield trying to find their way home, engages in ghost hunting, recounts sighting of such paranormal phenomena as "orbs" of light floating on the battlefield, or tape-records the night air to hear lost souls of soldiers speak. While such beliefs and practices are common, at the heart of the hobby is a sincere love of history and a desire to breathe life and relevance into this history through reenacting.

American Civil War reenacting groups are found in such unlikely places as Europe, Canada, and England (Hunt 2004), though most come from places close to where the war was fought. There are no reliable statistics on how many have participated in the hobby, with estimates ranging from fifteen thousand to over twice that number, at forty thousand reenactors nationwide (Cushman 1999: 52). According to Tony Horwitz, whose book *Confederates in the Attic,* written in the late 1990s when the hobby may have been at its peak, there are "over 40,000 reenactors nationwide," and "one survey named reenacting the fastest growing hobby in America" (1999: 126). A number of reenactors with whom I spoke claimed that the hobby has diminished in recent years, particularly post 9/11, speculating that it may not be as appealing to reenact during times of actual war. Others theorized that the popularity of reenacting can be linked to the influence of media, with Ken Burns' documentary series *The Civil War* and such feature films as *Gettysburg, Gods and Generals,* and *Glory* having fueled interest in the hobby in the 1990s. Whatever the reasons for its popularity, reenacting has grown considerably from its early days in the 1960s, around the time of Civil War centennial when the current form of the hobby is said to have begun.

Reenacting is a mainly male hobby (although at the more mainstream events whole families can participate), and most reenactments are "blindingly white affairs" (Horwitz 1999: 137) although there are some black reenacting groups, including an all-black Union regiment that regularly marches through Gettysburg on the anniversary of Lincoln's Gettysburg Address, or Remembrance Day, when thousands of reenactors parade through the town. Typically, however, the reenactor is a white male, though his socioeconomic background can vary. It is often pointed out that one can find people from very diverse lifestyles and careers reenacting side by side and that one's life outside of reenacting may not reflect one's position inside the hobby. As Horwitz was told by a reenactor during an event: "Se⟋ that general over there? He's probably pumping gas at Exxon during the week" (1999: 13⟋

Most reenactors concentrate on doing a specific "impression," typically that of e⟋ northern "Union" or "Federal" soldiers, commonly referred to as "Yanks" or Yankees⟋me southern "Confederate" soldiers, also referred to as "Rebs" or "Johnny Reb." ⟋ ⟋own reenactors are willing to portray both sides in the ⟋ ⟋ with e side. as "galvanizing," or switching sides—m⟋

One reason why some do not "galvanize" is simply the expense, since even entry-level outfits, like the typical infantry kit complete with replica Springfield rifle, cost over a thousand dollars. Civilian attire is also an option for reenactors, and people specialize in a range of period impressions, for example sutlers (shopkeepers and craft specialists), medical practitioners, and missionaries.

Authenticity is a big issue for reenactors, and there is a broad spectrum in terms of individual levels of commitment. At one extreme, there are the most devoted and serious reenactors, refereed to as "hardcore" or "campaigners," who go to great lengths to be authentic. At the other end of the spectrum are more family-oriented "mainstream" or "garrison"-type hobbyists for whom authenticity is less critical. When spending time with reenactors, one often hears the term "farb," or the adjective form "farby" (and various other derivatives, such as "farb fest"), both of which refer to anything that is inauthentic or modern. The term is commonly said to derive from the phrase, "far be it from authentic," though there are other suspected etymologies (Thompson 2004: 291). References to farbs and farby items are rampant in reenactor discourse, and it is a common insult among reenactors to call someone a farb. Farby items can be virtually anything that would not be considered period—whether this is the presence of a cooler, a vehicle, a filtered cigarette, or simply one's attitude or demeanor. For hardcore reenactors, even items out of sight, such as one's undergarments, may be criticized as farby.

Most reenactors come to Gettysburg as part of local regiments attending one of the various events, the largest being a three-day-long battle reenactment that takes place each year, usually around the time of the anniversary of the actual battle, July 1–3, 1863. This annual reenactment, held on private land, is a for-profit commercial venture that draws tens of thousands of paying spectators and thousands of reenactors, who also pay a small registration fee to participate and camp on site. During the prominent anniversary years, such as the 140th anniversary of the battle in 2003, the event tends to draw larger numbers, and there is already a great deal of talk about the upcoming 150th reenactment in 2013. In addition to the private reenactment held away from the Gettysburg National Military Park, there is also a large regular gathering of reenactors that takes place in Gettysburg each year in November, commemorating the anniversary of Lincoln's Gettysburg Address. Finally, there is a steady trickle of reenactor groups who come to Gettysburg throughout the year, in cooperation with the Park, to offer Living History demonstrations.

For Civil War enthusiasts—reenactors and non-reenactors alike—Gettysburg is a place of great emotional significance, with the battle there considered a decisive turning point in the Civil War. For many, coming to Gettysburg and visiting Civil War battlefields can be seen as a pilgrimage experience. Gatewood and Cameron, who did research on tourists who visit the park, have noted religious-like elements in the experience of many battlefield tourists. Those who initially came with a casual interest are increasingly drawn to the emotional power of the landscape as "impressions of the site become more complex and more layered with repeated visits" (Gatewood and Cameron 2004: 213). It was precisely these pilgrimage-like characteristics of battlefield tourism and reenacting that drew me to this anthropological research, having previously looked at the phenomenon of religious pilgrimage elsewhere (Amster 2003).

The main purpose of this article is to give voice to reenactor stories and viewpoints in ~nderstand what motivates people to participate in this hobby. Research was done over a three-year period, during 2004–2006, mainly during the summer months. Methodology included participant observation and interviews with dozens of reenactors. Most of my interviews took place immediately before or after reenactments, when I would spend time in reenactor camps. Interviews were conducted with individuals from a broad cross-section of the hobby—men and women, young and old, experienced and inexperienced, and, most importantly, Union and Confederate reenactors. Unfortunately, I have not had the opportunity to interview reenactors from African American regiments, as the regiments they portray did not fight at the battle of Gettysburg and similarly do not tend to appear at Gettysburg reenactments. Each year, I attended both the annual commercial reenactments and a range of Living History demonstrations in the park, including the one where I myself participated, as a Union infantryman. By joining a reenactor group and "going native," I got my most vivid glimpse of "the life"—as some reenactors call it—and the unforgettable chance to "feel the itch of the wool."

"Civil War Moments"

When asking Civil War reenactors why they reenact, one is invariably told a number of "official" sounding answers: to educate the pubic, to commemorate and honor those who died, for love of country, and to better understand details of history. While all of these are, to a certain extent, true, there seems to be an unspoken agreement that when reenactors interact with the "public," a certain façade must be maintained to shield their motives. It does not take much probing, however, to learn that there are a host of other reasons why people choose to reenact, most prominent among them being that it is fun.

So, *why* is reenacting fun? Reenactors often stress an intense camaraderie that accompanies involvement in the hobby: the good friends and people they meet, the pleasure of telling stories around the campfire at night, singing Civil War songs, drinking, and the deep bonding with others who share their interest in history. During my own participation in firing demonstrations, I could not help but notice how much the men enjoyed simply using their weapons. In such firing demonstrations, as well as battle reenactments, actual gunpowder is loaded in the rifles, though no bullets are used. At one point, after a particularly intense round went off and the smoke cleared, the man next to me, sporting a wide grin, commented blissfully to himself, "Love the sound. Love the feel." As Jim, a Navy reserve officer in his mid-forties, put it:

> It's the ultimate guy hobby. You've got camping, firearms, and the occasional beer, you know, weekends out with nature. It all makes sense. You have guys giving you all those fancy, you know, honor-my-great-granny-type stuff and some of them might believe it, but most of them are just here because it's a good time. You hang out with your friends, you do something that's somewhat interesting, and you learn a little bit, maybe you help someone learn a little bit, and you have a good time doing it.

Jim, who resides in the Philadelphia area, has a passion for both military history and firearms, and he readily admits that these interests, rather than some abstract altruistic desire to educate the public or honor the dead, are what motivate him to do this. Having done Civil War reenacting for more than a decade, Jim is also now among a growing group of reenactors who have become involved in reenacting other wars. World War I, for example, has recently increased in popularity (Thompson 2004).

As I questioned Jim further about his particular motivations, he talked about how the hobby allows him to think concretely about the challenges of facing combat, something he has never actually experienced and does not want to experience. He said he often asked himself: "Could I have done what they did? Could I have spent time in the field the way they did? How would I have reacted in the same circumstances?" Jim was quick to point out that one can never really know what a soldier might have felt during a Civil War battle, but at least by doing some of the things reenactors do, one gets closer to the experience. "Whether it's eating hardtack or nasty salt pork or sleeping in the cold, marching in the rain," he said, "you know *they did it*."

Over and over, I heard similar comments about the deep experiential value of reenacting and the unique pleasure it brings reenactors. Wayne, a fifty-two-year-old Union reenactor from the Baltimore area, described his special moments in the heat of battle:

> You get into certain reenactments or certain times and it's only milliseconds, it might last a few seconds. You're in a long line of battle, the breeze is a' blowing, the flags are a' fluttering, the smokes coming up, they're yelling commands, and for those small seconds you are almost transported back in time and [you] say 'I'm living this.' It gives you a time capsule, a time machine, to come back in time and experience something, even if it's for a little part of time. You almost put yourself back in that time period. Of course, you're not having the bullets go past your ear, you're not having blood splattered on you, you're not having bombs exploding in the air, but it's just small periods—you can blot out everything and you're there, you're actually there. So that's what pulls me. I enjoy it, I enjoy it immensely.

Bruce, aged fifty-one, from the Lancaster, PA, area, expressed similar reasons for why he was drawn to reenacting. He also cited family connections that drew him to the battle of Gettysburg specifically, including a great uncle killed by friendly fire and another relative who drowned while on guard duty. As a deeply committed Christian, Bruce saw no conflict between his love of reenacting and his religious beliefs and, indeed, merged them in his work, teaching history at a Christian school. He had been reenacting for five years and traced his love of the Civil War back to his childhood, when he began collecting Civil War artifacts at five years old. For Bruce, reenacting is a kind of "men's club" for people who like history. "I get personal satisfaction because it is fun. I like to camp, I love the camaraderie. I think the relationships that we build with our fellow reenactors come the closest to understanding what a soldier's heart is." He also brings students to Gettysburg and pointed out that this is an effective way to teach history. "A person standing out there in a hot uniform, with a smoking pole, is gonna grab somebody's attention, and hopefully they are going to learn from us what they don't learn from their teachers at school."

For many people I interviewed, their interest in reenacting was linked to personal experiences in the military, memory of combat, or simply a proxy for their fantasies about military life. As a teenager from Central New Jersey commented, through reenacting "you go into the military without paying the consequences of being in the military." For some veterans, reenacting can provide a kind of alternative to combat and perhaps even have a therapeutic effect. Keith, a professor at a major research university, became a reenactor because it helped him process some of his memories from Vietnam and offered him a place where he could proudly wear an American military uniform without feelings of shame. While many of his academic colleagues could not relate to his military past or his interest in reenacting, he had much in common with friends in the reenacting community. Simply carrying a rifle and marching in formation evoked a powerful bodily memory that allowed him to think about his relationship to the military and his own, otherwise muted, patriotic feelings.

Jerry, a reenactor from Virginia in his late forties, first became involved in reenacting in his teens and then later joined the army for two years, a career choice he attributes to his prior involvement in reenactment. But Jerry far preferred Civil War reenacting to being in the actual military. He has been reenacting for twenty-five years and estimated that he had been to over three hundred reenactments and experienced roughly seven hundred battles, pointing out that it was starting to get mundane and he was considering stopping. For Jerry, the camaraderie around the campfire at night was by far the best part of reenacting, although what kept him coming back most of all was his sense of commitment to the group he founded and the men who depend on his leadership. For him, having "Civil War moments" (or "time bubbles," as he called them) was no longer important, and such experiences were fewer and farther between.

"Civil War moments" can be both individual and shared. One group of men told me about a collective moment when they were simultaneously affected by what sounded eerily like actual bullets whizzing by their ears. After the fact, they speculated the sound was caused by an echo off a nearby barn. One of the men called this a "Civil Wargasm," bringing up jokes about "multiple Civil Wargasms," a term that was used in the book *Confederates in the Attic* to describe a whirlwind tour of Civil War sites (Horwitz 1999: Chapter 10). Another man told me that his first Civil War moments occurred prior to becoming a reenactor and that he first experienced this moment as a spectator watching a battle, leading him to become involved in the hobby.

Cushman lists commemoration, instruction, and entertainment as the three main reasons why people reenact, adding the kind of special moments on which I have focused here as a fourth reason. "Reenactors also reenact in order to lose track of time, to fool themselves, to experience a mystical moment when the seemingly impermeable boundary between the present and the past suddenly dissolves" (Cushman 1999: 62). A common characteristic of these moments is that they are chaotic and confusing, which fits many reenactors' preconceptions about actual battle. Such moments are thus marked psychologically by a temporary loss of orientation, one that mimics what reportedly happened to soldiers in battle at Gettysburg.

> One of the most prevalent themes among soldiers who did record their thoughts in diaries and letters around that time is confusion. Men were stupefied by the experience of battle—the deafening noise, the whirlwind of pain and death, the numbness of shock and horror—and had no idea what had just happened. Even the more sober and clearheaded would only have seen and remembered what occurred within a few feet of them, as that is as far as their vision and consciousness allowed them to record. (Desjardin 2003: 14)

It is thus the small and often chaotic details of battle, rather than the broader tactical view, that make reenacting seem realistic. Sitting down with Jason, a fifty-year-old Confederate soldier from Indiana I had met earlier the same day, after he had just come back from a long hot reenactment, it was clear he was overwhelmed with emotion. He described the event in which he had just participated as incredibly "real," in part because of the utter chaos. "We pushed the Yanks back, and they pushed us back, and then we pushed them back and it was just so totally real." Slumped over on the rough ground, wiping the sweat from his brow, he spoke of his feelings, particularly toward his fellow soldiers:

> Going up that hill elbow-to-elbow with your guys, it's just being full of worry for them and, you know, everything that goes through a soldier's mind. You think about home in a heart-beat, and you think about your buddy next to you, and you think about getting the job done for your officers. And then at the same time you gotta think, "Am I gonna make it?" You know, I don't know if I'm gonna make it. And then you make it! And the jubilation is just incredible. We weren't in somebody else's footsteps but we recreated somebody else's hard fight today. We didn't feel the bullets enter, but we felt the rest of the pain they felt, we felt the rest of the fear they felt, the anxiety, you know, "Am I going to be OK today?" By that I mean, am I going to do right by my fellows today? You know, what it really all boils down to is you're fighting for the guy next to you, you're not fighting for the officers, you're not fighting for the President whether he's in the White House, or in Mobile, or in Richmond; you're fighting for the guy next to you. And you know at the end of the season—there's no doubt in your mind at the end of a season—that if you had to kill somebody to protect your buddy, you would, for real . . . not just powder.

Referring to the same battle, a group of Confederates from Delaware told me. "It was so real it was incredible. It had us all torn apart."

For many Confederate reenactors, their involvement in the hobby is often linked to their political views. As one told me, "The war is still on, the war is still on," launching into a scathing assault of contemporary American politics and asserting that "the issues haven't changed . . . it's the same song, just a different choir." As Horwitz points out, for many people from the South, "remembrance of the War had become a talisman against modernity, an emotional lever for their reactionary politics" (1999: 386). Similarly, Strauss (2003), who did participant-observation research among Confederate reenactors, points out that while one will not normally hear overtly racist comments, Confederate reenactors "had more in common with their Neo-Confederate counterparts than they were willing to admit" (160), including views that he describes as "symbolically manifesting discomfort with the eroding state of white hegemony in the United States" (159). Strauss also found that Confederate reenactors were often "adamant in their refusal to galvanize" (2003: 155), which I also found to be true of many Confederate reenactors, including those of southern heritage who live in northern states. When I asked a group of Confederates from New York State if they ever galvanized and portrayed Union soldiers, they told me in all seriousness that it was sac-rilegious, in their view, to don a Union uniform, citing their "rebel blood," and adding, "Nothing but Dixie. Won't catch me in a blue suit."

Union reenactors, for their part, tend to portray Confederates as fanatical and would point out that Confederates take reenacting "too seriously," citing the cliché that for some the war has never ended. While there is some truth in these observations, I noted far more similarities than differences, and, I would argue, playing up these differences is part of the performance and fun of reenacting. Confederate reenactors often told me that Union reen-actors were more disciplined in terms of their military formations and procedures, which the Confederates said reflected actual differences, though this is historically questionable. Confederate reenactors also claimed that Union camp life was "cold." In both Union and

Confederate camps at the commercial reenactment, however, there is a surprisingly strong family orientation and the differences between these enemies are more subtle than most reenactors admit. Indeed, some even refused to set foot in the other camp, though a family-friendly atmosphere prevailed in both camps. For Jason, who was divorced, reenacting provided him a venue to spend time with his fourteen-year-old son Dylan, who was in his second year of reenacting. Jason talked about the values he hoped to instill in his son at these events, not to mention the lack of video games. "You know, fourteen is where you lose a kid. He's not gonna get lost," he said, nodding toward his son. "Not while he's out here doing this with us. It consumes your focus."

Despite the carnival-like mood and commercialized aspects of Gettysburg reenactments, many people claimed to have experienced profoundly special moments, even with blaring loudspeakers and a large presence of spectators in the grandstands. After a major battle, a group of teenage reenactors from Central New Jersey described how the crowds completely disappeared as a group of them shot off a volley and three men across from them suddenly went down (known as "taking a hit"). "I felt it right there for at least five seconds," one said, pointing out that this was enough to make the whole weekend worthwhile. Others with whom I spoke said they preferred smaller events, especially those without spectators, where things "can get a little more intense." Describing an event at a remote Living History farm in upstate New York, a reenactor noted how "you can time warp a little bit better, or time travel a little bit better, because there's really nothing around you other than what is there in the camp."

Many women reenactors also described similar experiences of period rush. Carol, in her late thirties from San Antonio, had just come back from the thick of battle, where she had been serving for the first time as an "ice angel," bringing ice chips to soldiers. She was glowing with excitement: "It was overwhelming, I almost cried 'cause you just *almost* feel it. You feel like you're actually out there trying to fight for your ground." Julie, an experienced reenactor in her late thirties who comes to Gettysburg each year with her husband and two children, described her relationship to reenacting as an "addiction" that allows you to "leave the twenty-first century behind." She herself portrays a Union soldier. "It's so funny," she told me, "I can't wait to get out into ninety-degree weather in wool and shoot at each other, and smell the gunpowder, and campfires." Similarly, her seventeen-year-old daughter Megan said, "When I went out the first time, I came back and I went 'Mom, I'm never putting on a dress again.' I had black powder all over my face, but it was absolutely wonderful. I was sweaty, I was sticky, but it was fun." Another young woman in her twenties, who had just gone into battle as a Confederate soldier, told me: "It's such an adrenaline rush while you're out there. You forget everything in the world and you're just marching to the beat of the drum, climbing over fences and walls. It's fun. I love it."

Ultimately, part of the allure of such Civil War moments is their rarity. As one reenactor told me, "I've done this event so many times . . . man, I'm all out of magic moments." Another reenactor, in response to my question about whether he had experienced anything "special" or "magical" in a battle that particular day, said:

> No, I didn't go through the bubble, I'm afraid. That truly is a rare thing. You can't psych yourself up for it, you can't put yourself in the mood, it's just something that happens. You know when it's real when you suddenly catch yourself, and you jerk back to reality and say

"what, am I going psychotic or something?" You can't pretend to do it and make it happen. It's 'cause it really is that true experience, as though, in your mind anyway, that you are really there for that split second. It's a beautiful moment.

As powerful as such occasional experiences are, they always remain partial. And, as Cushman points out, "No matter how completely they identify with their roles, contemporary Civil War reenactors do not come away from reenactments with post-traumatic stress disorder caused by their reenacting" (1999: 56). While many take the hobby very seriously, I never got the impression that reenactors *really* believed they were capable of time traveling or that they became another person, though it is clear that they enjoy the illusion of being in such moments, the ultimate pay-off for the hard work of living as soldiers of the era did. As Bruce, the history teacher from the Lancaster area, said: "While we're not facing the bullets and the shrapnel and guts flying all over the place, there are some things that I believe are very similar, like the friendships, the experiences, the heat, the smell." Finally, as a sixty-year-old Union officer told me, "We only do an impression. We don't live like it really was. I wouldn't want that anyway. I don't want diarrhea, I don't want lice, I don't want fleas. And, of course, there weren't too many soldiers pushing sixty years old running around there either, unless they were generals on a horse."

Authenticity and Experience: Some Final Thoughts

As a discipline, cultural anthropology places great emphasis on the value of participant-observation fieldwork as a key methodology through which anthropologists gain access to other people's perspectives. In a sense, reenactors also use and gain from this methodology, although, since "informants" from the Civil War are long dead, reenactors can only participate and observe via recreating the experience. While my own immersion in reenactor culture was brief, I emerged with a better grasp of what motivates reenactors to pursue this hobby and with an appreciation of the sincerity, passion, and even the fun involved.

I also began to see reenacting as having characteristics similar to those in cultures around the world, particularly in their religious and ritual aspects. Throughout history, human beings have performed rituals to express and reaffirm key values of their cultures, and reenactors, too, can be seen in this mold, carrying out their activities to maintain links to history, forebears, and sense of place. Whenever people hold auspicious rituals—whether part of a world religion or a remote indigenous culture—there is often an implicit understanding that in repeating acts believed to have been passed down for generations, one gets closer to something essential or primordial. By recreating the past through acts of remembrance, reenactors may have more in common with ritual practitioners who call up ancestors and divine spirits, Sunday churchgoers, and New Age pagans than they do with other hobbyists, such as those who might be passionate about sports, become devoted to coins or stamps, love to shop, or spend all their spare time maintaining the perfect lawn.

In a very real sense, then, what reenactors do when they come out for a weekend and put on their uniforms is not simply have fun, make good friends, and escape the modern world, but also reaffirm links to their heritage as Americans. This experience is heightened, as I have described above, within the seemingly authentic circumstances and performances that result in intense and powerful bursts of emotion that are part of what keep people coming back. When such bursts occur, reenactors are like religious pilgrims traveling to a sacred site, as both groups seek to connect to something beyond their everyday circumstances. As such, reenacting has a quasi-religious (and perhaps civil religious) element. Of course, like any religious ritual or cultural practice, elements will change over time, and authenticity is always illusory (Amster 1999). This brings me to the topic of the Gettysburg National Military Park and its efforts to restore the landscape of the original battlefield.

In recent years, the park administration at Gettysburg has committed to a major project of battlefield restoration—what they call "rehabilitation"—with the aim of returning the landscape to its 1863 condition. Virtually every reenactor I spoke with applauded the park for its vision, which includes the current ongoing removal of 576 acres of "nonhistoric" trees, demolishing and removing structures that were not on the site at the time of the battle, and restoring fence lines and other features of the viewscape that can impact how tourists experience the battlefield. All of this is a reenactor's dream, as it allows him to better experience the actual locations of battles as the soldiers might have seen them and improves tactical understandings of military events. As Bruce pointed out, removing trees helps one learn about the battle in a multisensory way: "You're seeing it, you're feeling it, you're smelling it. You know, it's one of those things—the more senses you bring in to learning, the better you're gonna learn it. So I don't have any problem with what they're doing right now." Another reenactor described how a large stand of trees that had recently been removed from the lower end of Little Round Top allowed him to get "a whole new perspective" on specific events. "When you see that opened up like that," he said, "then you can understand, then you get a better picture of why and how things transpired in there." His only complaint about the project was that "unfortunately, it is going to take ten years to get it complete."

Another move by the park is to remove nonperiod architecture from the battlefield, such as the current Visitor Center and Cyclorama building, the latter constructed at great expense and with much fanfare in the 1960s and located near the heart of the battlefield. The current park administration now wants to remove these buildings, in part because they sit on "sacred" ground and interfere with seeing the battlefield as it was at the time. These recent attempts to provide a more "authentic" tourist experience, which have increasingly drawn in input from reenactor groups, represent a new approach to heritage and memory. As Jim Weeks points out, this trend has "pulled away from the family-friendly Gettysburg of the earlier era to create an authentic experience for enthusiasts" (2003: 187). Gettysburg, he observes, is now starting to resemble "a kind of giant hobby set for middle-class white America" (2003: 198). Critiquing this mindset, Weeks cites an example of a newspaper report by a black male who visited Gettysburg and had the uncomfortable experience of coming across a Confederate reenactor, pointing out one of the more obvious pitfalls that can accompany the obsessive pursuit of authenticity. One of my colleagues recently asked me, "What happens if Asian Americans want to get involved in reenacting? Would they be accepted?" These are good questions. There were, in fact, some Asian Americans who fought in the battle of Gettysburg, but it is telling that I have not yet seen an Asian American reenactor, nor black reenactors outside of an all-black reenacting group. Thus, in seeking to create accurate impressions, reenacting and battlefield "rehabilitation" both run the risk of promoting forms of exclusion, not just by implicitly limiting the participants in a reenactment,

Trees being removed near Little Round Top, Gettysburg National Military Park, January, 2005 (photo by Matthew H. Amster).

but by neglecting the possibility of other forms of commemoration, such as might be reflected in nonperiod architecture or allowing nonhistoric trees to stand as a different type of tribute on the battlefield.

Coming full circle, then, I return to my first day of reenacting and the events immediately following my own brief Civil War moment, described in the opening passages. As our group left the dusty path and crossed a modern road, we immediately encountered a group of tourists who stopped to take our picture. By then, I was fully back to present-day reality. Then, marching past General Meade's Union Headquarters on one side and the soon-to-be demolished Cyclorama building on the other, one of the men in my line, chatting idly, glanced over at the building and said, "It will be nice to get that off the battlefield." It was clear that his desire to see a more authentic battlefield landscape was entirely heartfelt, even though I find such views extreme, having some sympathy for the architectural preservationists who see this building as a valuable piece of our history as well. In any case, being there in formation on the battlefield with reenactors gave me a better perspective on what was taking place from both the reenactor and the park administrative perspective, now converging on the idea of the battlefield as "sacred ground" that is best commemorated through accurate historical representation. Having been freshly jarred out of my own brief time bubble by "farby" elements—the road, cars, tourists, the modernist building—in that moment I could more fully appreciate the ever-present challenges of achieving authenticity for such pilgrims to the past.

Questions for Further Discussion

1. Why do reenactors feel so strongly about issues of authenticity in trying to achieve authentic impressions? How does this relate to their personal feelings about the reenacting experience?

2. In what ways do the recent efforts to rehabilitate the battlefields in the Gettysburg National Military Park resemble the aims of reenactors? Is it appropriate or desirable for a federal park to try to recreate the authentic landscape of 1863, even when it entails the removal of trees and buildings? What should take precedence when the mission of historic preservation is at odds with protecting the physical environment?

3. In what ways might reenacting as a hobby exclude some groups of people? Consider the ways people of different backgrounds might respond to the reenacting community.

References

Amster, Matthew H. 1999. "Tradition," ethnicity, and change: Kelabit practices of name changing. *Sarawak Museum journal* 54(75): 183–200.

———. 2003. New sacred lands: The making of a Christian prayer mountain in Highland Borneo. In Ronald A. Lukens-Bull (ed.), *Sacred places and modern landscapes: sacred geography and social–religious transformations in South and Southeast Asia,* 131–160. Tempe: Southeast Asian Studies Monograph Series, Program for Southeast Asian Studies, Arizona State University.

Cushman, Steven. 1999. *Bloody promenade: reflections on a Civil War battle.* Charlottesville: University Press of Virginia.

Desjardin, Thomas A. 2003. *These honored dead: how the story of Gettysburg shaped American history.* Cambridge, MA: Da Capo Press.

Gatewood, John B., and Catherine M. Cameron. 2004. Battlefield pilgrims at Gettysburg National Military Park. *Ethnology* 43(3): 193–216.

Horwitz, Tony. 1999. *Confederates in the attic: dispatches from the unfinished Civil War.* New York: Vintage Books.

Hunt, Stephen J. 2004. Acting the part: 'Living History' as a serious leisure pursuit. *Leisure studies* 23(4): 387–403.

Strauss, Mitchell D. 2003. Identity construction among Confederate Civil War reenactors: A study of dress, stage props, and discourse. *Clothing and textiles research journal* 21: 149–161.

Thompson, Jenny. 2004. *War games: inside the world of twentieth-century war reenactors.* Washington: Smithsonian Books.

Weeks, Jim. 2003. *Gettysburg: memory, market and an American shrine.* Princeton: Princeton University Press.

3

Mining History: Small Town Histories and Celebrations Among the Nacirema

Barry P. Michrina
Mesa State College

Recognizing that the centennial of small mining towns can act as an impetus for cultural events, Barry Michrina has studied memorialization, celebration, memory, and the construction of histories among rural Nacirema. As an anthropologist who lived his early life in one of these towns, he is drawn not only to study the events but also to construct history himself. What do people choose to remember? How do they want to be perceived? What constitutes historical fact for these people? And whose voice is heard?

Barry Michrina is a Professor of Anthropology at Mesa State College, where he has been teaching since 1990. He has authored three books: Pennsylvania Mining Families: the Search for Dignity in the Coal Fields, Person to Person: Fieldwork, Dialogue, and the Hermeneutic Method *(with Cherylanne Richards) and* Mines, Memories and More, *the book that resulted from the work described below.*

The Nacirema experiences what Sorenson has called "supraliminal consciousness" (1996). Members of this nation are characterized by having abstract ideas of space, time, property, and kinship, and thus both obsess over future possibilities and dwell on past occurrences. Because of this they have a custom of recording the past, both informally and formally.

The topic of using history as a resource is very important to understanding Nacirema behavior. History to the Nacirema must be legitimate, accurate, and meaningful, but with the recent trend for common people in industry-related enclaves to record their own town's history, the nature of legitimacy, accuracy, and meaning has changed. Trained historians who have addressed the small town past have concentrated on the conflictual relations between workers and industry owners. However, Bodnar (1989), Frisch (1989), and Basso (1996) have each foreseen how common people might create narratives with themes different from exploitation and class struggle. Small rural enclaves celebrate their past and use history as a resource to improve self-image, create nostalgia and sentimentality, and appear as part of generalized mass society.

The Nacirema have intermixed and intermarried with explorers and fortune seekers from other cultures, and some have created regional populations which have lived in the same area for several generations. One such group is that of the rural mining families in the coal fields of the Allegheny Plateau. Small towns, largely built with industrial capital, have existed for decades, and those who live there have recently celebrated their towns' centennials.

Insiders and outsiders alike have sought to use the image and memory of coal miners to achieve present goals. The residents of many towns have recently celebrated their centennial year, and some individuals have written books to coincide with these events. The UMWA (United Mine Workers of America) as well celebrated its centennial in 1990. With the closing of mines, communities such as Colver and Bakerton chose to build memorials for former miners. What types of histories were written? What images are being portrayed or cherished? Outsiders such as historians, anthropologists, and National Park Service personnel have used the life history and the symbolic miner to reach outside audiences. What images are arising here? I will begin by examining the residents' use of history.

The coal company towns of Hastings and Bakerton celebrated their centennials in 1989, Portage in 1990, and St. Benedict in 2001. Of these, Bakerton seems to serve as the best case for analysis. During the year 1989, three events marked the one hundredth year of its existence: a written history, a celebration, and a monument to miners. Bakerton differs from the other mentioned towns in that it is a linear town—houses mostly line the main thoroughfare that stretches for miles as it winds through the hollow cut by the West Branch of the Susquehanna River. As the road heads north, the creek lies to the left and the railroad to the right. Bakerton is a patchwork of former company houses and owner-built residences. It has no fire company and shares a police officer with the town of St. Benedict. Bakerton has had "boney piles" at both ends and at the center of town. These mine refuse piles, which gave off a sulfurous odor for years as they burned, gave the town an unrefined and dirty appearance. In contrast, Portage and Hastings were laid out in a cross-hatch of streets, they have had fire companies and police forces, and the mines and boney piles lay on the outskirts of town. In further contrast, St. Benedict was a true "company town," having been built by Peale, Peacock and Kerr Co. in 1901.

Mary Frances Inzana, the author of Bakerton's history, said that her purpose in writing the book was to honor her deceased father who had been a coal miner in Bakerton for most of his adult life. The chapters detail the town's former mines, former businesses, school, and important personalities. Except for a piece written by a one-time resident who served a short stint in the mines as a young man, there was little written about miners themselves. Any details of conflict were also left out. For example, the 1927 coal strike with its strikebreakers and coal and iron police was not included. Also missing were details of the Ku Klux Klan. Ms. Inzana would have liked to explore the Klan issue further, but she also wanted to avoid disturbing descendants of Klansmen who still live in the area. So her book takes on a rather sanitized appearance—Smalltown, U.S.A., a great place to have lived. The book does include a detailed account of Tony Callabria, who helped organize area miners when the unions came back upon the election of Nacireman leader Nilknarf Tlevlesoor. The purpose that these histories serve is one of unifying and celebrating a shared past—experienced directly or through their ancestry. Nostalgia would understandably be preferred to criticism as a theme for such histories.

The Bakerton centennial celebration was motivated largely by the desire of townspeople to win the admiration and respect of people in surrounding towns, as well as that of critical columnist Charlie Reese. Ms. Inzana, to whom most Bakerton residents referred as the "sparkplug" of the centennial celebration, spent her years in grade school and high school hearing derogatory jokes and stories about Bakerton from students from other towns.

This motivation explains one of the major themes of the celebration: "Many Bakerton residents went on to become successful." A former resident, and now a brigadier general, came back to aid in the celebration. A bank executive, who was a former resident and short-term miner, acted as the master of ceremonies for the miners' memorial dedication. He stated this "successful son" theme clearly:

> I wonder who would dare say that coal miners don't amount to much in the professional and business world. I think coal miners are the backbone of building this country to where we are today, and they certainly are knowledgeable and experienced in any field they undertake.

This represented a clear conflict of themes, in that the master of ceremonies, dedicating a miners' memorial, failed to honor miners but rather honored those who successfully left mining. It seems to me that this followed from the lack of fit between the motive of the celebration and that of the monument dedication. This discrepancy did not displease those who came for the dedication or for the celebration; it was not mentioned by residents or local newspaper columnists (see, for example, Kaufman 1989).

Hastings, Portage, and Bakerton held similar celebrations: parades, queens, fireworks, game booths, and food concessions. This was in keeping with local traditions like fireman's and church festivals which are held in most of the local towns. The higher level of the events and the size of the crowd attending were the major differences. A cake under a tent in Bakerton, awaiting cutting after the memorial dedication, had icing which read, "Happy Birthday Bakerton." A true party was necessary with the town seemingly anthropomorphized.

Despite the remarks by the master of ceremonies, the monument dedication had elements of a funeral. In this region of mostly Catholics, a celebration often follows the solemnity of the funeral service. In this case the monument dedication preceded the centennial festivities. Clergy were present, and the large brick monument was like an oversized tombstone, dedicated to the miners who had passed away (perhaps even symbolizing the death of coal mining as an occupation). The monument continued to function as a funeral marker after the dedication. Ms. Inzana mentioned that wreaths have since been placed on it upon the death of local residents who had formerly been miners:

> every time there's a funeral—they used to take a basket maybe and put it on the war memorial—now they're putting it on the coal miners memorial. Niedemeyer was a veteran, I know—they had a military funeral. Yet, they put his flowers on the coal miners' memorial.

What does this example of Bakerton suggest about the residents' use of history? Most centennial towns used history as a theme for homecoming festivities. Their written histories described the town's businesses of the past, the prominent citizens, sports, schools, and buildings. It was a celebration of both continuity and change—a great place to live and to have lived. Missing is a sense of the dominant force the coal mine owners had represented. Missing also is the sense of conflict between classes and ethnic groups. The move to give history back to the people seems to have two goals: to provide a resource for the people themselves and to produce a somewhat less sanitized version than is noted in renditions by institutions such as museums and the National Park Service (Frisch 1989, Cohen 1989). The coal town histories are clearly being used as resources. However, the examples presented here would indicate that the product may not always be a version which includes conflict. In other words, the people's version may be sanitized for different reasons.

There is still more material to consider. What is the object of a local teacher's project to increase the appreciation of mining as an occupation and as history? Before the coal industry experienced its collapse, Dr. Irma Konitsky, an English teacher at Northern Cambria High School, advised her students in publishing several collections of essays and poems dealing with coal mining life of the past and present. The "Out of the Dark" series was aimed at building an appreciation for and pride in the area's major industrial occupations—those involving the mining of coal (Konitsky 1980, Yuhas 1975; 1977). Interestingly, there is a dearth of information about ethnic and labor conflict in the historical essays that dot these publications, an exception being Rocco's essay on Joseph Ploucha (Yuhas 1977). It is not due to Dr. Konitsky's lack of understanding of these topics. As a daughter and wife of a coal mine worker she has been aware of the struggles with the owners. In fact, she penned passionate letters to the editor of the *Barnesboro Star* (a weekly newspaper) concerning the miners' issues during the 1977 strike (Konitsky 1977; 1978). At the time when the books were written, there were many retired miners and their wives who would have remembered the great strikes of 1922 and 1927 and the Ku Klux Klan marches and cross burnings of the 1920s.

Her mission of teaching appreciation for the occupation of one's parents was likely more urgent than teaching labor history. It is also possible that older residents considered these topics inappropriate for such a publication. In any case, the "people's history" is again mostly devoid of these conflict topics.

"People's history" varies with the situation for which it is produced (Basso 1996: 52–55, Ortiz 1988, Bodnar 1989). Histories written to celebrate warm feelings for a hometown or to increase pride in an industrial occupation will most likely exclude details of conflict. That does not mean that older residents have forgotten these conflicts nor that they are reluctant to describe them. However, the purpose of the history had to be properly defined. Although older residents wished to tell the world about the atrocities of the 1927 coal strike and the time without the union, they required the presence of someone who was perceived as a part of the "outside world" and who had the qualities, (e.g., scholarship, connections, and an appreciation for historical significance), to reach a wide audience with these accounts.

The lack of dissemination of local conflict history seems to explain the almost universal lack of knowledge of the 1927 strike by residents (other than those old enough to have experienced it). During the four-month strike of 1977, local news reporters and mineworkers referred to it as the "longest strike in the history of the UMWA" (Kotrick 1978a, b). Perhaps if more residents had known of the two-year strike in non-union Somerset county in 1922, or the strike of 1927 that lasted a year-and-a-half, they could have used it as a source of inspiration and pride.

Authors such as Smith (1999) have suggested that a new ethnography (and by implication, history.) be encouraged—one created by regional natives who are trained in modern social science methodology. Thus scholarly members of a culture (or regional subculture) would write about the population of their origin. Can coal mining history be written both to include conflict and to appeal to the mining towns' residents? In the late 1980s and early 1990s an anthropologist named M. Yrrab, who was also a regional native, wrote about historical and cultural studies of the coal mining people of the Allegheny Plateau. His projects resulted in the publication of two books—a regional labor history and a pictorial history of the town of St. Benedict.

The older residents, then in retirement, saw themselves as more a part of the Nacirema mass society, and their children and grandchildren having educations and career options not available even two generations earlier. Then there was no shame in admitting the injustice and exploitation at the hands of the coal companies. The avoidance of these topics came partially from embarrassment of one's station in life. There's had been at one time a life at the bottom of the ladder. They know that class had existed among the Nacirema, and they became proud to point to their abilities to struggle against the industrial powers and to have survived. Perhaps the most frequent, and certainly the most noteworthy, response of the oldest generation of coal mining families was a desire to tell Yrrab and the world about the way things had been for them. Sometimes this involved their obtaining a new appreciation for their own lives and history. Often this seemed to take place in the glow of their feeling appreciated and of being taken seriously as an equal.

> Other people might have started this and quit because it was too much work . . . It's sad—this generation knows less about the way things were like in the past. They don't care.

Others felt like authorities or teachers; for example, one informant told Yrrab upon his third meeting: "You didn't have to bring me an apple" (meaning an apple for the teacher).

At other times the new appreciation occurred during the telling. What had appeared to them to be mundane, or perhaps embarrassing, took on new significance. "It used to be you was ashamed to admit that you came from a coal mining family. Now the story should be told—after all, it's a part of our heritage." This allowed them to resolve old feelings which lay in the back of their minds like mementos in the bottom of a cedar chest. In one case of a woman whose husband died in the 1940 Sonman Mine Disaster, the process literally involved a cedar chest: "Many times I would open up that cedar chest and take stuff out until I saw the ribbons from the flowers. Then I'd start cryin' and cryin'." It was necessary for her to cancel her scheduled meeting with Yrrab until she could bear removing the contents of the chest in order to get newspaper clippings of the event for him. At the interview she told him:

> My son was only 13 months old at that time. Now it's 48 years later, and I think it's time for him to see [the clippings] . . . I used to pray to God to keep me alive until my son grew up. After he got married I said "OK, now you can take me."

The process also facilitated communication with her son about those times. Two years later, the two of them attended the memorial service for the miners killed in that blast.

Not only intergenerational but peer communication was also facilitated. One retired miner said: "I was talkin' to an old man in Heilwood, and we were talkin' about where the old spotlight [used by the company police to spot curfew-breakers] used to be." Some informants gained new insights into their past lives. For example, one man was surprised by the number of dangerous situations he had encountered after he had reflected on it. Others gained insights regarding their spouses, such as a woman who, after hearing her husband's explanation for fearing a return to the mines after having worked elsewhere, exclaimed: "you must be superstitious. I'm hearing this for the first time. You should trust God more."

For many of the informants, talk of the past aided in their interpretation of the present. This was particularly true of politics. Most of the informants were "Tlevesoor Starcomed" who explained their thinking about the then-current political campaign couched in terms of the past. Yrrab exhibited a strong empathy for their political views, a quality which they appeared to greatly appreciate.

Another topic which could be interpreted by explanation from the past was the (then current) miners' strike against the Pittston Coal Co. People told Yrrab:

> after 1927. Every other pay we would have a ten percent cut because of competition. The coal companies tryin' to break the union today should learn from that—it hurts them, too, with competition.

> They're killin' the union. I lived to see the same thing before. They say that history repeats itself, and it's true. It happened before, and it's happening now. The mine owners wasn't makin' enough money because of competition, and the miners wasn't makin' enough to live on. If they don't have togetherness they don't have nothin'.

> Don't forget to tell 'em that I took a dollar fifty trip to [Tsew Ainigriv]. Just like those guys went now, we went to [Tsew Ainigriv][to picket].

> In the conclusion of your book you should write about how quite a few of the companies today are involved with union busting. People from this area are going to Pittston, and they said there are company police there. It's starting to sound like it's going to happen again. We're going back to the same thing. It's kinda scary!

An almost universal response of informants was an appreciation of an anthropologist taking interest in them. This was expressed verbally and in the many gifts which he received: garden produce, freshly baked bread, copies of the *UMWA Journal,* meals, and home-canned foods. Even excluding the books written, there was much which they expressed as gaining. The same was true for responses to early chapter drafts for the book.

Yrrab was in the unique position of being able to circulate chapter drafts to several informants. There was a universal eagerness to read what he had written, several people reading it immediately, practically ignoring his presence. One informant said: "I read it before supper. In fact, supper was a little late [because of reading it]."

Everyone appreciated being included in early readings and in making comments. One former miner who took care to correct what he thought were misinterpretations told Yrrab: "I'm really going to enjoy reading this. I feel like I'm a part of it now." One reviewer, a wife of a retired miner, told of promoting the book.

As an author, Yrrab had to choose an audience for whom to write, and since he wanted to be recognized as a Nacirema anthropologist, he needed to appeal to the academic audience despite his wishes to provide a meaningful product for his informants. To a certain extent his text satisfies the demands of both audiences. The many quotes from informants constitute a text embedded within the academic text. A retired miner, his wife, or his children could feel that a proper representation of the past was presented by reading these quotes.

The unfortunate aspect of this is that the book's formal language held from their scrutiny his explanation for what has occurred in their lives. In reading the quotes they may have gotten the false impression that he has presented their information at "face-value." In a positive vein, some of the informant-reviewers shared the chapter drafts with their offspring. This process doubtless enhanced intergenerational communication about the region's history:

> My daughter read those chapters you wrote. She was out here late readin' them. I went to bed, and she stayed up a coupla more hours, so I know she read them carefully. She told me, "This is good, Dad. Boy, you better not lose him as a friend."

> I don't think that my grandchildren would believe the way that things were. [My parents] are always telling me about this guy who comes around. They're happy that someone is taking an interest in their lives and now writing about it.

> We have nephews and nieces who have left this area and gotten college educations. You'd be surprised how interested they are in this.

> I have a nephew who lives in Texas. He wants to know what coal is. I went and picked him a box of it.

> Reviewers were also stimulated to talk among peers about the books and their issues. In some cases, the drafts were shared among them. All of the first audience expressed their good wishes for Yrrab and the project. Perhaps these are best summed up by a retired coal miner: "We hope something comes of this for you."

Exercise

Writing a town history is very much like writing ethnography. Not only do you have to make decisions about what to write and how to write it, but these decisions are not entirely your own, in that they will affect the people who have trusted you to render what they have told you accurately and fairly. What events would you expect to see commemorated in a history of your own hometown or urban neighborhood? How would they be represented? What likely would not appear in such a volume and why?

References

Basso, K. 1996. *Wisdom sits in places*. Albuquerque, NM: University of New Mexico Press.

Bodnar, John. 1989. Power and memory in oral history: workers and managers at Studebaker. *Journal of American history*, 75(4): 1201–1222.

Cohen, L. 1989. What kind of world have we lost? Workers' lives and deindustrialization in the museum. *American quarterly*, 41(4): 670–681.

Frisch, Michael. 1989. What do you do with oral history: moving beyond the supply side. Paper presented at "Discovering Our Past: Oral History and Industrial Heritage," Indiana University of Pennsylvania, July 12.

Kaufman, D. 1989. *Barnesboro Star,* July 26.

Konitsky, E. 1977. UMWA not a bank account – but a brotherhood. *Barnesboro Star,* 73(49).

———. 1978. What do coal miners want? *Barnesboro Star,* 74(7).

———. 1980. *Work: out of the dark, a coal area model for high school English class.* Dissertation. Indiana, PA: Indiana University of Pennsylvania.

Kotrick, P. 1978a. We are united. *Barnesboro Star,* 74(8).

———. 1978b. Longest coal strike in nation's history ends. *Barnesboro Star,* 74(8).

Michrina, Barry. 1993. *Pennsylvania mining families, the search for dignity in the coalfields.* Lexington: University Press of Kentucky.

———. 2001. *Mines, memories and more, the people and history of St. Benedict, Pennsylvania.* St. Benedict, PA: The Rembrandt Club.

Ortiz, Alphonso. 1988. Indian/White relations: a view from the other side of the "frontier." In F. E. Hoxie, ed., *Indians in American history.* Arlington Heights, IL: Harlan Davidson, Inc.

Smith, Linda. 1999. *Decolonizing methodologies, research and indigenous peoples.* London: Zed Books Ltd.

Sorenson, E. Richard. 1996. Sensuality and consciousness IV: where did the liminal flowers go? *Anthropology of consciousness,* 7(4): 9–30.

Yuhas, T. ed. 1975. *Out of the dark.* Indiana, PA: A. G. Hallding Publishing Co.

———. 1977. *Out of the dark 2: mining folk.* Indiana, PA: A. G. Hallding Publishing Co.

4

Metakinesis: How God Becomes Intimate in Contemporary U.S. Christianity

Tanya M. Luhrmann
Stanford University

Shamans are spiritual experts who develop intensely personal relationships with divine figures, often through the use of consciousness-altering practices and substances. Tanya Luhrmann, in this article, illustrates how American evangelicals attain a similar level of intimacy with God, employing such consciousness-altering means as language, prayer, intensifying technologies, and ideologies of personhood that have emerged from the alienating experience of modern sub/urban life.

    How do people know what is real? Tanya M. Luhrmann has carried out a good deal of research on this question, among modern-day witches in Britain (Persuasions of the Witch's Craft, *Harvard 1989), the self-critical postcolonial elite of India* (The Good Parsi, *Harvard 1996), and American psychiatrists who come from different "cultural" backgrounds within the profession* (Of Two Minds, *Knopf 2000). The members of each of these groups have come to believe something utterly that may not in fact be recognized as "real" by others, and it is the development of conviction—an anthropological process producing a psychological result—that Dr. Luhrmann has illuminated through her work to date. She directed the Clinical Ethnography project for the Committee on Human Development at the University of Chicago, and subsequently moved on to a position in the Anthropology Department at Stanford University.*

In the last thirty or forty years, middle class U.S. citizens have begun to worship their God(s) in a markedly different manner than before. Mainstream churches have seen their

Luhrmann, Tanya. "Metakinesis: How God Becomes Intimate in Contemporary U.S. Christianity." *American Anthropologist* 106.3 (2004): 518–528. © 2004 American Anthropological Association. Reprinted by permission.

congregations dwindle; evangelical, New Age and other more demanding faiths have seen their membership explode. And what U.S. citizens seem to want from these new religiosities—and from evangelical Christianity in particular—is intense spiritual experience. We in the academy have focused on evangelical Christianity's claim that the Bible is literally true. That claim is undeniably important (Crapanzano 2001). But it is at least as important that the new U.S. religious practices put intense spiritual experience—above all, trance—at the heart of the relationship with God. The most interesting anthropological phenomenon in U.S. evangelical Christianity is precisely that it is *not* words *alone* that convert: instead, congregants—even in ordinary middle-class suburbs—learn to have out-of-the-ordinary experiences and to use them to develop a remarkably intimate, personal God. This God is not without majesty. But He has become a pal.

How does God become real to people? A recent, widely read book—Susan Harding's (2000) *The Book of Jerry Falwell*—argues that in evangelical Christianity, what makes God come alive to people is the mastery of God's word. This book is an attempt to understand the compelling power and appeal of Jerry Falwell's brand of evangelical fundamentalism. The book is specifically cast as an account of conversion and from the beginning presumes an identity between the culture and practice of Christianity, on the one hand, and its language on the other. Harding describes her book as an attempt "to show how Bible-based language persuades and produces effects" (2000: xii). She dismisses the "considerable literature, both popular and academic, on how various ritual practices and psychological techniques trigger experiences that result in conversion" (2000: 35). Those experiences may "pave the way for radical shifts in belief and commitment" (2000: 35), but, she says, they are not necessary. The appropriate question, she says, is this: "How does the supernatural order become real, known, experienced, and absolutely irrefutable?" (2000: 36). And her answer is that it can do so through language alone.

> Among conservative Protestants, and especially among fundamentalists, it is the Word, the gospel of Jesus Christ, written, spoken, heard, and read, that converts the unbeliever. The stresses, transitions, influences, conditioning, and techniques scrutinized by many social scientists do not in themselves "explain," do not "cause," conversion to Christ. All they do is increase the likelihood that a person might listen to the gospel; they may open or "prepare a person's heart."

Harding agrees. The first chapter's title and its concluding sentence (2000: 60) state the basic argument: "Speaking is believing." "Generative belief, belief that indisputably transfigures you and your reality, belief that becomes you, comes only through speech" (2000: 60).

Yet the patterns of new U.S. religious practice suggest that ritual practices and psychological techniques are not ancillary, but central, to contemporary spirituality. At least, congregants seem to want to experience the Gospel in intensely bodily ways that seem to make the message of the Gospel come alive for them in a way it has not previously. The demographic shift in U.S. religious practice since the late 1960s is remarkable. Two-thirds of the generation referred to as the "baby boomers" who were raised in religious traditions—and nearly all were—dropped out of those traditions as adults; and just under half of those now seem to be returning to religious practice—but not in the style in which they were raised (Ostling 1993). Across the board they have joined groups that demand more in religious practice and encourage more in religious experience. Evangelical and fundamentalist Christianity has exploded as a cultural phenomenon, as has the New Age, in all its many forms (like modern witchcraft and modern Santeria): In 1996, 39 percent of U.S. citizens described themselves as "born again" or "evangelical" (Gallup and Lindsay 1999: 68). Even Judaism, whose traditional and reform rabbis look askance at intense spirituality because it distracts the faithful from the obligations of their practice, has seen an enormous increase in the interest in an immediate spiritual experience of divinity, from new centers (such as the Kabbalah Centre in Los Angeles) that teach kabbalah as a practice accessible to all (a heretical idea in the past) to Chabad and Hasidic shuls that teach an experience-centered religiosity to ever-expanding crowds (e.g., Kamenetz 1997). There are many explanations for this shift and many anxieties about its political and social implications (e.g., Fogel 2000). But its behavioral implications are clear: These religions greatly value intense religious experience. As a group, they encourage participants to experience the divine vividly, immediately, and through unusual moments of altered consciousness (Wuthnow 1988).

Harding is certainly accurate when she reports that evangelical Christians often say that they are converted by the word alone. But conversion is a complex process, and above all else a learning process. Converts do not make the transition from nonbeliever to believer simply by speaking—by acquiring new concepts and words. They must come to believe emotionally that those new concepts and words are true. And this, as Saba Mahmood points out in an Islamic context, is a matter of "skills and aptitudes acquired through training, practice and apprenticeship" (2001: 844). As many anthropologists have pointed out, those skills are often bodily and the training often emotional (Csordas 1994; Whitehead 1987; Desjarlais 1992; Mitchell 1997; Lambek 1981; Boddy 1989; see also the rich discussion in Rambo 1993). What is striking about U.S. religion since the 1960s is that it not only emphasizes bodily phenomena, but uses those experiences to create remarkably intimate relationships with God.

When we take an ethnographic look at what these converts actually learn in the process of becoming evangelical Christians, we see that their new cognitive/linguistic knowledge is embedded within other kinds of learning that not only make that new knowledge real but also make this God as gritty as earth and as soothing as a summer breeze. New believers do indeed acquire what Harding calls a "shared elementary language" (2000: 19) of faith (see also Keane 1997). That linguistic/cognitive knowledge can be described more precisely, perhaps, than Harding has done: There are words or phrases to describe their new life in Christ (their "lexicon"); themes which structure the logic of their new understanding (their "syntax"); and a common plot-line which describes the way they decided to join this way of life (their "conversion narrative"). This new knowledge is important; it is necessary to the convert's conversion.

But it is not sufficient. For these converts, in these new and intensely experiential U.S. evangelisms, God becomes an intimate relationship—a buddy, a confidante, the ideal boyfriend. It is not mere words that make Him so, but learnt techniques of identifying the presence of God through the body's responses—particularly in the absorbed state we call "trance"—and learned techniques which frame that responsiveness into the experience of intimate relationship. This is not to say that every convert has these intense experiences of absorption. But the religion models the practices which produce these experiences as central to the experience of God.

We can describe this process as *metakinesis,* a term used in dance criticism to depict the way emotional experience is carried within the body so that the dancer conveys the emotion to the observer and yet does it by making the expressive gesture uniquely his or her own (Martin 1983: 23–25). New believers learn to identify bodily and emotional states as signs of God's presence in their life, identifications which imply quite different learning processes than those entailed by linguistic and cognitive knowledge. Then, their new linguistic/cognitive knowledge and bodily experiences are put to use through new relational practices. Through prayer and Bible reading, worshippers report that they learn to experience themselves in an intimate interpersonal relationship with their God; they do so not only by acquiring new knowledge but also by using that knowledge to relate to what might be psychoanalytically termed an inner "object" (cf. Lester, forthcoming). These are relational processes that are yet again another kind of learning process.

These three different kinds of learning—cognitive/linguistic, metakinetic, and relational—are psychologically distinct. Linguistic/cognitive knowledge tends to be the domain of cognitive science; emotional and altered states tend to be studied by developmentalists and those interested in psychopathology; relationship practices tend to be studied by attachment theorists, often with a psychoanalytic bent. Together, they enable the new believer to do something quite remarkable—to construct, out of everyday psychological experience, the profound sense that they have a really real relationship with a being that cannot be seen, heard, or touched. The learning process used by these U.S. evangelicals teaches us that new religious practices are giving us a God more intimate, more personal, and in some fundamental sense more tangibly real than the God of our fathers. We have yet to come to terms with this enormous social fact.

The Ethnography

Horizon Christian Fellowship in southern California has the no-frills, ordinary-folks approach characteristic of the "new paradigm" Christian churches (Miller 1997). Like other such churches, Horizon has a rock band on Sunday morning, not a choir; the pastors have an informal, anti-intellectual style; many congregants meet in small home Bible fellowships during the week; they hold their large worship meetings in a gym; and they call themselves "Bible-based," by which they mean that the written Bible is literally true and the only decisive authority. They are also entrepreneurial, well organized, and extremely effective. Horizon is an offshoot of perhaps the prototypical new paradigm church, Calvary Chapel, which began to grow in the mid-1960s by reaching out to the countercultural Jesus movement on southern California beaches but now has over 25,000 members and nearly a thousand "seeded" churches around the country. These days Horizon serves about five thousand mostly white congregants at its main church campus. It has seven associated churches in San Diego and claims eighty offshoots around the world. Horizon runs a preschool, an elementary school, a junior high, a high school, a school of evangelism with a master's program in divinity and pastoral studies, outreach evangelism in this country and abroad, youth programs, summer camps, and constant concerts, "getaways" and social events. The specific and much-reiterated goal of this busy institution is to lead each worshipper to have a vividly personal relationship with Jesus (see also Ammerman 1987).

How does God become so real for people? The great majority of U.S. citizens (96 percent) say that they believe in God—or, at least, in a power "higher than themselves"—when asked in a Gallup survey. The number has remained more or less constant for fifty years (Gallup and Lindsay 1999: 24–25). At the same time, those who have come to Horizon have usually developed a faith quite different from that in which they were raised (Miller 1997). Most congregants say that they believed "intellectually" in Christ in their childhood, or not at all, and that as adults they discovered a "new" life in Christ. How does a new congregant learn to turn an amorphous, often intellectual belief in God into the rich personal experience modeled in these religious sites?

Seen from another angle, this ethnographic puzzle is the central practical issue for a church like Horizon. Congregants at Horizon are acutely aware of their newcomers; after all, the point of an evangelizing institution is to convert them. And yet learning to be a true Christian is understood as a lifelong goal. As so many tracts say, faith is a journey in which the believer aims always to grow in the knowledge and love of God. While sermons talk of accepting Jesus as a one-time commitment (come, today, to the altar to be saved), they speak in the same breath of a long-term process of "dying to self" so that gradually and with difficulty you learn to put God's desires above your own. Being "saved" is both a singular event that people celebrate like a birthday and an on-going process.

As a result, there is no sharp distinction between newcomers and longtimers in actual practice. At Horizon, newcomers learn about the faith in two institutional settings. The first is the service. There are as many as five services throughout the weekend, each often packing the gym. They are usually led by different pastors and are sometimes structured differently, but they all focus on an hour-long sermon structured around a particular Biblical text. The services have the anonymity of all large groups. During the week, however, congregants often attend a more intimate home fellowship gathering in someone's home, where they participate in the small group worship Robert Wuthnow (1994) finds to be so characteristic of contemporary U.S. religion. Despite variation, each home fellowship meeting will involve personal testimony about Jesus and Biblical teaching.

Books are also an important vehicle for learning about the faith. The well-appointed church bookstore sells an impressive array of Christian goods. Many of their items are obviously intended as learning tools: there are over a hundred guides to prayer and Bible study, with prominent displays for what are seen as basic manuals. Each sermon, or message, is taped and sold for a nominal fee so that congregants can listen to them again in their cars. There is a wide selection of Christian novels, videos, and music. The music section has a chart that helps you to identify what mainstream music you already like and, thus, what Christian music you will like. The music ranges from folk to disco, its difference from the mainstream only in its lyrics. The wider commercial success of these products is stunning.

For three years, from 1997 to 2000, I carried out fieldwork with a colleague, Richard Madsen, to try to understand how adults create a personal relationship which feels to them authentic, intimate, and mutually reciprocal with an intentional being who does not exhibit any of the normal signs of existence. We studied four of the growth points of U.S. religion: (1) Horizon as an example of evangelical Christianity; (2) a charismatic Catholic church; (3) a New Age Santeria house; and (4) a *baal tschuva* (newly orthodox) shul. In each group, we attended services for months, in most cases nearly a year, bought the books and tools described as helpful to new converts, and to the extent that was feasible, tried to understand and to do what new converts did when they entered these groups. For each group, we formally interviewed the leader of the group and ten of its congregants. Using the formal interviews and casual conversations as our guide and drawing only from fieldwork at Horizon, I now describe (in brief) at least three kinds of learning that took place: (1) cognitive/linguistic; (2) metakinetic; and (3) relational. The cognitive/linguistic learning actually contains its own analytic triad—the lexical, the syntactic, and the specific conversion narrative—which reflects the more clearly differentiated kinds of learning that take place under the rubric of the cognitive and linguistic.

Cognitive/Linguistic Knowledge: The Lexicon

At Horizon, not all of the knowledge presented in the written material is taken equally seriously by congregants, at least to judge by the content of their conversation. Few congregants spoke in their interviews about "the Rapture" and "the end of time," concepts which are central to an enormously best-selling fantasy series called the Left Behind series, (e.g., LaHaye and Jenkins 1995) which was planted front and center in the bookstore, and which many congregants seemed to have read. But certain phrases did reverberate through the manuals, the church services, other books, and the transcripts of our interviews. As newcomers became members of the community, these phrases became part of their speech patterns.

The most important phrase was "to walk with God." Sometimes a noun—"my *walk*"—and sometimes a verb—"learning to *walk*"—this phrase describes the daily experience of living your life as this kind of Christian. As the manuals use the term, "to *walk* with God" refers both to learning to develop a relationship with God and to managing the everyday challenges to your faith: temptation, frustration, disappointment. This, for example, is the way one congregant uses the term when she describes her goal for a women's Bible Study group she started with students in Horizon's School of Evangelism, where she works. "It's really just interacting with them so that they can get to a different level of their walk with God" (all quotations are taken from a series of taped interviews conducted in May, 2000; fieldwork spanned a considerably longer period of time). To "walk with God" describes the way you incorporate God into your life, and people accept that there are different degrees of that incorporation, more being better. To "walk with God" also captures something about the sense of the intimacy of God's presence in your daily life. As another congregant said, "To me, well, now that I am walking with the Lord I know that, like, I feel that God talks to me all day long. . . . I just think God's with me all the time."

Another common phrase in the lexicon—and there were many others—is the "Word of God." The phrase refers overtly to the written Bible, but it connotes the loving, personal, and unique relationship congregants believe God has with each individual Christian. One man said, "I went [to church] for several weeks in a row and I heard the Bible and it was addressing me and speaking to me personally. . . . I was realizing that it is a love story, and it's written to me." This is a remarkable claim, the more remarkable in that it was made by a sober man in his forties: that the written Bible, a text which is the same for all who read it (issues of translation aside) was at the same time written uniquely and with love for each of us individually. "The Bible says," he continued, "that the word of God is actually written on the tablets of your heart."

Cognitive/Linguistic Knowledge: Syntax

By *syntax,* I mean an underlying logic that knits together different phrases; syntax organizes the narratives around meaningful phrases like "my walk with God." While by *lexicon,* I mean to denote the new words and phrases which participants begin to use, by *syntax,* I mean to denote the themes of this kind of religious commitment, what one could metaphorically describe as the grammar of this religious life. The sermons at Horizon, along with the books and videos sold by the church, model the kind of people Christians are, what they struggle with and to what end. New congregants are not so much learning a specific, concrete story as they are learning ways to tell a range of stories. Albert Lord (1960) famously distinguished "formula" and "theme" as building blocks for the great stories told by singers of tales, the Homeric bards among them. Such singers, he argued (with Milman Parry), did not memorize and precisely reproduce the thousands of lines of text found in the great epics. Instead, they composed anew each time in what Parry and Lord called the "oral-formulaic" tradition. They became familiar with large and small plots that could be elided or elaborated as the occasion demanded, and they learned to use common phrases associated with the tale. "Rosy-fingered dawn" is a formula, a phrase often evoked to describe the Iliadic morning; the tragedy of Achilles and the deception of the Trojan horse are themes. The new congregant to Horizon becomes familiar with formulaic phrases like "walking with God," and part of what it means to be a Christian is to use those phrases in describing your daily life. Another part of being a good Christian is to become familiar with the themes—the syntactic knowledge—that organize the way the life is understood and experienced.

Horizon's syntactic themes are well represented in its sermons, or "messages." Here is one such sermon, not recorded and transcribed but captured in my notes from the service one morning in May.

> Someone, somewhere, has to start a revolution, the pastor said. The people of this government, they've been to Harvard and Yale, they just passed a law saying that pornography can be shown on television at any time, because it's protected by the freedom of speech. But that's not what free speech is about, he said; we all know that free speech is about having the freedom to criticize the government, not to allow rubbish on television . . .
>
> Remember, he said, that we are the children of God. You ladies [and here the room got very silent], you are the daughters of God. . . . Lift your head out of the gutter. You are noble. . . . [When] you realize this, and you say to God, I'm here in a place full of body odor and bodies, a fleshly material place, and can You please help me, He will help you. Even when you want to pray so badly and you can't really get it out, it's okay because there's a spirit inside of you helping it to come out. And if you are praying and being with Jesus, the devil won't distract you. He'll say, she's got the helmet of righteousness on. She can't be reached. And he'll move on. Because his time is short. Short. And your time is infinite. So don't numb your feeling, don't dull yourself with alcohol and drugs. Feel good. Reach out. Start living. Smell every flower. Live like that, live with God. Be alive. He loves you. (field notes, May 28, 2000)

In a sermon like this, the pastor is teaching a way of thinking about how to live in the world as a Christian: what it is to be a person (you need to be responsible; you are noble, a child of a mighty Lord); what the world is like (full of rubbish, full of people who have been to Harvard and Yale but can't see what's morally obvious, a place of bodies and odors); who God is (He's responsible, He's pure, He loves you); and why a Christian person needs God (to keep you pure, to give you armor for protection from the devil, to help you be fully alive). Interwoven with these more general spiritual themes are some remarkably concrete politics. It is also worth noting that a good Christian might "want to pray so badly and you can't really get it out." These Christians expect that prayer does not come easily and naturally. It is a skill that must be learned, as a relationship to God must also be learned. That is part of the logic of the faith.

Cognitive/Linguistic Knowledge: Conversion Narrative

While congregants learn specific phrases to depict their new religiosity and thematic plots to describe God's human world, they also learn a specific personal narrative to depict their own entry into committed evangelical Christianity. This narrative form stands out from these other kinds of narratives, like the sermon above. It is both more personal and more stereotyped. This combination of the very personal and the stereotyped is hardly unique to evangelical Christians. The anthropologist Christopher Crocker (1985) describes the recruitment of Bororo shamans as exhibiting a similar combination of cultural expectations (everyone knows that the shaman-to-be must see a stump or anthill or stone move suddenly in the forest; catch a small wild game animal like a wild turkey; dream of attempted seduction; and so forth) and intensely personal experience. "Their details and sequences are standardized almost to the point of collective representations, known by most adult non-shamans. Yet the shamans I knew best spoke of them with vivid sincerity, adding variations and personal reactions at once idiosyncratic and consistent with the general pattern" (1985: 206; see also Crapanzano 2001: 102ff).

In these accounts, congregants said that they knew God, or knew about God, in an abstract way or as children; then they had a wild ride through drugs, sex, alcohol, and depravity; they hit bottom; they realized that their life was empty, unsatisfying, and unfulfilled. They accepted Christ (often as a result of coming to a Bible-believing church on a whim) and were filled with love, acceptance, and forgiveness. A male congregant, who worked in construction for Horizon, told us that he grew up in a house without religion, although he knew the commandments and that "there was someone I was accountable to, and that was God." By the time he was thirteen, he had already experimented around and realized that "it all amounted to emptiness." He continued to lark around. The sense of emptiness, he said, "really hit when I was 38." He tried drugs, what he called "Buddhism," existentialism, one romance after another but never apparently a Christian church. "I had tried everything and, because of drugs, lost everything. I lost my business, lost my place, lost my hope. Absolutely rock bottom." Homeless, he moved in with friends, and someone invited him to Horizon. When he went, he said, "I just knew it. Without a doubt." Eight of the ten people we interviewed formally gave us some version of this story of self-destruction, despair, and redemption.

Should we trust these stories? If accurate, they are an alarming glimpse into the U.S. (or at least, Californian) experience. It is possible that some congregants at Horizon learn, like Augustine, to stretch their little sins until they become an abyss of wickedness. It is also possible that a church like Horizon offers the structure to enable an addict to abandon his addiction, just as the fast-growing Pentecostal church offers women a tool with which to detach their men from drink (e.g., Brusco 1995). In any event, the message of the narrative is clear: I was lost, so deeply lost, so lost that no one could love me—and then God did, and I was found.

Metakinesis

I use the term *metakinesis* to refer to mind–body states that are both identified within the group as the way of recognizing God's personal presence in your life and are subjectively and idiosyncratically experienced. These states, or phenomena, are lexically identified, and indeed, the process of learning to have these experiences cannot be neatly disentangled from the process of learning the words to describe them. A congregant must use language to describe, and thus to recognize, the moment of experiencing the state. Yet congregants do not use the phrases the way they use phrases like "my walk with God," which is used to denote a general orientation toward life. In identifying metakinetic states, congregants identify—and thus psychologically organize—bodily phenomena that seem new and distinctive to them, which they come to interpret in ways which are congruent with the group's understanding of evidence of God's real reality in their lives. They seem to be engaging a variety of bodily processes that are integrated in new ways and synthesized into a new understanding of their bodies and the world. Some of these processes could be called "dissociative," in which attentional focus is narrowed and manipulated to produce noticeable shifts in conscious awareness, so that individuals feel that they are floating or not in control of their bodies. Others involve sensory hallucinations, where people see or hear things that observers do not. There are specific and dramatic mood elevations, in which individuals are self-consciously and noticeably happier for extended periods of time. As a result of these phenomena, congregants literally perceive the world differently and they attribute that difference to the presence of God.

Horizon and the Calvary Chapel movement, more generally, do not place doctrinal or ritual emphasis on what Christians often call the "gifts of the Holy Spirit" (see Robbins 2004). No one speaks in tongues in public ritual, and spiritual authority is understood to rest in the Bible, not in private experience. Yet the singular point of the services, sermons, Bible study groups and prayer manuals, repeated with such maddening insistence that it becomes the texture of the religious life, is that one should build a personal relationship to God through prayer. *Prayer* is a commonplace word, tinged with the mystery of the sacred but ordinary in a way that words like meditation, visualization, and trance are not. And still the act of prayer demands that we focus our attention inward and resist distractions. Most of us remember the prayer of childhood service. I would bow my head, and my mind would wander to my dress's scratchy collar and what I would do that afternoon. In mainstream Christian and Jewish services, that is what prayer often is: a dutiful, closed-eyed silence while the leader intones, followed by a period of quiet in which it is all too easy to remember items you need to add to the shopping list. Horizon sets out to change those habits by modeling a relationship to God as the point of life—and incidentally, of going to church—and modeling prayer as the practice on which that relationship is built. And with this emphasis, prayer becomes the conduit of anomalous psychological experience it was for the nineteenth-century reformers, the medieval ecstatics, and the early pastoralists who sought to be still and hear the voice of God.

The taught structure of this prayer is deceptively dull: Prayer is about talking with God. But the taught practice asks the congregant to turn inwardly with great emotional attention. In the service, in the early period of worship before the pastor speaks, people start singing songs to God—songs *to* God, not *about* God. People shut their eyes, hold out their hands, and sway back and forth, singing of how much they love Him and yearn for Him. Some will have tears on their cheeks. Then the music will fade, and congregants will remain standing, eyes shut, deeply absorbed in their thoughts. Sometimes the bandleader will pray out loud here, softly describing "how much we seek to glorify You in our hearts." Prayer, says a popular manual, is a yearning for God (Burnham 2002). That private, absorbed yearning is visible on the faces of those who pray here.

There are perhaps a hundred prayer manuals and books about prayer at the Horizon bookstore. These books, the sermons, and home fellowships insistently and repeatedly assert that none of us pray as seriously as we can or should; all urge you to pray more intensely. And despite Horizon's literal interpretation of the Bible and its overt hostility to charismatic phenomena, in fact the practical theology invites the congregant to assume that truth is found inwardly and not from external experts. God is to be found in personal experience, as He speaks to you directly in your prayers and through His text. Pastors hasten to say that anything He says to you in private must be confirmed through His word, but in fact the Bible is learned not as a text to be memorized but as a personal document, written uniquely for each.

This emphasis on prayer has, I believe, two effects. First, it encourages people to attend to the stream of their own consciousness like eager fishermen, scanning for the bubbles and whorls that suggest a lurking catch. And perhaps, because memory is adaptive and perception obliging, they begin to note the discontinuities that are natural to our state and actually to interpret them as discontinuous, rather than smoothing them over with the presumption of a simple integrated self. Second, it demands that people engage in practices that help them to go into trance. *Trance* is an ominous-sounding word, but I mean something relatively straightforward by it: that one can become intensely absorbed in inner sensory stimuli and lose some peripheral awareness (Spiegel and Spiegel 1978). Trance is the consequence of shifting the streetlamp of our focal awareness from the external to the inward. We do this naturally when we daydream, play, or read, and we seem to vary somewhat in our spontaneous ability to ignore the distracting world. But for many, probably most of us, that ability is also a learnable skill. Prayer, as it is taught at Horizon, encourages trance because it focuses the worshipper's attention inward, away from external stimuli, and it can be learned because mental concentration responds to practice (Luhrmann 1989). There are no known bodily markers of a trance state, but as the absorption grows deeper, people become more difficult to distract, and their sense of time and agency begin to shift. They live within their imagination more, whether that be simple mindfulness or elaborate fantasy, and they feel that the experience happens to them, that they are bystanders to their own awareness, more themselves than ever before, or perhaps absent—but invariably different. In addition, trance practice appears to encourage the wide variety of anomalous phenomena (hallucinations, altered states, mystical awareness, and so forth) often called "spiritual" (Roche and McConkey 1990; Tellegen 1981; Tellegen and Atkinson 1974; Luhrmann 1989).

Whether because they pay new attention to their awareness or whether because these new practices alter their conscious experience, all congregants spontaneously associated the process of "getting to know Jesus"—which one does through prayer and reading the Bible—with occasional experiences which involved heightened emotions and unusual sensory and perceptual experiences—and which they identified, labeled, and discussed.

One of the less dramatic of these metakinetic states was "falling in love with Jesus." People said that you could tell when someone was a newly committed Christian because they got "this goopy look" on their face when you asked them if they loved Jesus. They repeatedly spoke of Christ as their lover or their greatest love and described this love in physical terms. Even the men did so, although for them He was more buddy than boyfriend. When I asked John (a construction worker) whether the phrase "falling in love with Jesus" made sense to him, he said "Absolutely . . . the closer you get the more of his love you feel and it is undeniable. You become flooded. You become absolutely radiant." Is that different from falling in love with a woman? "He will never disappoint me. He will never let me down. He'll tell me the absolute truth, and He will never push me. He will never force me to do anything. He will always encourage. Granted, he's perfect."

"Falling in love with Jesus" is an emotional state, not a general way of being in the world, as "walking with the Lord" denotes. People spoke about this experience as if it were indeed the intense love of early adolescence, with the confidence that the beloved truly is perfect and that his perfection is a kind of miraculous confirmation of one's self. You were not necessarily in prayer when you felt it, but it emerged through the process of establishing a relationship through prayer. One woman compared her relationship with God "to a relationship with the man of my dreams." Another spoke for an hour about her love of God and ended our interview by talking about people who might tell her that God was selfish to want her exclusive love. "And you know what? They're right. They are right. He wants to be loved." Falling in love with the Lord was a giggly, euphoric experience—a breathless, wonderful high. Because of this, it could also be seen as merely the first step on the road to true Christianity. A pastor spoke scoffingly to us about people who had fallen in love with Christ but didn't realize that there were rules and responsibilities to being Christian. He went on to compare the experience of being a true Christian to being married: Sure, you fell giddy in love and there was all the romance, but you had to get past that and do the dishes and pay for the car.

Then there was "peace"—the "peace of God that passeth understanding." Like "falling in love with Jesus," *peace* had a bodily quality and was treated as an emotional state or a mood. People often spoke of this peace as something God gave to them. They felt sad for those who did not feel it, and often used the word in the context of turning responsibility for some decision they needed to make over to God, with a kind of relief that He would make the decision. These emotional states were clearly understood as the result of creating a relationship with God through prayer. "Falling in love" was the first phase of that relationship; what one evangelical writer describes as the "first love" years (Curtis and Eldredge 1997: 30). A person "new in Christ" may experience "peace" immediately, but it is also associated with mature Christian faith. Peace is the result of the engagement of the yearning, sometimes anguished spirit; the true prayer may begin in pain but it ends in peace. Peace is the sense of being spiritually heard and emotionally met, of being calmed through the act of relating to God. While the concept and its evocation are shared by all Christian traditions, at Horizon the word was likely to be used to evoke the shape of a feeling, rather than a political goal. One man said, "I almost stopped [on his way down to the altar during an alter call] but I felt peace, so I went forward."

In addition to these emotional phenomena, nearly half of the congregants also report a variety of what a psychologist would call sensory hallucinations—phenomena of thought, not mood. These are not everyday events for these Christians. They are not, however, as rare as one might think even in the wider population. Many people (in the United States, roughly one in ten; see Bentall 2000) literally hear an apparently hallucinated external voice at least once, and for most of them, this is not a symptom of illness. The congregants do seem to experience hallucinations: individuals were very clear about the difference between hearing God's voice "inside" and "outside" their heads. One congregant, making that distinction, remarked, "There are rare times when I hear a definite voice, but . . . it's hard to explain. Like just a small tiny push or something, like a thought in your mind." It is possible that the trance-like practice of prayer may evoke such hallucinations: that would be in accord with what we know scientifically about the relationship of concentration practices and anomalous experience (e.g., Luhrmann 1989; Cardena et al. 2000). Whether their prayer induces such phenomena or not, individuals do seem to learn to pay attention to the fragmentary chaos of conscious awareness in a new way. To some extent, we impose coherence on our conscious experience retrospectively (Gergen 1991; Kunzendorf and Wallace 2000). These congregants learn to identify and highlight these moments of discontinuity, and they come to understand those moments as signs of God's presence in their lives.

Sometimes the term *Holy Spirit* is used to indicate such moments, although that term is also used more broadly than to describe hallucinations. But even moments too trivial to be glorified as the Holy Spirit are reported and associated with God nonetheless. A man who served as one of the many associate pastors called them "these quirky things that happen that there is no scriptural support for. Every person I talk to," he continued, "has some oddball supernatural experience that sounds crazy, unless you're a Christian." The story that prompted his comment was this:

> I'm pretty much a new believer at this point and I'm driving and I hear the evangelist say on the tape, "Dennis, slow down. You are going too fast." It certainly wasn't something on the tape; it was something I heard. So, I slowed down and immediately a cop passed me and pulled over another guy who was also speeding, in front of me. I thought, God is really doing something here.

Congregants also reported tactile sensations, as this woman did when I asked her how she sensed God:

> One time I was praying for this woman who had dated this guy who was into this Satan worship and she felt like there were demons in her. We were praying for her and stuff and I felt like there was a hand on my head. . . . And sometimes I just feel when I'm driving along, sometimes I can feel it on my body and sometimes it's just more inside. He is just such a comfort to me, and it's just so great.

Again, what a psychologist would call "sensory hallucinations" are not everyday events for these Christians, but they are clearly significant, meaningful enough for nearly half of our interviewees to bring up in a comparatively short formal interview and common in many evangelical accounts of prayer and divine relationship (e.g., Burnham 2002; Curtis and Eldredge 1997).

Other moments are more complexly constructed. Answering the altar call is described by many congregants as an emotionally overpowering experience accompanied by a conscious loss of bodily control. Congregants remember that God took over their body (this can be described as submission to God's will) and carried or pushed them up to the altar. One said that "it was like someone had lifted me up out of my seat and I pretty much ran down there. I was walking real fast down there. It was like it wasn't me; it was kind of like he was pushing me up there. It was kind of cool. And I was just crying. . . . I was weeping. I was crying so much. I was so happy." These memories recall moments which are both bodily and profoundly emotional, which stand out sharply from everyday experience, which are identifiable by bodily sensations, and which for those who experience them mark God's spiritual reality in their lives.

Relational Practice

At Horizon, the goal of worship is to develop a relationship with God. Developing that relationship is explicitly presented as the process of getting to know a person who is distinct, external, and opaque, and whom you need to get to know in the ordinary way. "Acquaint thyself with God," says a classic evangelical guide; "God is a Person and He can be known in increasing degrees of intimate acquaintance" (Tozzer 1961: 116). This is a remarkable characterization, the more so at Horizon because the intimacy is modeled so concretely. God is not only first principle, an awesome, distant judge, a mighty force, although congregants quickly say God is these as well. Nor is He only *spouse,* a formal term. He is *boyfriend* (for women), *buddy* (for men), and *close friend* and *pal* (for both). Several congregants explained the process of developing a relationship with God by asking me whether I had a boyfriend. Congregants describe God and Jesus as people you need to meet personally, as if you were out for coffee and had to figure out what the person across the table from you really meant. As one congregant said, "It's just like any relationship. If I had a best friend and we never hung out, where would our friendship be?" Another remarked: "The closer you get to a human being, the better you can get to know them. It's the same with Jesus, the more time I spend reading the Bible, the more time I spend praying, the closer I get to Him and the better I get to know Him."

As that congregant suggests, the two practices thought to create that relationship are Bible reading and prayer. They are taught as two sides of a personal conversation: The worshipper speaks to God through prayer and receives His answer through His Word. But the printed text of the Bible is the same for all, of course. A congregant's relationship with God is supposed to be unique, private, and personal; he or she is meant to understand that this common text is a "love story . . . written to me," as the congregant put it. What seems to enable congregants to experience this personalization of a common text is their ability to identify their own bodily reactions as indicating God's responsiveness as they read the Bible, and as they pray.

At Horizon reading the Bible is modeled as an interactive process, a way to know God better and to learn what he has to say specifically to you in this love letter that he has written. God is understood to be communicating when, as one congregant put it, "a verse just jumps out at me," or when you have a powerful bodily feeling—you feel peace, or intense joy, or suddenly you feel very tired as if a burden has been lifted and now you can sleep. Another congregant told this story:

> All of a sudden I was in the Book of Isaiah. . . . I felt that the Spirit was leading me. . . . I started reading about what the chosen fast was, which was to break the bonds of wickedness. And something about it made me think about my family members and how I wanted to pray for my family members. Like that was the answer for me. I really felt that God brought me to that Scripture and that this is where I need to be. . . . It was just such an amazing thing. It was like 2 o'clock in the morning, and I remember reading it wide awake, and as soon as I read that it was a relief, and then I felt really sleepy. It was comforting. And so that's an example of how I think God speaks to me through the Word.

She knows that God "speaks" to her because she feels different when she reads a particular scripture: that scripture then becomes what he "says" specifically to her.

Metakinetic states—when God gives you peace, speaks to you outside your head, when you feel that he carries you down to the altar—give a kind of real reality to God because they create the experience of social exchange between opaque individuals, between individuals who cannot read each other's minds and must exchange goods or words in order to become real to each other, in order to know each other's intentions. Adam, then a college undergraduate, told a story about how he did not understand what a pastor was talking about when he spoke of being filled with the Holy Spirit. Then he went on a trip to Acapulco with his friends and got high (as was his wont).

> And this night I was laying on the bed over to the side and all these guys were talking and stuff and I was quiet. I hadn't said a word in like over an hour because I was communing with Him again, and He was telling me all these things. . . . Usually when I'm high I'm kind of tingling and stuff, but this time I felt a wave going through me, though all my body. . . . I felt like I was floating. I was like, *dude*. . . . Overwhelmingly I knew that it was Him and He said, this is Me, filling you up. For the first time it was like I was being filled with the Holy Spirit and I knew what that meant because I was filled with it and I was floating.

He was, of course, high. But at that time, he was often high. He experienced this high as different, as identifiable through bodily sensations, and as proof of God's spiritual presence in his life.

Congregants seem to use more dramatic experiences as a model for their experience of everyday interaction. Later in the conversation, Adam went on to describe the way he experienced prayer on a daily basis: "When we worship we sing songs and I just close my eyes and it's like I'm talking to Him again and communing with Him. *It's the same experience I had in . . . Acapulco*. It's like me and Him talking. He knows me, He knows my name, and we just talk back and forth. . . . It's so cool" (emphasis added). It was not, of course, the same experience: Adam only felt the body wave once. But he uses that dramatic initial experience as his mnemonic marker for his ongoing experience of his relationship with God.

Dramatic experiences like hallucinations do not, in fact, seem to be nearly as central to the process of building that on-going relationship as metakinetic states like "peace" and emotional responses that congregants come to interpret as God's participation in a daily personal dialogue with them. People say that you learn to know God by having a relationship with Him through His text, and part of that involves just getting to know the kind of "person" He is. Texts and sermons constantly discuss some Biblical passage and ask how God is reacting and why. "How is God feeling at this point?" a book asks when describing the Eden story (Curtis and Eldredge 1997: 79). People read Biblical passages over and over, noting their thoughts about particular verses, or what others have said about them. Bibles are accreted with the personal history of reading; the typical congregant's Bible is stuffed with notes and post-its, its pages marked up in different colors and papers from past meetings stick out from the unbound sides. But a significant part of developing that relationship with God is learning to *feel* God actually interacting, and that demands that worshippers pay attention to their own bodily states as they read, as memories of previous readings wash over them, as they think about the associations of particular verses for their lives, and to use those experiences to build a model of who God is for them in their relationship with Him. A guide for Bible Study begins with this how-to advice: "This Bible Study has been created to help you search the Scriptures and draw closer to God as you seek to understand, experience and reflect his grace. . . . Before you begin each chapter, pray for attentiveness to how God is speaking to you through His Word and for sensitivity to His prompting" (Heald 1998: v).

Adam describes his on-going relationship with God here:

> I wake up in the morning and I thank Him for nothing bad happening throughout the night because you never know what can happen. I thank him for letting me sleep well and I ask that he blesses my day, that it will go okay, and I'm not hurt, and whatever He wants me to learn that day I'll learn. When I talk to Him, He's always listening. He doesn't talk to me verbally like, "Adam, this is God." It's more like a feeling I get inside of me that I know He is listening. Or when I go to bed at night . . . I'll read some scripture. Like now I'm studying Acts. . . . I'll pray that he opens my heart so that I can kind of be transported back into that time so it makes sense to me. . . . By reading the Bible, that's His Word. That's where He talks to you.

Adam knows from "more of a feeling I get" that God is listening. He is used to that feeling. From his personal history, he has many memories of prayers where he spoke to God and felt familiar emotions that made him confident that God was listening and answering. Adam develops through this a comforting familiarity with who God is in the relationship and who he, Adam, is in that relationship. And Adam experiences that relationship as intimate and good.

This is a viscerally intimate God, a God who cares about your haircut, counsels you on dates, and sits at your side in church. One congregant talked about the fact that God speaks to her through His word on the page, but He also interacts in a more personal manner, when He "puts a thought" into her mind. Then she talks to Him the way she talks to anyone—just more intimately. "Sometimes I feel a real closeness to Jesus . . . I just talk to Jesus through the day." As another congregant said, "You start to know the fulfillment and comforting feeling that God gives you. Sometimes, sitting in church, I have this overwhelming feeling that God is speaking to me and sitting right there with me. . . . It's just so much peace." A congregant I call Alexis said that at first it was a great struggle for her to pray. She couldn't bring herself to kneel. She still can't. But now, prayer is easy for her. I can see from the way she prays that she has learned to interpret God's presence through her own bodily experience and she has,

I think, learned to integrate that awareness of an external being with her ideas about who she is and who God is within the relationship. And for her, that relationship is real. She did not, she said, ask the Lord whether she should paint her toenails. Then she seemed to hesitate, as if she wondered whether she wouldn't. She experienced Him as a person deeply involved in her everyday life, like a husband. And that, she knew, was amazing. "It's a very humbling experience, because you're talking to the Creator, and you're an ant. . . . You know, He created the human race so that He could have fellowship and He could have a relationship with us. It's almost like—I wonder whether he's lonely, or was lonely. . . . It just kind of blows my mind."

Discussion

Why now? What is it about late-twentieth-century U.S. life that has led people to search out psychologically anomalous experiences and to use them metakinetically to build a relationship with God? Two tentative explanations present themselves.

The first is the rise of television and modern media. The literary scholar Mark Hansen (2000) points out that the radical technological innovations of our time have fundamentally altered the conditions of our perception. Technology, he argues, changes the very way we experience with our bodies. Television, the virtual reality of the Internet, and the all encompassing world of music we can create around us seem clearly to be techniques that enhance the experience of absorption, the experience of being caught up in fantasy and distracted from an outer world. We play music to create the shell in which we work or to soothe ourselves from a daily grind. We put on headphones on buses and subways specifically to create a different subjective reality from the frazzled one that sways around us. We park our children in front of videos that they will be absorbed into their own little universes, and we can cook or clean around them undisturbed. A classic book on trance says that "the trance experience is often best explained . . . as being very much like being absorbed in a good novel: one loses awareness of noises and distractions in the immediate environment and, when the novel is finished, requires a moment of reorientation to the surrounding world" (Spiegel and Spiegel 1978: 23). Not all people have that experience of absorption in a good book, and even for those that do it may not be that often. Television, with its gripping images and mood-setting music now provides that experience every night and for hours each day.

The second is what one might call the attenuation of the U.S. relationship. This is a controversial issue, but a great deal of sociological data suggests that the U.S. experience of relationship is thinner and weaker than in the middle of our last century. Robert Putnam's (2000) massive analysis of the decline of civic engagement in the United States argues powerfully that U.S. citizens have become increasingly disconnected from friends, family, and neighbors through both formal and informal structures. Union membership has declined since the 1950s. PTA membership has plummeted. Fewer people vote in presidential elections (except in the south). And with data collected since 1975, one can see that people have friends to dinner less often (and they go out with them no more often): "The practice of entertaining friends has not simply moved outside the house, but seems to be vanishing entirely" (Putnam 2000: 100). Time diary studies suggest that informal socializing has declined markedly. Between 1976 and 1997, family vacations (with children between eight and seventeen) nose-dived as a family practice, as did "just sitting and talking" together as a family (Putnam 2000: 101). Even the "family dinner" is noticeably in decline.

Putnam uses this data to argue that social capital is on the wane in the late-twentieth- and early-twenty-first-century United States. It also suggests, however, that U.S. citizens might feel more lonely. They are certainly more isolated. More Americans live alone now than ever before: 25 percent of them compared to 8 percent in 1940 and none in our so-called ancestral environment (Wright 1995). It is possible that this increased isolation contributes to a putative increase in mood disorders (Wright 1995), as isolation is a leading risk factor for depression. Isolation certainly increases morbidity and mortality (Cacioppo and Hawkley 2003).

What may be happening is that these congregants and others like them are using an ease with trance-like phenomena supported by our strange new absorbing media and using it to build an intensely intimate relationship with God to protect them against the isolation of modern social life. After all, the most striking consequence of these new religious practices is the closely held sense of a personal relationship with God, and this God is always there, always listening, always responsive, and always with you. In this evangelical setting, congregants learn to use their own bodies to create a sense of the reality of someone external to them. That learning process is complex and subtle: it involves developing a cognitive model of who the person is in the relationship; a metakinetic responsiveness which can be interpreted as the presence of another being; and many repetitions of apparent dialogue through which a person develops an imagined sense of participation and exchange. And the experience of faith for these Christians is a process through which the loneliest of conscious creatures comes to experience themselves as in a world awash with love. It is a remarkable achievement. In the end, Harding's (2000) question—how does the supernatural become real, known, experienced and absolutely irrefutable?—is the deepest question we ask of faith.

Acknowledgments

It is a great pleasure to thank Jennifer Cole, Joel Robbins, and Richard Saller for their comments on an earlier draft of this manuscript. Thanks also are due the University of Chicago's active Interdisciplinary Christianities workshop for a lively and productive meeting on the paper.

Questions for Further Discussion

How is the experience of evangelical Christians, described in this article, similar to other spiritual experiences, both within and outside of Christianity, with which you are familiar? How is it different? Try to place these similarities and differences in cultural context; that is, what encourages religious adherents to become totally committed to the reality of their beliefs?

References

Ammerman, Nancy. 1987. *Bible believers*. New Brunswick: Rutgers University Press.

Bentall, Richard. 2000. Hallucinatory experiences. In Etzel Cardena, Steven Lynn, and Stanley Krippner, eds, *Varieties of anomalous experience,* 85–120. Washington, DC: American Psychological Association.

Bickel, Bruce, and Stan Jantz. 1997. *Bruce and Stan's guide to God*. Eugene, Oregon: Harvest House.

Boddy, Janet. 1989. *Wombs and alien spirits*. Madison: University of Wisconsin Press.

Brusco, Elizabeth. 1995. *The reformation of machismo: evangelical conversion and gender in Colombia.* Austin: University of Texas.

Burnham, Sophy. 2002. *The path of prayer*. New York: Viking Compass.

Cacioppo, John, and Louise Hawkley. 2003. Social isolation and health, with an emphasis on underlying mechanisms. *Perspectives in biology and medicine* 46 (supplement 3): 39–52.

Cardena, Etzel, Steven Lynn, and Stanley Krippner, eds. 2000. *Varieties of anomalous experience.* Washington, DC: American Psychological Association.

Crapanzano, Vincent. 2001. *Serving the Word*. New York: New Press.

Crocker, Christopher. 1985. *Vital souls*. Tucson: University of Arizona.

Csordas, Thomas. 1994. *Sacred self*. Berkeley: University of California Press.

Curtis, Brent, and John Eldredge. 1997. *The sacred romance*. Nashville: Nelson.

Desjarlais, Robert. 1992. *Body and emotion*. Philadelphia, PA: University of Pennsylvania.

Fogel, Robert. 2000. *The Fourth Great Awakening and the future of egalitarianism.* Chicago: University of Chicago Press.

Gallup, George, and D. Michael Lindsay. 1999. *Surveying the religious landscape.* Harrisburg, PA: Morehouse Publishing.

Gergen, Kenneth. 1991. *The saturated self*. New York: Basic.

Hansen, Mark. 2000. *Embodying technesis: technology beyond writing.* Ann Arbor: University of Michigan Press.

Harding, Susan. 2000. *The Book of Jerry Falwell*. Princeton: Princeton University Press.

Heald, Cynthia. 1998. *Becoming a woman of grace*. Nashville, TN: Thomas Nelson.

Kamenetz, Rodger. 1997. Unorthodox Jews rummage through the Orthodox tradition. *New York Times Magazine,* December 7: 84–86.

Keane, Webb. 1997. Religious language. *Annual reviews in anthropology* 26: 47–71.

Kunzendorf, Robert, and Benjamin Wallace, eds. 2000. *Individual differences in conscious experience.* Philadelphia: J. Benjamins.

Lambek, Michael. 1981. *Human spirits*. Cambridge: University of Cambridge Press.

LaHaye, Tim and Jerry Jenkins. 1995. *Left behind: a novel of the Earth's last days*. Wheaton, Il: Tyndale House Publishers.

Lester, Rebecca. Forthcoming. *My name is Jerusalem*. Berkeley: University of California.

Lord, Albert B. 1960. *The Singer of Tales*. Cambridge: Harvard University Press.

Luhrmann, Tanya Marie. 1989. *Persuasions of the witch's craft*. Cambridge: Harvard University Press.

Mahmood, Saba. 2001. Rehearsed spontaneity and the conventionality of ritual: Disciplines of Salal. *American Ethnologist* 28(4): 827–853.

Martin, John. 1983. Dance as a means of communication. In R. Copeland and M. Cohen, eds, *What is dance?* 22–27. New York: Oxford University Press.

Miller, Donald. 1997. *Reinventing American Protestantism*. Berkeley: University of California Press.

Mitchell, J. 1997. A moment with Christ: the importance of feelings in the analysis of belief. *Journal of the Royal Anthropological Society* (n.s.) 3(1): 79–94.

Ostling, Richard. 1993. The Church search. *Time*, April 5: 44–49.

Putnam, Robert. 2000. *Bowling alone*. New York: Simon and Schuster.

Rambo, Lewis. 1993. *Understanding religious conversion*. New Haven, CT: Yale University Press.

Robbins, Joel. 2004. Globalization of Pentecostal and Charismatic Christianity. *Annual Review of Christianity* 33: 117–143.

Roche, Suzanne, and Kevin McConkey. 1990. Absorption: nature, assessment and correlates. *Journal of personality and social psychology* 59: 91–101.

Roof, Wade Clark. 1993. *A generation of seekers*. San Francisco: HarperCollins.

Spiegel, David, and Herbert Spiegel. 1978. *Trance and treatment*. Washington, DC: American Psychiatric Press.

Tellegen, Auke. 1981. Practicing the two disciplines for relation and enlightenment: Comment on "Role of the feedback signal in electromyography biofeedback—the relevance of attention." *Journal of experimental psychology: General* 100: 217–226.

Tellegen, Auke, and G. Atkinson. 1974. Openness to absorbing and self-altering experiences ("absorption"): a trait related to hypnotic susceptibility. *Journal of Abnormal Psychology* 83: 268–277.

Tozzer, Aiden Wilson. 1961. *The knowledge of the Holy*. San Francisco: Harper San Francisco.

Whitehead, Harriet. 1987. *Renunciation and reformulation*. Ithaca: Cornell University Press.

Wright, Robert. 1995. The evolution of despair. *Time,* August 28: 50–57.

Wuthnow, Robert. 1988. *The restructuring of American religion*. Princeton, New Jersey: Princeton University Press.

———. 1994. *Sharing the journey*. New York: The Free Press.

———. 1998. *After Heaven*. Berkeley: University of California Press.

5

Paradise is for Pussies: Star Trek *and the Myth of the Bad Mother*

Clare L. Boulanger
Mesa State College

In his famous article on the Nacirema, Miner implies that Americans are reluctant to consider themselves in the same terms they freely apply to others. For instance, we expect that such peoples as the Utes or the Yanomami adhere to myths, but in our own society the word "myth" has come to refer to something that is patently untrue. We believe we labor to dispel *myths, not abide by them. This line of thinking takes us away from the anthropological meaning of myth, which, as Middleton put it, is: "a statement about society and man's place in it and the surrounding universe" (1967: x). From this vantage point, it is clear that if we look for myth only in the guise of sacred text (which Americans do* not *generally call "myth"), we will fail to comprehend one of the primary means through which the vital process of enculturation—the learning of one's own culture—is accomplished.*

As a graduate student in anthropology, Clare L. Boulanger pursued a concentration in American Studies and wrote her M.A. papers from two ethnographic projects carried out in the United States, the first on political decision-making in Vermont, the second on class symbolism in western Massachusetts. While she went on to conduct her dissertation research in Malaysia, a country that remains her primary geographical focus, she continues to have an interest in Americanist work. In the article below she hopes to justify her lifelong dedication to Star Trek *through a (mostly) serious anthropological treatment of the series. Currently she is a professor of anthropology at Mesa State College in western Colorado.*

An earlier version of this paper, "The United States and the Power of Myth," was read at the 102nd Annual Meeting of the American Anthropological Association in November of 2003. An abridged version of the conference paper was published in the FOSAP Newsletter (Bulletin of the Federation of Small Anthropology Programs) *11, 2 (Fall 2004): 15–17.*

The great anthropologist Clifford Geertz (1973: 448) famously assayed the cockfight among the Balinese as "a story they tell themselves about themselves." "Stories we tell ourselves about ourselves" is an apt definition for the term "myth," and many scholars have taken up the phrase in this capacity. However, it should be remembered that for Geertz, culture itself was "an ensemble of texts" (1973: 452), and hence all cultural phenomena, not merely those we recognize as myth, could be "read" to gather the sort of meaning one might receive from a story.

This principle can be helpful in fashioning an anthropological understanding of a people I call "Usans," after the abbreviated name of their country. Formerly, anthropologists referred to this group as the Nacirema, although Usans tend to refer to themselves as Americans. Since "American" could rightfully be applied to the denizens of all the countries in the Americas, for Usans to reserve "American" strictly for themselves would seem somewhat audacious. It should be mentioned, however, that Usans have been prone, historically, to audacious behavior and that such peoples as the Canadians and Mexicans may just as soon cede any claim to "American" to avoid being identified with Usans.

There is much to be read, following Geertz, in Usan culture. Montague and Morais (1976), for instance, subjected the game Usans call football to the same sort of treatment meted out to the Balinese cockfight. At first glance, games would not seem to have much in common with myth. If football is a story Usans tell themselves about themselves, the story would seem to have countless variations, as no two matches are alike in terms of who does what and how the points are scored. But Montague and Morais note that beyond the details of each match, the game does in fact tell a story, over and over again, and it is a success story. Usans can gain from football the conviction that self-sacrifice is necessary for a team to function effectively and that teamwork eventually reaps rewards. Since this conclusion is not so easily reached when one performs what seems to be a minor task for a large corporation, what transpires on the football field, like any good ritual, renders the point obvious. Diligence in the office cubicle is bound to serve some greater end, even if it is not readily discernible on the level of the individual.

Usan society is steeped in mythology of this sort, no less so than any other society and perhaps more so, given the plethora of channels—radio, television, billboard, World Wide Web, church pulpit, classroom, and so on—through which it can be disseminated. What emerges is a huge and disorderly mythological corpus, but the latter condition does not solely result from the former. Mythology, like culture itself, is often contested, and a myth may be less a charter for right behavior, *à la* Malinowski (1926), than a battleground where oppositional elements are unmasked and forced to fight. In the same article in which they describe Usan football, Montague and Morais offer as counterpoint a second icon of the era—the rock star. While the football player is self-sacrificing, the rock star is self-indulgent, but each attains success in Usan society. The larger issue is that every society wrestles to establish an appropriate balance between the group and the individual, and no society resolves the matter absolutely. Rather, myths can clarify that such a struggle exists and stake out the end-points of a continuum within which actual human conduct is continually adjusted relative to what often can be portrayed as a common goal despite the disparate means used to attain it.

Individuals within societies also vary a good deal as to the extent they invest belief in mythology. Most Usans are aware that George Washington never chopped down a cherry tree, but they appreciate the moral of the story nonetheless. Many Usans believe in the Bible, but not necessarily literally in all instances—they may doubt, for example, that there was ever an Adam and Eve or a worldwide flood. Still, they take to heart what they see as the lessons of the Bible without necessarily taking the Bible at its word. Other myths have become part of what Bourdieu has termed the "habitus" (featured in, e.g., Bourdieu 1977). They are so firmly embedded in our consciousness that we are barely aware of their existence, even though they may guide what we think and do. Only an irritant like an anthropologist, whose discipline demands a degree of personal dislocation from the habitus, may occasionally be able to dislodge others as well, hopefully to worthwhile effect.

My favorite Usan tale of this sort is what I call "The Myth of the Bad Mother," which I introduce in my course on Usan culture under the rubric, "Manifest Destiny—It's a Guy Thing." As these titles indicate, the Bad Mother myth is overtly about gender. The Bad Mother stands in contrast to the Good Mother, who expeditiously individuates her child. The Bad Mother, however, refuses to release him (masculine pronoun intended) to become his own person. She may keep him shrouded in infancy, and/or she may feminize him, jealously preventing him from attaining his rightful manhood by misdirecting him toward inappropriate pursuits. The climax of any retelling of the Bad Mother myth is when the hero breaks away from his mother's stifling influence and becomes productive not only on his own account but on behalf of others beyond his immediate kin (Figure 1).

Like so many Usan phenomena, as Linton (1937) elegantly pointed out many years ago, the Myth of the Bad Mother has its origins elsewhere. Indeed, it seems to reach into the most ancient strata of Indo-European thought. For example, in one version of his life story, the Greek hero Heracles undergoes a period where he is taken in by Queen Omphale (whose name refers to the umbilical connection). He dresses as a woman and does women's work until such time as he realizes he must resume his adventures. Similarly, Odysseus is distracted from his voyage home by the nymph Calypso, who detains him in a womblike cave. Gilmore (1990: 39) reminds us of the German legend of Tannhäuser, who escapes the indulgent care of Venus to return to noble, manly battle. But the retelling that addresses most specifically the notion of masculinity as it has been celebrated in our society is that of the master mythographer Sigmund Freud, in, among other sources, *Civilization and Its Discontents* (1961). According to Freud, there is nothing the (male) infant desires more than cathexis with a love object, that is, his mother, at least in the earliest stage of his life. For the sake of civilization, however, it is imperative this desire remain unfulfilled. This is because the dyad of mother-and-infant is a sterile one; it is only when the infant is thwarted in his quest to unite with the love object that he learns to channel his productive energies outward, toward the needs of society. Hence civilization is tragically but necessarily founded on the defeat of this most basic form of self-gratification, and only a Bad Mother would interfere with such an essential process.

The Bad Mother mythic formula is central to the plot lines of many classic Usan books and films. The renowned WWII romance *Casablanca,* for example, can be "read" thus. Rick, an able-bodied and intelligent expatriated American, could be contributing substantially to the war effort but instead languishes in Morocco, running a seedy café. Any greater ambitions on Rick's part are scuttled by the memories of a love affair from which he has never fully recovered. His love object is Ilsa, a Bad Mother who haunts him because she has not been effectively rejected. Circumstances conspire to bring Ilsa back into his life, thus

FIGURE 1   The Myth of the Bad Mother.

giving Rick a second opportunity to win his freedom, but not before it seems he might once again succumb to the blandishments of cathexis. In the long run, however, he manages to shake off his ill-starred attraction and nobly restores Ilsa to her husband's side. Only then is Rick able to undertake his own manly share of battle, and the conclusion to the film implies that he, in concert with his (male) partner-in-crime, will go on to frustrate many a Fascist design.

Like all myths, the Myth of the Bad Mother is subject to variation. The Bad Mother, for instance, is not always represented as female or even as feminine, though the effect she has on her victim remains the same. Mind-altering substances, machines, and socialist systems of government have also been cast in the role of the Bad Mother, depriving men of their individuated masculinity. Beyond Freud's belief that rejection of the love object is a key component in the making of civilization, in some media products civilization is depicted as *over*elaborated, and hence itself takes on the qualities of a Bad Mother. In *One Flew Over the Cuckoo's Nest,* for instance, McMurphy and his asylum mates are beset by an especially oppressive civilization, represented by the avatar of castrating bitches, Nurse Ratched. When McMurphy and his merry band contrive to escape from the asylum, it is hardly coincidental that their outing involves drinking, whoring, sailing, and other hyper-masculine pastimes. *The Shawshank Redemption* echoes the plotline of *Cuckoo's Nest,* although *Shawshank* is less obviously misogynist and ends far more happily.

In my class, I touch on these examples briefly, saving time for a full examination of my favorite source of Usan mythology, *Star Trek.* In considering *Star Trek* a worthy object of anthropological analysis, I am in good company; see, for example, Claus (1976), Kottak (1990: 101–5). The *Star Trek* phenomenon began in the late 1960s, when what has become known in Trekker circles as The Original Series (TOS), chronicling the adventures of the starship *Enterprise,* was aired. Though TOS lasted only three seasons, it had a tremendous impact on Usan popular culture, and long pent-up demand ensured the six-season success of *Star Trek: The Next Generation* (TNG) eighteen years later. A plotline introduced on TNG gave birth to both *Star Trek: Deep Space Nine* and *Star Trek: Voyager.* Finally, there was *Enterprise,* a prequel to the other series. *Enterprise* was canceled in 2005, and there are currently no realistic plans for reviving it or spawning yet another series, though given *Star Trek*'s extraordinary history and still-extant fan base, no one can say definitively that this phenomenon has run its course.

It is perhaps unsurprising that Bad Mother figures abound in TOS. In the name of eradicating the scourge of Communism, the United States had become embroiled in a bloody and dispiriting conflict in Southeast Asia, and citizen support for the war effort had tailed off dramatically. Indeed, during this era Usans were questioning virtually the gamut of traditional ideals. In such troubled times, the appeal of myths that renew faith in one's society and culture may be enhanced. For Usans, the Myth of the Bad Mother amply serves this need.

The pilot episode of *Star Trek,* where Captain Pike rejects an idyllic life of fulfilled fantasies, sets the tone for the entire run of TOS (ironically, the pilot was not aired, but became the story-within-a-story for a two-part episode of TOS called "The Menagerie," in which Pike actually takes up the proffered fantasy life, but only after it becomes clear that his years as a productive man are over). Other episodes that more or less fit the Bad Mother mold include "The Return of the Archons," in which a machine strictly regulates the behavior of its humanoid subjects; "The City on the Edge of Forever," in which Captain Kirk must allow the woman he loves to die so that the timeline that leads to the glorious conquest of space can be restored; "The Apple," in which a machine maintains a population of infantilized humanoids in a sterile environment; and "The Paradise Syndrome," in which Kirk, stricken with amnesia, settles into marital bliss with a comely Indian maiden (I kid you not) until First Officer Spock rudely recalls him to duty through a Vulcan mind meld.

Arguably, however, "This Side of Paradise" (written by Dorothy Fontana) provides us with the purest rendition of the Bad Mother myth. In this episode, the Bad Mother is a consciousness-altering substance, known as "spores," but there is a distinct feminine cast to the evil involved here in the person of Leila, a woman from Spock's past who lures him into spore use. Leila belongs to a contingent of humans charged with setting up an agricultural colony on Omicron Ceti III, but well after the colony had been established, it was discovered that the planet was uninhabitable due to chronic radiation. Kirk and the *Enterprise* crew had been assigned the unhappy task of retrieving the bodies of the colonists. Upon reaching their destination, however, they are astonished to find the colonists alive and well, though not living in the way proper humans should—they engage only in the amount of agricultural activity necessary to sustain them, and there has not even been any population growth from the time they arrived. It turns out the spores are responsible for this steady state, because while they protect the humans from radiation, they also strip a man of his drive to achieve. Eventually everyone from the *Enterprise* falls under the spell of the spores, and the crew happily prepares to abandon its mission to join the colonists. Kirk, however, recovers the strength of will to throw off the spores and then induces the others to do the same. The colonists suddenly realize they have been deterred from their aspirations; the first words uttered by their leader, Sandoval, as he regains his presence of mind, are "We've done nothing here. No accomplishments, no progress." Since the colonists cannot survive on the planet without the spores, they are evacuated to a new planet where, as Sandoval says, they can "get some work done." Back on the *Enterprise,* as Omicron Ceti III recedes from view, Dr. McCoy compares the ship's departure to a second exile from Eden. Kirk counters with a stirring speech on how men were not meant to live in Paradise, how they must "struggle, claw their way up, scratch for every inch of the way." Spock's final assessment of his experience was that he was happy for the first time in his life. But this happiness, of course, had to be displaced by the necessary discontent that accompanies the state of being civilized.

The popularity of Bad Mother mythology waxes and wanes, and in TNG, whose post-Vietnam scriptwriters were evidently more reflective regarding the pitfalls of imperialism, such themes are somewhat less pronounced, although the eventual archvillain of the series, an alien group known as the Borg, is a Bad Mother *par excellence*. The Borg is made up of members of a variety of species, "assimilated," via prostheses whose mechanical function is regulated by a Queen, into a collective entity. The Borg appear in both *Voyager* and *Enterprise* as well, and they are germane to the plots of the first two *Next Generation* films. *Deep Space Nine* featured a number of scurrilous species, but the ultimate enemy, the Dominion, is governed by a race of Founders whose individuality is drowned in a collective pool called the Great Link; when the Founders need to generate a humanoid representative, she takes female form. If Bad Mother imagery, despite these examples, can be said to recede in TNG through *Voyager,* it returns to prominence in the last *Star Trek* series.

Enterprise is situated squarely on a Bad Mother premise—after the Vulcans land on Earth, they try to suppress the human ambition to explore space, believing humans to be at an infantile stage of species development. The Enterprise is only allowed to take flight with Vulcan supervision, in the person of the female Commander T'Pol. The series arc eventually moves away from this opening gambit, but the first season of *Enterprise* is remarkable for its misogyny (see Minkowitz 2002).

Bad Mother mythology surfaces in the *Star Trek* film series as well. The film that serves as the bridge between TOS and TNG movies, *Star Trek: Generations,* features a classic Bad Mother story line: Kirk must be retrieved from a dreamlike state where all of his wishes come true to perform one last manly, heroic act. In *Star Trek: First Contact,* the Borg Queen appears as a temptress, seducing Enterprise officers into the Borg collective. *Star Trek: Insurrection,* wherein the Enterprise crew defends a seemingly backward people against its enemies, might at first glance appear to repudiate the Bad Mother myth, but during the course of the film we learn that the persecuted villagers are actually technological sophisticates who have deliberately chosen their "primitive" lifestyle. These people, then, have not subverted "progress," but have in fact become so "advanced" that their everyday lives can be lived more simply.

On the face of it, the prevalence of Bad Mother mythology in *Star Trek* and other Usan sources would seem to bode ill for women in Usan society. How are actual women and men affected when they see the feminine so consistently demonized? Clearly the Bad Mother myth strengthens stereotypes that are deployed against women in a number of ways. Men may chafe against the "limitations" they complain are imposed upon them in marital relationships, employers may regard an aggressive female employee as a "ball-buster" and undermine her quest for promotion, and men and women alike scorn the "mama's boy" and deride his mother for thwarting his achievement of manhood. However, in today's United States, a decades-old drive to achieve gender equity has shifted acceptable female behavior toward what was once solely the masculine norm, resulting in a culture where the individuation of girls is treated scarcely differently from the individuation of boys. In this historical moment, then, the version of gender laid out by Bad Mother mythology bears less and less resemblance to real life, and hence the Bad Mother has perhaps become, as Stoler (1991: 54) has put it, more iconic than pragmatic. Still, Usans who prefer gender as it is currently constructed in our culture should not rest easy, since Bad Mother imagery remains at large and has been applied to other gendered purposes with the intent of denying human rights. I suggest, for example, that the Bad Mother reared her ugly head in the 1992 campaign to pass Colorado's notorious Amendment 2, a measure designed to overturn local laws protecting homosexuals from discrimination. A conservative Christian organization, Colorado for Family Values, put out several pamphlets identifying (male) homosexuals as vampiric, sucking away life-giving semen while returning only death, in the form of AIDS. In a tract entitled *The Psychology of Homosexuality,* the anonymous pamphleteer claims that throughout history, "homosexuals have been considered non-productive and hence inimical to the well-being and even the survival of the community." Discrimination against homosexuals, far from being wrong, was rather a social imperative, "like discrimination against the able-bodied who refuse to work." Hence male homosexuals, like a Bad Mother, were shown not only to deprive men of their masculinity (in a variety of horrifying ways) but to deny civilization the vital labor that true men contribute. Doubtless swayed by such arguments, a majority of the Colorado electorate supported Amendment 2, although it was later deemed unconstitutional by the U.S. Supreme Court (see Boulanger 1995).

The Bad Mother myth does what Ortner (1974) has claimed all human societies do—align female with nature and male with culture. Women are shown to retard cultural progress, at best achieving only a level of subsistence—"mere" survival—that any animal can achieve. Such an alignment may certainly constitute a disadvantage for women, but it also denigrates subsistence production. And if, at this moment in Usan history, it has become socially unacceptable to cast such aspersions on women, there is and has been no such moratorium on derogatory remarks levied at those few humans remaining on the planet whose ambitions and technologies consign them, in our terms, to backwardness. Indeed, the idea that hunter-gatherers and subsistence horticulturalists must be modernized is barely questionable outside of subversive anthropological circles. The Myth of the Bad Mother, then, accomplishes two related aims: it valorizes men who escape the clutches of women and it valorizes human *endeavor* over animal *existence*. In pursuing the latter aim we humans seek to lay down a vast buffer zone between culture and nature. Nonetheless, even in our currently "advanced" state, we remain haunted by nature—we contract disease, we die, and on a societal level our greatest works are destroyed by the vagaries of earth and sky. So long as we renew the paranoid vision of nature as a malevolent force that seeks to subdue the human spirit, there can never be too much space between nature and culture, and hence we continue to widen the gap.

A less conspicuous but still related aim of Bad Mother mythology is to displace the self-sufficiency of subsistence-oriented society with the *faux* individualism of self-reliance. Usans tend to conflate individualism with independence, but as Hsu (1972) once pointed out, the Chinese peasant village of his day could readily provide for itself, whereas Usans, enmeshed in vast networks of interdependence, could not on their own satisfy even the most basic daily needs, a helplessness that has only been exacerbated in these times when globalization has intensified. The irony, Hsu noted, is that the Chinese peasant will brag about how well his sons care for him, while the Usan tends to minimize the considerably greater dependency he has on a much larger group of people. Bad Mother mythology helps to obscure these economic connections by reducing them to a psychological parable where the hero, entirely in accord with the designs of the industrial/post-industrial state, makes the "choice" to fulfill ends beyond the fundamentals of survival.

But how motivational is the Bad Mother myth? Can it be, as I have indicated in Figure 1, "the key to Western 'success'?" In concert with other Usan myths and the way they are operationalized economically, socially, and politically, I believe the Myth of the Bad Mother is in fact an effective call to action. Henry (1963) once identified all culture as absurd, and the secret to maintaining a culture is to prevent its adherents from fully recognizing that fact. In the United States we accomplish this through a very well-integrated set of institutions, along with a ruthless suppression of alternatives (see Hall 2002), although enough of these are allowed to exist in the margins to cull off troublemakers. Those contradictions that occasionally emerge in the mainstream become objects of ridicule, as Usans, perhaps more so than other peoples, deploy a cutting sense of humor to force those aspects of Usan life that make us most uncomfortable into a conceptual cage where they are less threatening (Robbins 1993: 66–7). In this environment, the Bad Mother story, as often as it might be consciously recognized in the works of Freud or the writers of *Star Trek,* also operates effectively as a hidden template on which our subconscious actions may be modeled.

Exercise

Arensberg and Niehoff once wrote, "Whether in the conduct of foreign affairs or bringing up children or dealing in the marketplace, Americans tend to moralize" (1971: 215). This is no less true of our television series, and in fact, *Star Trek,* especially in its original incarnation, exemplifies this tendency. Discuss another television series (do not neglect sitcoms and talk shows) with an eye toward its moral message—How are Americans supposed to behave? What are they supposed to value? What happens to them if they refuse to adhere to these behaviors and values? Can they return to a righteous path after they have strayed? How?

References

Arensberg, Conrad M. and Arthur H. Niehoff. 1971. *Introducing social change: a manual for community development.* Chicago: Aldine Atherton.

Boulanger, Clare L. 1995. *Imagining the anti-community: the demonization of the homosexual in Colorado.* Paper read at the 94th Annual Meeting of the American Anthropological Association.

Bourdieu, Pierre. 1977. *Outline of a theory of practice,* trans. Richard Nice. Cambridge: Cambridge University Press.

Claus, Peter J. 1976. A structuralist appreciation of "Star Trek." In W. Arens and Susan P. Montague, eds, *The American dimension: cultural myths and social realities,* 15–32. Port Washington, NY: Alfred Publishing Co.

Freud, Sigmund. 1961. *Civilization and its discontents,* ed./trans. James Strachey. New York: W. W. Norton & Co.

Geertz, Clifford. 1973. *The interpretation of cultures.* New York: Basic Books.

Gilmore, David D. 1990. *Manhood in the making: cultural concepts of masculinity.* New Haven: Yale University Press.

Hall, John A. 2002. A disagreement about difference. In Siniša Malešević and Mark Haugaard, eds, *Making sense of collectivity: ethnicity, nationalism, and globalisation,* 181–194. London: Pluto Press.

Henry, Jules. 1963. American schoolrooms: learning the nightmare. *Columbia University Forum:* 24–30.

Hsu, Francis L. K. 1972. American core value and national character. In Hsu, ed., *Psychological Anthropology,* 241–262. Cambridge: Schenkman.

Kottak, Conrad Phillip. 1990. *Prime-time society: an anthropological analysis of television and culture.* Belmont, CA: Wadsworth.

Linton, Ralph. 1937. One hundred per cent American. *The American Mercury* 40: 427–429.

Malinowski, Bronislaw. 1926. *Myth in primitive psychology.* New York: W. W. Norton & Co.

Middleton, John.1967. Introduction. In John Middleton, ed., *Myth and cosmos: readings in mythology and symbolism,* ix–xi. Garden City, NJ: Natural History Press.

Minkowitz, Donna. 2002. Beam us back, Scotty! *The Nation* (March 25): 36–37.

Montague, Susan P. and Robert Morais. 1976. Football games and rock concerts: the ritual enactment of American success models. In William Arens and Susan P. Montague, eds, *The American dimension: cultural myths and social realities,* 33–52. Port Washington, NY: Alfred Publishing.

Ortner, Sherry B.1974. Is female to male as nature is to culture? In Michelle Zimbalist Rosaldo and Louise Lamphere, eds, *Woman, culture, & society,* 67–87. Stanford: Stanford University Press.

Robbins, Richard H. 1993. *Cultural anthropology: a problem-based approach.* 1st ed. Itasca, IL: F. E. Peacock.

Stoler, Ann Laura. 1991. Carnal knowledge and imperial power: gender, race, and morality in colonial Asia. In Micaela di Leonardo, ed., *Gender at the crossroads of knowledge: feminist anthropology in the postmodern era,* 51–101. Berkeley: University of California Press.

6

Being vs. Doing in International Sports

Conrad P. Kottak
University of Michigan

Why do Americans win so many medals at the Summer Olympic Games? We Americans may not even ask ourselves this question, since we are so accustomed to thinking we are the best at everything. If pressed, we might mention the better training facilities to which our athletes have access, or we might give a more obviously ethnocentric answer, along the lines of "Americans just naturally excel in whatever they do." Anthropologists are known for digging under such phrases as "just naturally," and thus the answer that Conrad Kottak provides, in this article, will explore such seemingly varied aspects of the question at hand as media exposure and ideologies of self.

Conrad P. Kottak, who has taught at the University of Michigan since 1968, is what we call a general anthropologist. He has published a great deal in his capacity as a cultural anthropologist, but his expertise in the other subdisciplines of American anthropology—archaeology, biological (physical) anthropology, and anthropological linguistics—is sufficiently well developed to write popular textbooks covering these areas as well. While he has carried out field research in Brazil and Madagascar, he clearly sees the United States as an appropriate venue for anthropological study, as his recent work with the University of Michigan's Center for the Ethnography of Everyday Life attests. In 1999 he received the American Anthropological Association/Mayfield Award for Excellence in the Undergraduate Teaching of Anthropology. (For more on contrasts between Brazil and the United States, especially with reference to media, see Kottak's 1990 book Prime-Time Society: An Anthropological Analysis of Television and Culture.*)*

At the close of the 1988 Winter Olympics in Calgary, where "Team USA" had not excelled, it was announced that New York Yankee owner George Steinbrenner had been hired by the U.S. Olympic Committee to head a panel to determine how American athletic performance on the international level could be improved. Many Americans were asking how our "free-enterprise" athletes could have been bested so often by "Communists." Had we lost our "national will to win"?

A broad and objective analysis of determinants of success in international sports would ponder several general questions unlikely to be considered by Steinbrenner's panel and would recognize that the Olympic Games provide excellent case study material for the understanding of cultural contrasts as applied to sports and the values they express. Why do countries excel at particular sports? Why do certain nations pile up dozens of Olympic medals while others win only a handful, or none at all? Cross-cultural comparison demonstrates that it isn't simply a matter of rich and poor, developed and underdeveloped, or even of the virtual "cradle-to-medal" government support that was provided to promising athletes in such places as East Germany and the former Soviet Union. It isn't even a question of a "national will to win," for, although certain nations stress winning even more than Americans do, a cultural focus on winning doesn't necessarily lead to the desired result. Indeed, cross-cultural comparison shows that an overemphasis on winning may actually *decrease* its likelihood.

This article will examine several ways in which cultural values, society, and the media influence international sports success. As primary examples I shall use the United States and Brazil, the national giants of the western hemisphere, with populations around 300 million and 200 million, respectively. These countries both have continental proportions and large, physically and ethnically diverse populations with roots in Europe, Africa, Asia, and Native America. Each is the major economic power of its continent. However, they offer striking and revealing contrasts in Olympic success: In the 1984 Summer Olympics the United States won an impressive 174 medals, while Brazil managed only 8. In 2004 the comparable figures were 102 and 10.

Part of the explanation for variable success of nations in international sports competition lies in the availability, extent, variety, and sophistication of media sports coverage. Americans' interest in sports has been honed over the years by an ever-growing media establishment, which provides us with daily examples of individual and team accomplishments, self-definition through activity and achievement, and, presumably, payoffs from hard work—all of which are highly valued by our culture. In addition to our tripartite structuring of local "news" broadcasts into news, sports, and weather, there is a steady stream of televised events, matches, games, playoffs, and championships. By 1985, our commercial television networks were broadcasting 1500 hours of sports annually, double the 1960 figure. Today, cable and satellite TV, which reach almost 90 percent of American homes, provide almost constant sports coverage. In 1984, the last full Olympic year prior to the appearance of the original version of this article, two sports programs ranked first (Super Bowl) and tenth (Summer Olympics Closing Ceremony) in total TV viewership, and the Olympic games attracted extensive coverage and substantial (if not overwhelming) audiences, as the Winter Olympics also did in 1988.

Brazilian television, which I have been studying since 1983 (with support from the Wenner-Gren Foundation, the National Science Foundation, and the National Institute of Mental Health), has much less sports coverage than does American TV, and the coverage that is offered is amateurish. There is no apparent technical reason for this—Brazil has a high-quality commercial television network (Rede Globo), which during the 1980s drew some 70 million people—60–90 percent of the national nightly audience—to locally produced programs, and regularly produces expertly made dramatic and documentary shows. But with respect to media conduits for sports, during the 1980s Brazil had no cable channels, and sports were a regular part of neither local nor national news. There was no regular nationally televised sports event comparable to the Superbowl or the World Series. The (soccer) World Cup, held every four years, is the only sports event that ever draws audiences comparable to those of Rede Globo's most popular regular programs, the *telenovelas* or locally produced "soaps," broadcast nightly in three slots—6, 7, and 8:30 p.m.

Despite the fact that for decades soccer has been a Brazilian national obsession, engendering fierce team loyalty and passionate interest, regularly scheduled soccer matches weren't televised very often, so that fans had to either attend local games or follow them on the radio. Nor were championships and major hometown games, such as the traditional rivalry between Rio de Janeiro's Flamengo and Fluminense (Fla–Flu) clubs, which routinely attracts 200,000 people to Maracanã, the world's largest soccer stadium, shown on TV. In this context of meager overall television sports coverage, it is perhaps unsurprising that in the Olympic year of 1984, no sports event—not even the Summer Olympics, to which Brazil sent more than 150 athletes—attracted much of a TV audience.

The Olympics is an international event in which much of the world can participate via television. The games are supposed to unite nations (symbolized by the interlinked rings of the official logo), providing a peaceful context for competition between them. However, given flags, anthems, Olympic history, and the tally of medals by country, nationalism is unavoidable, and the media fuel the international competitive aspect of the games. In summer 1984, ABC was criticized for stirring up undue nationalist fervor because its cameras seemed rooted to the Los Angeles spectators, largely U.S. citizens, and their victory chants of "U.S.A., U.S.A." To many, ABC's coverage was too jingoistic. It irritated athletes and coaches from other countries, many of whom didn't realize that their fans back home were seeing different reports, and led the president of the international Olympic committee formally to protest what he said was ABC's overemphasis on American athletes.

For the 1984 Summer Olympics, ABC actually produced not only the broadcasts seen by Americans and tailored to them but also a more neutral record of each event—about 1300 hours of coverage in all—available to be excerpted for broadcast throughout the world. Fascinating cultural contrasts are revealed when we consider how the Olympics were viewed and interpreted by television and the press in various countries. Cultural variation is obvious in the different ways in which the same film and events were scheduled, edited, cut, excerpted, explained, and evaluated in different nations.

In most nations, if no countrymen are participating, the media don't pay much attention to a sports event. This is an obvious reason why Brazilian television pays almost no attention to the Winter Olympics, because cold-weather sports are of little interest to Brazilians. However, it is much more surprising that Brazilian television pays so little attention to the Summer Olympics, to which Brazil routinely sends a large delegation. In 1984, the Globo network did not follow ABC's example of substituting Summer Games coverage for regular fare, nor did it plan to do so in 1988. Instead, Globo rigidly maintained its normal schedule, offering Olympic summaries outside of prime-time. Regular programming was interrupted only for a very few special events of strong interest to Brazilians, such as, in 1984, swimmer Ricardo Prado's performance in the finals of the 400 meter Individual

Medley (IM), which took place during the eight o'clock *telenovela*. Globo's strategy made sense, given the preferences of the Brazilian audience, which in 1984, when presented with a choice, opted for Globo's normal programming 7 to 1 over the Manchête network's broadcast of the Summer Olympic Games Opening Ceremony. ABC, on the other hand, had much fuller 1984 Summer Olympic coverage, despite the fact that the games cut into its profitable day-time soap opera schedule. But the level of interest in the United States was sufficiently high for ABC to meet its pledge to sponsors to deliver 25 percent of American households during prime-time (even as Globo was holding 60 percent of Brazilian TV households with routine *telenovelas*!).

To this American analyst, the Olympic coverage that did get broadcast in Brazil in summer 1984 can be criticized on several grounds. There was too little live coverage, focusing too exclusively on events in which Brazilians were participating, to the neglect of some of the most dramatic events, with certain key races never shown. For example, as far as I know, Brazilian TV never showed the tie between two American women swimmers for first place in the 100 meter freestyle. Nor did Brazilian TV provide "expert" commentators—so familiar to American televiewers—to explain sports events to novices. In fact, Brazilian sportscasters demonstrated poor knowledge of sports other than soccer. This was true throughout the media—press as well as television. One newsmagazine, for example, erroneously reported that West German swimmer Michael Gross had won the 200 meter butterfly and that he had beaten a previous world record time of 54.27 (a more plausible time for the 100 but impossible for the 200 meter event). Another missing element in Brazilian sports coverage was the human interest angle so typical of American reporting—obvious again in Winter 1988 in stories about skaters Debi Thomas and Dan Jansen, whose sister died just before he was to compete, and the rivalry between two skaters named Brian (Boitano and Orser). In Brazil, just the actual contest (if even that) was shown, with no commentary about the background, qualities, and prior challenges that got the competitors there.

Through visual demonstration, commentary, and explanation of rules and training, the media help introduce sports to people, stimulating interest in participation. *Time* magazine, reasonably, attributed 1984 American Olympic success in bicycling, in which American men won six medals, to the popularity of the film *Breaking Away*. Indeed, the media play a major role in stimulating interest in all kinds of sports—amateur and professional, team and individual, spectator and participatory. Until Brazil has more frequent, reliable, and varied sports coverage, it is unlikely that its international sports success, aside from soccer and car racing (which *is* televised), will increase much.

* * * * *

Aside from media neglect of sports, another reason for Brazil's poor overall Olympic performance is that *team sports and victories are emphasized too much* and—a related matter—there is too thin a line between professional and amateur sports. In the Brazilian sports establishment, (professional) team sports have overwhelming weight—with soccer as king. A strong personal connection between fan and soccer team begins on the local level, where the fan proclaims "I *am* Fluminense," or "I *am* Flamengo," and the fans yearn for their team's victories, which are perceived as their own. This habit fosters an intense personal identification of fan with athletes—professional or amateur—that Brazil's Olympic athletes find extremely oppressive.

The load is heavy because Brazilian athletes in international competition, such as Olympic gold medalist runner Joaquim Cruz, silver medalist swimmer Ricardo Prado—or *any* soccer player in the Olympics or World Cup—*represent* Brazilians, almost in the same way as Congress is said to represent the people of the United States. A win by a Brazilian team or the occasional nationally known individual athlete is felt to bring respect to the entire nation, but the Brazilian media are strikingly intolerant of losers. How is this internalized by Brazilian athletes? When Ricardo Prado swam in the finals of the 400 meter IM, during the eight o'clock *telenovela,* one newsmagazine observed, "It was as though he was the country with a swimsuit on, jumping in the pool in a collective search for success." Prado's own feelings confirmed the magazine, "When I was on the stands, I thought of just one thing: what they'll think of the result in Brazil." After beating his old world record by 1.33 seconds, in a second-place finish, Prado told a fellow team member, "I think I did everything right. I feel like a winner, but will they think I'm a loser in Brazil?" Leaving the pool, Prado rushed to phone home, to find out how the national audience had viewed his performance. Prado commented that he realized as he swam that he was performing in prime-time and that "all of Brazil would be watching," and he complained about having the expectations of an entire country focused on him. He contrasted the situations of Brazilian and American athletes. The United States has, he said, so many athletes that no single one has to summarize the country's hopes.

Fortunately, Brazil did seem to value Prado's performance, which was responsible for "Brazil's best result ever in Olympic swimming." Previously the country had won a total of only three bronze medals (in 1952, 1960, and 1980)—the last in Moscow for a relay. Labeling Prado "the man of silver," the media never tired of characterizing Prado's top event, the 400 meter IM, in which he had once held the world record, as the most complete, exhausting, and challenging event in swimming.

However, the kind words for Ricardo Prado did not extend to the rest of the Brazilian swim team. The press lamented the "succession of failures that Brazilian swimmers . . . accumulated in the first days of competition." "It was a disaster, nothing went right," said one swimmer. "For an underdeveloped country we did very well," rationalized another. Prado consoled the team, "You gave your best, and that's all you could do," and when he returned to Brazil he complained that the Brazilian sports establishment gives swimmers, and athletes in general, poor support. "They think all you have to do is to put athletes up for a week at a good hotel." The president of the Brazilian confederation of swimming countered that the swim team actually had been given considerable support but had disappointed the country—a statement to the press that violated the American canon that you shouldn't speak ill of young (amateur) athletes.

An article in the Brazilian newsmagazine *Veja,* written prior to Joaquim Cruz's unexpected gold medal in track, decried a "pallid performance" up to then, in which only Ricardo Prado stood out among Brazil's Olympic contenders. *Veja* speculated about whether the 1984 soccer team could "avenge" Brazil's loss of the World Cup in Spain in 1982. (It didn't—getting a silver to France's gold medal.) Knowing that the press (as is documented in the following quotes from the major newsmagazines) is ever ready to express "the nation's terrible disappointment" (as it did when the basketball team failed to defend the "national sports dignity"), it is no wonder that Brazilian competitors feel burdened. One yachtsman arrived in Los Angeles a month early so that his fears would diminish, but he still didn't win. "We're only going to relax," said a volleyball player, "with the medal in hand." (The men's volleyball team also had to settle for "the bitter taste of silver.") The eventual failure of the women's basketball team was attributed to tension and "apathy." Ricardo Prado expressed his feelings as a Brazilian athlete: "Success in swimming has changed me a lot, has left me harder, *less confident*. I need to relax. I don't intend to kill myself for anybody."

Expectably, during the 1984 Summer Olympics the Brazilian media focused on the team sports—soccer, basketball, volleyball, and on Prado's swimming success (always juxtaposed with the *team*'s overall failure). There was little interest in and coverage of individual performances, other than Prado and Cruz—Brazil's only gold medalists. For example, when eventual silver medalist Douglas Viera disputed the gold medal with a Korean judoist, only five Brazilians (one athlete, two coaches, two journalists) bothered to attend, while hundreds of Koreans were there cheering on his opponent. The judo matches, which resulted in Brazil's second, third, and fourth medals ever in that sport, and the first since 1972, were not televised live, even though all three athletes had previously enjoyed some international success, so that the medals should not have been unexpected. The media gate-keepers had simply decided that the nation was uninterested in their feats. The names of the three medalists (one silver, two bronze) were mentioned briefly on TV, but I never saw the film of their matches.

There is more, of course, to the development of sports than constant and supportive media attention. There must also be encouragement of participation on the local level. This is available in the United States through myriad clubs and public school athletic teams. In contrast, in Brazil, teams in such sports as swimming, gymnastics, and diving are usually associated with money-making professional soccer teams. Because of this association, the Brazilian sports establishment doesn't pay much attention to the professional–amateur distinction. As is routine now for most countries, Brazil's most successful athletes on the international scene—*professional* soccer players—play in the Olympics. Brazil's 1984 Olympic soccer coach told foreign journalists that his team had just two amateurs, with the others "beginning professionals." As a result, the media and fans alike apply the same standards and judgments to amateur athletes that are used for salaried professionals.

A general measure of a nation's sports maturity, underlying its international sports success, is the extent to which it provides wide public access to athletic facilities and opportunities—places and occasions for prospective athletes to practice, develop, and compete. Sports opportunities in Brazil (except for soccer, which is played in town squares and streets, in fields, and on beaches) are relatively few because Brazil has no well-developed public education system, with the teams, facilities, and schedules that foster athletic competition in the United States. The United States can afford to maintain the distinction between amateur and professional sports because it has one of the world's largest sports establishments. Our developed economy, voracious media, achievement orientation, competitiveness, and traditions of joining clubs and associations all provide fertile ground for the growth of all kinds of sports—team and individual.

Thus, because Brazilian athletes are expected not just to represent but almost to be the country and because team sports are emphasized, the media focus too exclusively on winning, to the detriment of overall athletic success. How different is the situation in the United States? Winning, of course, is also an important American cultural value, but particularly in team sports—as in Brazil. American football coaches are famous for comments such as "Winning isn't everything; it's the only thing" and "Show me a good loser and I'll show you a loser." However, and particularly for sports such as running, swimming, diving, gymnastics, golf, and skating, which focus on the individual and in which American athletes usually do well, American culture also admires "moral victories," "personal bests," "comeback athletes," and "special Olympics," and commends those who run good races without finishing first. In amateur sports, American culture tells us that hard work and personal improvement can be as important as winning.

Americans are so accustomed to being told that their culture overemphasizes winning that they may find it hard to believe that other cultures value it even more. But Brazil certainly does. Ricardo Prado, commenting on his massive press coverage when he held the world record for the 400 meter IM, observed that only winning athletes were noticed in Brazil—only number ones, never number twos. He blasted the press for neglecting the achievements of athletes who held no world records.

Indeed, Brazilian sports enthusiasts are preoccupied with world records, probably because only a win (as in soccer) or a best time (as in swimming) can make Brazil indisputably, even if temporarily, the best in the world at something. Ricardo Prado's former world record in the 400 meter IM was constantly mentioned in the press prior to the 1984 Olympics. Furthermore, the best-time standard also provides Brazilians with a ready basis to *fault* a swimmer or runner for not going fast enough, when they don't make previous times. On the basis of this, one would predict, correctly, that sports in which standards are very subjective would not be popular spectator sports in Brazil. Brazilians like to assign blame to athletes who fail them, and negative comments about gymnasts or divers are more difficult because grace and execution can't be quantified as easily as time can.

I think that Brazilians value winning so much because it is so rare. In the United States, resources are more abundant, social classes less marked, opportunities for achievement more numerous, poverty less pervasive, and individual social mobility easier. American society has room for many winners. Brazilian society is more stratified; a much smaller middle class and elite group makes up just 30 percent of the population. Brazilian sports echo lessons from the larger society: victories are scarce and reserved for the privileged few.

Values in Sports

Not only do favorite sports, the athlete's role, and emphasis on winning vary between cultures, contrasting values are also revealed in the interpretations that the media, as well as ordinary people, offer when they discuss particular performances. The factors believed to contribute to sports success belong to a larger context of cultural values. Particularly relevant in this context is the contrast that anthropologists draw between ascribed and achieved status. Individuals have little control over the ascribed statuses they occupy (e.g., age, sex), which depend on intrinsic qualities, what one *is* rather than what one does. On the other hand, people have more control over—more to *do* with—the achieved statuses (e.g., student, tennis player) they occupy. Since—in the eyes of American law, if hardly in reality—we start out the same, American culture emphasizes achieved status over ascribed status: we are supposed to make of our lives what we will and can. Success comes through achievement. An American's identity emerges as a result of what he or she does.

In Brazil, on the other hand, social identity rests on *being* rather than *doing,* on what one is from the start—a strand in a web of personal connections, originating in the extended family. Brazilians' social identities are based in large part on class background and family connections, which Brazilians see nothing wrong with using for all they're worth. Parents, in-laws, and extended kin are all tapped for entries to desired settings and positions. Family position and network membership contribute substantially to individual fortune, and all social life is hierarchical. Brazilian law accords privileged treatment to certain classes of citizens, such as university degree holders, who usually have privileged family backgrounds. No one doubts that rank confers advantages in myriad contexts and encounters in everyday social life. High-status Brazilians don't stand patiently in line as Americans do. Important people expect their business to be attended to immediately, and social inferiors readily yield. Rules don't apply uniformly, but differentially, according to social class. The final resort in any conversation is "Do you know who you're talking to?" The American opposite, reflecting our democratic and egalitarian ethos, is "Who do you think you are?" As has been discussed at length by Brazilian anthropologist Roberto DaMatta in his influential book *Carnivals, Rogues, and Heroes,* when Brazilians ask "Do you know who you're talking to?" they are conjuring up all the well-connected people included within their personal networks—whether relatives, in-laws, school chums, business associates, or friends.

The contrasting roles that different cultures assign to ascribed and achieved status extend to sports. The following description of one of Brazil's 1984 judo medalists (as reported by *Veja* magazine) illustrates the importance of ascribed status and the fact that in Brazilian life victories are regarded as scarce and reserved for the privileged few.

> Middle-weight Olympic bronze medalist Walter Carmona began judo at age six and became a São Paulo champion at twelve. With his fourth place in Moscow in 1980, and subsequent prizes, he is Brazil's winningest judoist. Carmona lives in São Paulo with his family (father, mother, siblings); he trains five hours a day and is in his fifth year of engineering at Mackenzie University. He is fully supported by his father, a factory owner. Walter Carmona's life has been comfortable—he has been able to study and dedicate himself to judo without worries. His situation brings great satisfaction to his father, who says that he is "proud to support a champion."
>
> Although satisfied with the Los Angeles result, the father thought his son "deserved more than a bronze medal." "We are certain he expected the gold," said his mother—who seems to have been right, since Carmona didn't bother to phone home after receiving his medal. His final match over, the athlete "took a vacation from his team" and toured Los Angeles, not bothering to attend the silver medal-winning match of his judo teammate Douglas Viera.

Although wealth often does contribute to sports success in the United States—albeit less so than in Brazil—it's hard to imagine *Time, Newsweek,* or American television running a similar account. Like our culture, our media prefer underdogs and rags-to-riches, but even when an athlete does come from a privileged family, reporters do their best to find some aspect of doing, some special personal triumph or achievement, to focus on. Often this involves the athlete's struggle with adversity (illness, injury, pain, the death of a parent, sibling, friend or coach)—and helps depict the featured athlete as not only successful but noble and self-sacrificing as well.

However, given the opposite focus on ascribed status in Brazil, *the guiding assumption in sports as in society is that one cannot do more than what one is.* For example, the Brazilian Olympic Committee sent no female swimmers to Los Angeles because none had made arbitrarily established cutoff times. This excluded a South American record holder, while swimmers with no better times were attending from other South American countries. The attitude was that only swimmers with these arbitrary times had any chance to place in Los Angeles. No one seemed to imagine that Olympic excitement might spur swimmers to extraordinary efforts.

In contrast, achievement-oriented American sports coverage dotes on unexpected results, illustrating adherence to the American sports credo originally enunciated by Yogi Berra: "It's not over till it's over." American culture, supposedly so practical and realistic, has a remarkable faith in coming from behind—in unexpected and miraculous achievements.

The contrasting portraits of the United States and Brazil that emerge from media coverage of the Olympics pose an achievement-oriented society where "anything is possible" against an ascribed-status society in which it's over before it begins, and athletes internalize these values. Illustrating some of the factors believed to contribute to sports success in American culture, one 1984 Summer Olympic issue of *Newsweek* focused on three athletes—Australian swimmer John Sebin, who scored an *upset* win; American gymnast Mary Lou Retton, a gold-medal winning "piston-driven *pixie*"; and Japan's Koji Gushiken, who finally won the all-round male gymnastics title through *tenacity*. Although these winners were the products of different nations and had followed different paths to Olympic success, American values (summarized by the italicized words) were used to explain their achievements. These athletes were considered newsworthy in American culture because they embodied three American hero types: the underdog (Sebin); the giant killer (Retton); and the tenacious worker (Gushiken). Most obviously, Retton and Sebin, pixie giantkiller and underdog kid from out of nowhere, appealed to the characteristic American preoccupation with the unexpected. Their achievements were especially interesting to Americans because they were in some sense extraordinary and unforeseen. Given Sebin's twenty-fifth place world ranking prior to the event, the odds against his winning his race were "almost overwhelming." (Brazilians might have discouraged him from entering key races, or even kept him home.) Even Gushiken's victory was interpreted by the American media as the end to a "quest" that had spanned three Olympics. At 27, he would be *ordinarily* be considered all but decrepit by the standards of his sport. *Newsweek* proclaimed that "things like this don't happen in real life, only at the Olympics."

The credo that anyone can do anything is rooted in the doing—achievement—orientation of American culture. Unexpected results, virtually ignored by the Brazilian media, are considered some of the "brightest" Olympic moments by the American press. Not only did "unheralded" swimmer Sebin score "a stunning upset" over Michael Gross in the 200 meter butterfly, "against all odds" an American swimmer with a much slower seed time than Gross anchored the U.S. team to victory in a relay that the West Germans "had seemed destined to win."

However, the upset nature of these wins wasn't even mentioned in Brazil—because Brazilian culture has little interest in the unexpected. Brazilians assume that if you go into an event with a top seed time, as Ricardo Prado did, you've got a chance to win a medal. Prado's second-place finish made perfect sense back home, since his former world record had been bettered before the race began. Brazilian culture also criticizes failures to perform as well as expected—given what one was at the outset. However, it doesn't anticipate unexpected success through sudden bursts of achievement during final competition. Because of this, the Brazilian media didn't quite know what to do with runner Joaquim Cruz's unexpected gold medal, and he received less coverage than Ricardo Prado. However, an American newsmagazine ran a cover story using Cruz's humble upbringing on the outskirts of Brasília, to illustrate classic American values.

Given the overwhelming value that American culture places on work, it might seem surprising that our media devote so much attention to unforeseen results and so little to the years of training, preparation and competition that underlie Olympic performance. It is probably assumed that hard work is so obvious and fundamental that it goes without saying, or perhaps the assumption is that by the time athletes actually enter Olympic competition all are so similar (the American value of equality) that only mysterious and chance factors can explain variable success. The American focus on the unexpected is applied to losses as well as wins, so that factors encompassed by such concepts as chance, fate, mystery, and uncertainly are viewed as legitimate reasons for defeat. Runners and skaters fall; ligaments tear; a gymnast "inexplicably" falls off the pommel horse.

Americans thus recognize chance disaster as companion to unexpected success, but Brazilians place more responsibility on the individual, assigning personal fault. Less is attributed to factors beyond human control. When individuals who should have performed well, on the basis of what they are, don't, they are blamed for their failures. Accepting their body's failures, it is culturally appropriate for Brazilian athletes to invoke poor health as an excuse for losing. An American track star, Carl Lewis, could assert that "at the Olympics, it's 100 percent mental, because there's nothing you can change physically." Brazilians would disagree: you can always get sick. Indeed, Brazilian athletes routinely mention colds or diarrhea as a reason for a poor performance.

For example, because of a cold, runner Joaquim Cruz, Brazil's only gold medalist, withdrew from his second event, the 1500 meter race, in which he was favored, almost certainly because there is so much pressure on Brazilian athletes to win, and he was afraid he wouldn't. The newsmagazine *Veja's* report of his explanation for withdrawing illustrates some of the contrasting national values about the role of illness in sports.

> The night I ran in the finals of the 800 meters, I ate badly, almost didn't sleep, and was awakened at six A.M. by a phone call from "Uncle" [Joao] Figueiredo [then President of Brazil]. I was already weak from running four races in four days. Then I saw I had caught a terrible cold. I went to see the doctor supplied by Nike [the sport shoe company], had acupuncture and massages, and spent a night at the Santa Monica Holiday Inn to see if I could rest better, but it was impossible to recover my form.

Cruz withdrew because he "had no interest in running and placing last," was flying to Europe to compete again the following week, and wanted to "save himself" to set world records later in the year. Cruz's decision to forgo the 1500 meter race was accepted by his countrymen. He was right to withdraw, I was told in Brazil, because he probably wouldn't have won anyway since he was sick.

Poor health is used differently by American and Brazilian athletes, and particularly by the media and publics that must interpret and evaluate their performances. Brazilians use illness negatively, as an excuse, whereas Americans use it positively, as a challenge that often can be met and bested. As an illustration of this, contrast Cruz's behavior with that of top-seeded American breaststroker John Moffet, who sprained a leg tendon during his qualifying heat, then finished fifth on "arm power and guts," in a performance the American media called "unbelievable." Or consider the English runner David Moorcroft, whose last-place finish in the finals of the 5000 meter run served as the opening human-interest story for the American film *Sixteen Days of Glory,* which focused on the fact that Moorcroft (whose previously set world record survived the 1984 Olympics) had been plagued with a litany of illnesses and injuries. Moorcroft ran well in qualifying, then faltered during the finals because of leg pain. Realizing that he would finish last, Moorcroft's personal triumph was completing the race without being lapped by the winner. He accomplished that goal and finished his "long painful journey" with "pride" and "honor," according to the film.

Despite its characteristic focus on doing, American culture does not insist that individuals can fully control outcomes, and it's not as necessary as it is in Brazil for people to explain their own failures. As a result, the American press gives little space to unsuccessful athletes' explanations for less than optimal performances. The Brazilian media, in contrast, feel it necessary to assign fault for failure—and this usually means blaming the athlete(s). To avert this, Brazilian athletes try to find culturally appropriate excuses. This contrast in fault-finding reflects a combination of factors: the lesser pressure placed on any given American athlete to win for his country, recognition of the role of chance, and the sheer number of American successes—rendering discussions of failures somewhat ungenerous. Perhaps Americans are also more optimistic than Brazilians, preferring to focus on "the thrill of victory" rather than "the agony of defeat." Indeed, the American press talk much more about the injuries and illnesses of the victors and finishers than those of the losers and quitters. Thus, American culture, applied to sports, uses poor health not mainly as an excuse but as an obstacle for individuals to overcome, as in the Moffet and Moorcroft cases.

Illustrating the supreme American value of achieving against the odds is a 1984 *Newsweek* article by Pete Axhelm. "On very special occasions, there appears a quality in sport that defies all plans and diagrams. The athlete's "quest" is a "moving celebration of the potential of the human spirit," the article continued. Near Hollywood, the dream capital of an achievement-oriented society, the American athletes who stood on the victors' stand in summer 1984, displaying their medals, may have felt like *Star Wars* heroes, living a dream, fulfilling a quest, hurdling obstacles, winning out on their own. The closing week of the Olympics "was given to surprises of the spirit." After the 1980 boycott it had not been easy for Americans to return to their grinding training schedules. "I wasn't sure if the sacrifices were worth it," said swimmer Nancy Hogshead. But, proclaimed Axhelm, in the mood kindled in Los Angeles athletes demonstrated that they could not merely endure, but overcome.

While the Americans spoke of spirit, dreams, quests, and victories, Brazilian television found humor in failure, as chronicled in a montage of Olympic mistakes—pratfalls and stumbles by riders, weightlifters and runners—which ABC distributed along with its documentary footage. In the United States these "lighter moments" were used to illustrate that stunts aren't as easy as the best performers make them seem and that no matter how hard an athlete has trained, the unexpected can always happen, sometimes affecting the final result. In Brazil, the pratfalls were hugely popular on the nightly news. First, they showed the nation that people besides Brazilians could make Olympic mistakes. The film conveyed a second, less explicit, message. It suggested the futility of trying, or even hoping, to win in a cultural universe in which chances for success are so limited.

Cross-cultural comparison shows, therefore, that a focus on team sports, records, and winning is not the most certain route to international sports success. It raises the question of whether the United States Olympic Committee might better have invited a successful runner, swimmer, diver, gymnast, or skater to head its panel, rather than one of our nation's best-known advocates of winning at any cost.

Exercise

Locate the results for the most recent Pan American Games or Olympic Games. How well did the Americans do? How did the media cover the winners, and the losers? What phrases were used to describe the reasons for success or failure?

Part III

Economy, Society, Power

7

Consuming America

Richard Wilk
Indiana University

The archaeological anthropologist has a problem—how does one reconstruct the richness of human life from the things that humans leave behind? Cultural anthropologists can help with this problem, since they have the opportunity to study the ongoing interaction of people with things, and yet this is seldom the explicit focus of ethnography. As Richard Wilk points out in this article, this dearth of research is apparent even in the United States, where people are arguably more involved with more things than people in any other society. Dr. Wilk uses a history of the La-Z-Boy chair to demonstrate that a greater awareness of the everyday can yield a wealth of knowledge.

Richard Wilk is Professor of Anthropology and Gender Studies at Indiana University. He has done research in the rainforest of Belize, in West African markets, and in the wilds of suburban California. His most recent books are Home Cooking in the Global Village *(Berg),* Off the Edge: Experiments in Cultural Analysis, *co-edited with Orvar Lofgren (Museum Tusculanum Press), and the edited* Fast Food/Slow Food *(Altamira).*

The hardest thing to see, according to George Orwell (1968 [1946]: 122–126), is something right in front of your nose. Anthropologists have always had an easier time focusing on the distant and exotic. We have been less successful in finding the exotic close to home, especially in those mundane and vulgar symbols of the middle class that surround and frame everyday life, which millions take for granted. But the things middle-class Americans consume in such abundance, which they also take very much for granted, have fascinating social histories. Finding out how these things became so ordinary can be an engrossing intellectual journey. It may also be one of the most important contributions that anthropologists can make to help solve the global environmental crisis.

The Comforts of Home

The North American middle-class way of life is centered on the home. In houses which are growing in size every generation, Americans now consume more resources per capita than any other people in the history of the planet. But instead of seeing themselves as living a life of almost unimaginable luxury, the word Americans use to describe their standard of living is *comfortable*. Where did this notion of comfort come from? And how did it become so focused on material culture, the basis of constantly rising levels of consumption?

One way to answer these questions is to learn the social histories of the peculiar things that have come to furnish the American dream. Following the theme Ralph Linton (1936) pioneered in his famous essay on the American Breakfast, we can disclose the cultural nature of consumption in the average home by tracing the origins of mundane items back to their exotic origins. Take, for example, the reclining chair.

The Seat of Power

In 1996 the La-Z-Boy Company was the third-ranked manufacturer of furniture in the United States, with $947 million in sales. Introduced as "novelty furniture" in 1927, intended for outdoor use in the backyard, the La-Z-Boy recliner did not find a market niche until it became a symbol of working-class domesticity and respectability. It was advertised as a way to lure a man home after work; furnishing the nest where the upwardly mobile male relaxed from his daily struggle. Sales took off after WWII, when the "recliner lounge chair" became part of the domestic dream of single-family suburban homes full of nuclear families. When television, the electronic hearth, took over the domestic evening, Dad's recliner often landed the best spot.

There were no clear cultural antecedents for the recliner chair; early American furniture was known for its spare simplicity. From the perspective of symbolic boundaries, the big soft chair could be seen as dangerous and transgressive. It is, after all, furniture for the public part of the house that transforms into something very much like that most private of places, the bed. In a culture that values hard work and conviviality, the recliner encourages dozing and sleep, even while others in the room stay awake. Elite social critics fastened on the recliner as a symbol of an overstuffed, morally-lax working class, the "couch potatoes" who actually used their leisure time in a leisurely way, instead of uplifting themselves in museums or other cultural pursuits. In the 1960s the middle class was exhorted by the *New Yorker* magazine to "get out of your La-Z-Boy long enough to do something!"

The La-Z-Boy was accepted, despite its ambiguity, when it became part of a radical reformulation of American leisure, attitudes toward work, and engagement in the home and family as a cultural project. It was enmeshed in a movement that built a country around the polarities of work and home, undercutting all the civil spaces and social groups in between.

Together but Separate

In the eighteenth and nineteenth centuries, middle-class family life was not built around shared leisure. Working days were long, and even on the farm there were separate male and female work groups. When work was over, people wanted to party, talk, drink, ride, do something active, usually in all-male and all-female groups in setting like bars, sewing circles, social clubs, sports, churches, and lodges. Despite today's nostalgic images of Victorian parlor conviviality, families rarely spent their evenings sitting around the fireplace together, except perhaps on holidays and other special occasions (Hawes and Nybakken 2001).

Until the twentieth century, Americans never imagined that the reward for hard work was lying still and passive on an overstuffed chair for hours, surrounded by members of the nuclear family. When at home they were always doing something—knitting, playing cards, crafts, or some kind of assembly work. The idea that work and stress requires long evenings of passive relaxation is a recently invented tradition. It was part of a program of nuclear family togetherness and shared leisure pushed on the rest of the country by twentieth-century social reformers. They waged war upon what they saw as the unruly and destructive entertainment, and the informally mixed-up family arrangements of the "lower classes." As with so many dramatic changes in American life, the "wedge" issue was health. Extended families and sex-segregated raucous public amusements were labeled unhealthy and pathological. A healthy society of thriving individuals could only be built in a conjugal setting in which the nuclear family rested daily from the rigors of disciplined work.

The Good Life?

The reclining chair, like any other piece of material culture, is not just a passive reflection or indicator of social change. Major advances in the anthropology of consumption, in the hands of theorists like Appadurai and Bourdieu, have shown us that objects are much more deeply embedded in social process. Material culture has been part of a major transformation of middle-class family life over the last thirty years.

Leisure is now a project for the whole family, engaging more and more time and energy. Home furnishings are tools of transformation, and manufacturers have responded with new images and designs. In the 1980s and 1990s, recliner makers embraced the new label, "motion furniture." Gliding across increasingly blurred class distinctions, the overstuffed chairs were no longer exiled to the den, TV room, or rec room. "Motion Modular Furniture Groupings," in which several sections of a sofa-group recline separately, now include fold-down trays, pull-out drawers, phones, and a "multiple motor massage system" with optional heater. Advertising and marketing, once focused on Dad after a hard day at the office, now puts Mom and the babies together in a chair, and a whole happy family reclining together in their living-room module. Popular kid-size recliners promote true family democracy and "personalized comfort." There are special chairs for fat and thin, and units can be "customized to match any décor, family size, or lifestyle" (from La-Z-Boy's annual report). *Consumer's Digest* reports that, with all this diversity, one in four American homes has at least one reclining chair.

In a world where so many fashions begin with the elite and then trickle down the social scale, recliners stubbornly swim against the flow. At the high end of the scale, better chairs cost $800 or more, and the owners of La-Z-Boy "Galleries" report that expensive fabrics including cashmere and leather are extremely popular. There is even a market for an exotic imported Norwegian "stressless" recliner, which offers an "infinite number of positions." Prices start at more than $1000.

The transformation of middle-class domesticity has been anything but peaceful. Behind the happy advertising images that show harmonized living rooms, happy families, and the joy of togetherness, are millions of divorces, incidents of domestic violence, and other kinds of conflict. Some sociologists think that the allocation and spending of money in middle-class households has become a focus for highly charged issues of entitlement and authority raised by dramatic changes in work and gender roles (Cheal 1989, England and Farkas 1986). Consumer goods usually become emotionally and socially important as gifts, tools, and even weapons in negotiating and renegotiating domestic life.

Even La-Z-Boy advertisements acknowledge the problem of couples who are always "arguing about who gets the La-Z-Boy." In the working-class family, the recliner was "Dad's chair"; after all, Dad was the breadwinner and he deserved his relaxation. Advertisements in the 1940s showed Mom guiltily enjoying a rest in the chair while Dad was at work. Mom and the children may now have their own recliners, but this does not mean that Dad has given up his position. Men still tend to have the most elaborate models, and as a trade journal puts it, "These custom-built 'cocoons' become the director's chair in home theater ensembles." From his self-contained throne, Dad now rules by remote control.

Just Rewards?

Most Americans who own recliners do not see them as badges of potato-hood, sloth, or passivity. Instead, the theme word for reclining motion furniture is "relaxation." The folklore of the middle class is that life is hard and everyone needs compensation, times when they can "lie back and take it easy." That time in the chair becomes a virtue, a necessity for health in a world of business, stress, and the continuing drain of work and responsibility. La-Z-Boy imagines their customers as "people who have made it through the lean years and have earned the right to enjoy their success." They deserve a reclining chair, their "Grand Snuggler" or "Dreamland," or even their "Avenger." Motion furniture is sold as just compensation for the toils of "all the hard-working people who make America hum." But are there limits to how much material compensation Americans "deserve" for their hard labor? And, is material abundance, an overflowing cornucopia of consumer goods, really providing Americans with the happiness they expect?

Repeated surveys find, on the contrary, a negative relationship between wealth and self-reported happiness (see Princen 2002). According to Juliet Schor's book, *The Overspent American* (1999), many people feel trapped in a work-and-spend cycle, frustrated with technology, drowning in abundance. Voluntary simplicity groups and "simplicity circles," are spreading and expanding, while foundations like the Center for a New American Dream try to envision a less materialistic society.

American family consumerism is not just a moral or intellectual issue, it is one of the world's most pressing environmental problems, one of the most important fundamental causes of global warming and climate change. The average American, according to recent estimates by the Worldwatch Institute (2004), annually consumes 50–60 times more resources than an average resident of sub-Saharan Africa does. Americans consume energy and materials at a profligate rate unmatched by any other country, and as the energy crisis recedes into the past, our cars, houses, and bodies are once again getting more bloated every year. Yet the material lives of the American middle class are less known to anthropology than Trobriand jewelry.

Take a Chair

My example of the recliner chair is meant to make a simple point; the consuming world of middle-class Americans is rich in meaning, and bears much closer scrutiny by anthropologists. When Harold Wilhite and I began research on energy consumption and household decision-making in the middle-class of northern California in 1981, we found only one other anthropologist (Willett Kempton) doing consumption-related work in the U.S.A. While few anthropologists seemed interested, many in the energy conservation community found our ethnographic approach innovative and useful (Stern et al. 1997).

In Europe, particularly in England, anthropologists are key players in a renewed field of "material culture studies" that takes the consumer world of the middle class seriously. They have provided rich ethnographies of shopping, housing, and everyday material culture from the Sony Walkman to Woolen carpets. There is nothing like it here in the U.S.A., where few anthropologists work on middle-class consumer culture, and those who do find a much more receptive audience in the Association for Consumer Research than in the American Anthropological Association. Monographs like archaeologist Michael Schiffer's *The Portable Radio in American Life* (1991) are few and far between. Ironically, the key social theorists of American consumer culture are Europeans like Baudrillard and Barthes.

It is hard to explain this peculiar indifference to an important issue that is literally right in our faces (or perhaps under our buttocks). Isn't it striking that the very thing that most defines American culture, a love of technology and material abundance, is the thing we most stridently ignore? Over the years, graduate students in my seminars on consumer culture have produced fascinating, ethnographically rich work on topics like fishing tackle, lawn ornaments, ketchup, and mountain bikes. But then, facing the reality of the job market, they head off to do their dissertations on something more "exotic." Perhaps it is time for us to sit down, lean back, and pay some more attention to what is happening at home.

Exercise

Though wanton consumption can be hurtful, there are many positive ways that material goods figure in our lives. Two anthropologists did a study of favorite objects, comparing people in the United States with rural farmers in the country of Niger. They concluded that in the United States, favorite objects are most important because they are "symbols of other people and social experiences, rather than being enjoyed for their own attributes." In other words, favorite objects were important because they connected people to each other—they symbolize important relationships. They hold our memories of important people and social events in our lives. This was a surprising finding, considering how much we have been led to believe that Americans are materialistic and love having stuff because they enjoy the stuff itself.

Discuss your favorite object. Why is it important to you? What is the history of your relationship with the object? Does the observation above hold true?

References

Cheal, David. 1989. Strategies of resource management in household economies: moral economy or political economy? In R. Wilk, ed., *The household economy,* 11–22. Boulder: Westview Press.

England, P., and Farkas. G. 1986. *Households, employment, and gender: a social, economic and demographic view.* New York: Aldine.

Hawes, Joseph, and Elizabeth Nybakken, eds. 2001. *Family and society in American history.* Urbana: University of Illinois Press.

Linton, Ralph. 1936. *The study of man: an introduction.* New York: D. Appleton-Century Company.

Orwell, George. 1968 [1946]. *In front of your nose: the collected essays, journalism and letters of George Orwell.* London: Secker & Warburg.

Princen, Thomas, ed. 2002. *Confronting consumption.* Cambridge: MIT Press.

Schiffer, Michael. 1991. *The portable radio in American life.* Tucson: University of Arizona Press.

Schor, Juliet. 1999. *The overspent American: upscaling, downshifting, and the New Consumer.* Harper: New York.

Stern, R., T. Dietz, V. Rutan, R. Socolow, and J. Sweeney, eds. 1997. *Environmentally significant consumption.* Washington D.C.: National Academy Press.

Worldwatch Institute. 2004. *State of the world 2004: The consumer society.* Washington, D.C.: Worldwatch Institute.

8

The Button: Not a Simple Notion

Paul Grebinger

Rochester Institute of Technology

In the article below, Paul Grebinger, who began his professional life in anthropology as an archaeologist, asks you to see a world in a button. In the early twentieth century, button makers had to adapt to changes in American culture that threatened their industry. Applying the theory of human materialism, Dr. Grebinger draws out key connections between American immigration history, politics, economy, and technology.

    Paul Grebinger is a professor of anthropology in the College of Liberal Arts at Rochester Institute of Technology. He completed his undergraduate degree at Columbia University when Marvin Harris was chair, and Harris's theory of cultural materialism permeated the intellectual ether of the Department of Anthropology. On completing his Ph.D. at the University of Arizona in 1971, Grebinger specialized in prehistoric Southwestern archaeology. By the 1980s, however, he had refocused his interests on historical American material culture and technological change. He is currently conducting research into the role of horticultural industries in transforming the nineteenth-century American landscape.

The button is no mere appurtenance of costume. In the discussion that follows I treat it as a material reflection of change in American culture. It becomes a lens through which we can develop insight into dimensions of American life that otherwise might elude us. Although the manufacture of buttons is embedded in cultural contexts that are, strictly speaking, technical and economic, simple infrastructural determinism as set forth in cultural materialist research strategy does not provide satisfactory explanation of the transformations in button technology discussed here. Even an apparently "simple notion," such as the button, exhibits attributes of function *and* of style. It embodies cultural meaning that is not only technological and economic, but social and political as well.

    In order to explain transformations in button technology we must explore processes of change in American culture that reach back into the nineteenth century. The locus of change described here was Rochester, New York, a national center of both menswear manufacture and button production since the second half of the nineteenth century. The change was revolutionary in that the fundamental technology of button manufacture was transformed from mechanical to chemical and was so profound that there could be no return to the previous system.

Cultural materialism (Harris 1999; 2001), with modifications suggested by Magnarella (1993) under the rubric human materialism, is my framework for analysis. As Harris (2001: xv) notes, cultural materialism "is based on the simple premise that human social life is a response to the practical problems of earthly existence." Therefore, infrastructure will take precedence in human adaptive responses to the environment. In attempting to understand change in any human cultural system, an anthropologist should first look to perturbations in the technological and economic subsytems of culture. In cultural materialist analysis, infrastructure has causal priority. There are feedback links with structure (dimensions of social and political organization) and with superstructure (dimensions of political and/or religious ideology). Investigation of these links follows from careful identification of patterns of production and reproduction.

Proponents of a cultural materialist research strategy have tended to select subjects for analysis that lie at the very boundary of human interaction with the environment. For example, there is Eric Ross's "beef with Sahlins" (Ross 1980: 183–186). Marshall Sahlins has argued that human foodways are based on the logic of object versus human subject; hence, we do not commoditize what we tend to categorize as kin, for example, one's family pet. By contrast, Ross's materialist explanation is based on the cost/benefit analysis of cattle over dogs as a protein source; the herbivore is a much more efficient converter of energy into proteins than the carnivore. In another context, Harris and Ross (1987) analyze modes of reproduction among preindustrial and developing societies. Cultural mediation of birth and death rates in response to cost/benefit analyses of child rearing, given available food supplies, is a human adaptive response to environmental change.

However, when one's research happens to focus on cultural behaviors that are not so firmly embedded in infrastructure, as are foodways and population, the cultural materialist strategy presents problems. Further, Brian Ferguson (1995: 30–33) has argued that cultural materialism is weak when it confronts short-term historical change. And indeed, for Harris and Ross (1987: 2–3), "causal relationships [in synchronic or slice-in-time analysis] dissolve into an incoherent corpus of middle-range eclectic correlations linking infrastructural, structural, and superstructural components in infinite arrays." They seem to prefer working through broad evolutionary time frames while consigning the analysis of everyday minutiae to historians. Ferguson, however, sees "no reason to abandon the quest for causal regularity in normal historical process" (1995: 31). To deny the value of synchronic studies is to throw out the baby with the bath water. Feedback relationships among infrastructure, structure, and superstructure can be understood as a function of the special nature of the cultural thing and context of events under investigation.

Paul Magnarella (1993: 1–19) and Maria Palov (1993: 144–152) offer a useful alternative model. Magnarella recognizes the dynamic relationships among infrastructure, structure, and superstructure. However, he divides infrastructure into components: material (technology), human (demography, psychology, biology), and social (leadership and power). These are in feedback relationships among themselves as well as with social structure (kin, economic, and political organization) and superstructure (ideology). In other words, Magnarella embraces complex relationships in the form of general systems analysis. These are asymmetrical, in the sense that change in infrastructure has causal priority with impacts on social structure and superstructure. Further, they are open to change from the natural and sociocultural environment. Finally, Magnarella makes a plausible case for human teleology in these systems. People in power will maximize outcomes for themselves, even when the well-being of others or long-term adjustment to the natural environment is jeopardized.

I attempt to cast the results of my research on the button in a form consistent with the nature of the material under study and the cultural contexts in which it is embedded. A descriptive account of the technologies that changed provides insight into the material infrastructure of button manufacture in early-twentieth-century Rochester, New York. This is followed by an analysis of change within the general guidelines of human materialism as described above.

Technology of Button Making: Material Infrastructure

Before 1935 buttons manufactured in Rochester were handcrafted from vegetable ivory, the fruit or nut of the Tagua palm (*Phytelephas macrocarpa*). The Tagua nut is several times larger than, but similar in shape to, the Brazil nut, and when mature exhibits the color and texture of tusk ivory, hence its generic name vegetable ivory. The process of manufacture was subtractive. Material was removed from the original matrix in a carefully ordered sequence of steps that were readily adapted to a factory system for mass production. The process included: drying to loosen the nut from a flint-like shell casing; tumbling in a barrel or "shucker" with metal weights to crack the shell casing; "scabbing" upon hand inspection in order to remove minute bits of shell; sizing or sorting according to size; sawing individual nuts into slabs the thickness of a button using circular saws that ran at a speed of six thousand revolutions per minute; further drying to remove every bit of residual moisture; immersing in steaming hot water in preparation for turning at a lathe in order to produce the basic button shape; drilling the holes; dyeing, either in a bath or by spraying to achieve a mottled effect; final polishing and finishing; and carding, where buttons were sewn onto cards for demonstration or sale (Albes 1913: 192–208).

A different operative performed each major step. The machinery employed was simple: circular saws, polishing wheels, lathes, and drills adapted to the scale of the product. Each slice of the Tagua nut was manipulated a hundred times before it was finally carded or boxed. As a result, the labor investment in producing a vegetable ivory button was high—as much as 80.5 percent in some types (Simon 1949). This was a labor-intensive process.

Between 1930 and 1935 changes in the local industry were instituted that would shift manufacturing to capital-intensive processes. The entire technological transformation dates between 1931 and the end of World War II. During this period techniques for mass producing buttons from plastic materials manipulated by automatic machines replaced the hand labor and craftsmanship employed in producing buttons from vegetable ivory. Of three major or national manufacturers of vegetable ivory buttons operating in Rochester during World War I, only one continued operations following World War II. It became the leader of the national plastic button industry.

Among plastics of that time, "beetle" (an early compound of urea), phenolics like Bakelite, and casein were satisfactory substitutes that could be fashioned into machine-made buttons at considerably less cost than vegetable ivory. The synthetic materials from which plastic buttons were produced in the 1930s were actually several times more costly than the unprocessed Tagua nuts, but the reduced labor costs offset this disadvantage (Anonymous n.d.). Casein was in fact the plastic that figured in the early drama of change in the Rochester industry.

Casein is produced from the protein of skim milk, which, when treated with formaldehyde, produces a thermosetting plastic. One hundred pounds of new skim milk produces approximately three pounds of casein powder. An especially fine grade of casein is necessary in the manufacture of buttons. This grade at the time was only available from abroad and consequently expensive (Anonymous n.d.). Neil O. Broderson, President of Rochester Button Co. and the innovator responsible for most of the technological change described in this article, determined that he would have to create his own supply of button-grade casein. He established a processing plant near one of the largest creameries in the State of Wisconsin. At that location, 10,000 gallons of skim milk per day could be converted into casein through the application of rennet (Clune 1936).

Production of buttons involved extruding chemically treated casein from machines that compacted and forced the material through nozzles from which it emerged in the form of rods. The rods were then machined to uniform or standard sizes, and then turned on to automatic screw machines that produced buttons at the rate of two hundred buttons per minute. Or, in some cases in separate operations, the rods were cut into round discs and then faced and backed on automatic lathes. A subsequent formaldehyde bath strengthened the button and imparted a varnish-like sheen that in cheaper varieties substituted for polishing and other types of surface treatment. Since dyestuffs in the form of a bath do not penetrate the surface of casein buttons, coloring agents were added to the casein at the time that it was extruded in rod form (Anonymous n.d.). The reduction in the number of steps involved in the manufacturing process and the ease with which casein plastic could be adapted to automatic machine processing made it an attractive candidate for mass production of buttons. Its chief limitation was its tendency, although thermosetting, to absorb water, swell, soften and break in a hot-water wash, and to discolor and become pliable when subjected to moderately elevated temperatures such as those produced by an iron (Masson 1959: 14–15). Other more durable plastics such as urea-formaldehyde, melamine-formaldehyde, nylon, and polyesters would eventually replace casein in button manufacture.

An Industry Transformed: Human Materialist Analysis

In the summer of 1930, with signs of business slowdown everywhere, Neil Broderson had some doubt about the future of the button business. He took more than passing interest in a letter dated 22 July 1930 (Rochester Button Company Papers) from George Baekeland of the Bakelite Corporation offering to put him in touch with a friend who might be interested in buying Rochester Button Company:

> I do not want to meddle in your affairs, but I did get the impression that you want to get out of your present business. Otherwise I should not be bothering you.

Broderson responded with the candor typical of him in a letter dated 23 July 1930 (Rochester Button Company Papers):

> Your assumption that I am not particularly fond of the button business is correct. However, I realize that which one has is the best until something better is found. The button business is most interesting, the principal criticism is the fact that the entire industry is such a small one that a bright future could not be hoped for, unless we can develop something aside from buttons.

At that moment, and barely thirty years of age, Broderson was about to embark on a remarkable career as innovator in plastics technologies and button making.

Neil Broderson was an intuitive engineer with no formal training in chemistry. However, he had a network of friends in the nascent plastics industry upon whose advice he could rely. Between 1931 and 1935 he developed and installed a successful casein button manufacturing department in his plant in Rochester. This innovation, like many others in biological and cultural evolution, follows Romer's rule, where, in effect, "the initial survival value of a favorable innovation is conservative, in that it renders possible the maintenance of a traditional way of life in the face of changed circumstances" (Hockett and Ascher 1964). Plastic substitutes had already begun to replace vegetable ivory in the manufacture of largely functional buttons such as those used to attach suspenders to men's pants and fly buttons. There was a lucrative market in such mundane items. Plastic in general was not yet of a quality that would provide satisfactory substitutes for more stylistically crucial or visible buttons. Under pressure from his salesmen to rush to plastic alternatives, Broderson in a letter dated 19 October 1934 counseled (Rochester Button Company Papers):

> The longer we can preserve our ivory button business while building up our substitutes, the better it will be for us. It will be difficult to gain the same advantageous position in substitutes that we enjoy in ivory and it cannot be done in six months or one year's time.

Technological change as it plays out in the lives of real people is often undramatic. Broderson developed a conservative but successful strategy that led him to further success in plastic button technologies. Following World War II he chaired the button division of the Society for Plastics Industries. He saved his company from the extinction that overtook a rival vegetable ivory button maker in Rochester, the Art in Buttons Company. In his business papers, however, Broderson offers no analysis of the economic, social, and political forces to which he and the industry were responding. Here then is a role for the anthropologist who wishes to write culture history.

The economic perturbations of the Great Depression were only a catalyst that precipitated technological change in the button industry. Population growth was the mechanism driving transformations described in this paper. Vegetable ivory button manufacture grew up as a subsidiary of the ready-to-wear clothing industry, which was directly linked to the population boom of the late nineteenth century in North America. Between 1881 and 1924 more than 21 million immigrants entered the United States, most of them of peasant origin from eastern and southern Europe (U.S. Bureau of the Census 1975). Immigration, not natural increase, provided a market for cheap clothing. Poor immigrants required mass produced garments of uniform and undistinguished character. Once people were suited in such attire, ethnic distinctions based on dress were obliterated. This was the "democracy of clothing" described by the historian Daniel Boorstin (1973: 91–100).

Vegetable ivory as a raw material was ideally suited for buttons on such clothing. It was collected from palm trees growing under natural conditions in Ecuador, Colombia and Panama. The raw nuts were harvested by cheap and exploited laborers, Indian Taguaros (Albes 1913). Before the properties of Tagua as vegetable ivory were discovered, the nuts were used as ship's ballast (Simon 1949). In short, the cost of the raw material was low. Further, clothing designed to suit everybody did not require buttons in a dazzling array of form and color. Consequently, the subtractive technology for transforming the nut into a button was adequate for the need. Finally, with the exception of sawing, turning, and dyeing, relatively unskilled labor was sufficient for the other steps in the process of producing a vegetable ivory button. The immigrant consumer of these symbols of mass democracy became the cheap labor that produced them. The industry expanded along with the immigrant population, and flourished in the early twentieth century. By the 1920s there were 35–40 factories producing vegetable ivory buttons in the United States (Simon 1949).

The decline of the industry, to which Neil Broderson was responding through technological innovation in the early 1930s, had already set in just after World War I. The factors involved can be traced to feedback from the structural and superstructural subsystems. First, the immigrant boom was brought to an abrupt halt as national sentiment against the flood led to quota laws in 1921, 1924, and 1929 (Schaeffer 1984, 120–122). The fall-off in immigration between 1924 and 1925 was dramatic. In 1924, 364,399 immigrants from Europe were admitted, but in 1925 there were only 148,366 (U.S. Bureau of the Census 1975). The quota laws reflected the concern of organized labor that immigrants would lower wage standards. But, probably more important were general antipathy toward Europe following the war and jingoistic fears that southern and eastern European immigrants were not assimilating culturally. A eugenics movement, with considerable influence in both academia and government, played on fears that biologically inferior immigrants would weaken the American gene pool. President Calvin Coolidge signed the 1924 quota law with this admonition (quoted in Harris 1999: 68):

> America must be kept American. Biological laws show that Nordics deteriorate when mixed with other races.

In the button industry sales volume is critical. Impacts of these changes were immediate. Second, styles in women's fashion changed dramatically in the 1920s. The flapper attired herself in dresses with a draped and pinned look. Fashions of the previous decade were festooned with buttons from shoulder to hemline. Among Rochester manufacturers, Art in Buttons produced for both the men's and women's apparel industry and was hardest hit by this downturn in demand. The president of the company, Henry T. Noyes, was an uncooperative, even unscrupulous, member of the community of vegetable ivory "button men," as they referred to themselves. His schemes to undercut and undersell competitors were an additional factor in the cost/benefit analysis that led ultimately to a strategy of technological innovation. The annoying Noyes ultimately led his company to extinction.

Third, serviceable slide fasteners were first introduced as closures for money belts in 1917. In that year the Hookless Fastener Company sold 24,000 fasteners. In 1923

B. F. Goodrich began producing galoshes with slide fasteners and originated the name "zipper." By 1934 the Hookless Fastener Company sold more than 60 million slide fasteners (Weiner 1983: 132–133). Throughout the 1930s and 1940s the slide fastener would become a substitute for fly buttons and a frequent alternative to buttons on outerwear. Although it is clear from his business papers that Neil O. Broderson was not concerned about inroads from the slide fastener in 1930–1931, by the late 1930s this competing technology was reinforcing his earlier decisions to intensify in the direction of further plastics technologies. He quickly moved to compounds of urea and by the late 1940s, with assistance from professionally trained chemists in his employ, he developed a nacreous polyester button that literally drove natural pearl buttons out of the men's shirt market.

From 1924 through to the early 1930s the button makers were under assault from forces they did not fully understand. Politically influenced population shifts, style changes in fashion, and then the economic downturn of the Great Depression put the button men under stress. They responded through a process of intensification based on cost/benefit analysis. It is important to note that technological innovation was the last strategy they employed.

Initially the effects of competition among the leading producers were dealt with by price-fixing. The first and only attempt ended when one of the industry leaders excused himself from a meeting in which new wholesale prices had been set, to pass the information on to a confederate waiting in the men's room. The confederate, of course, contacted customers with offers to fill orders at below the new market price (Zimmer, Nelson, President of Shantz Associates. 1983. Interview by Paul Grebinger). All the evidence in this case points to Henry Noyes.

More effective as an intermediate strategy was merger. In 1926 two competitors, Rochester Button Company and Shantz Button Corporation (a Rochester company), merged with a third the Superior Ivory Button Company of Newark, New Jersey. By the early 1930s the Shantz and Superior companies had been closed, with all manufacturing operations concentrated in the single Rochester Button Company plant. Broderson was the son of the owner of Superior Ivory Button Company and had become the manager of the New Jersey plant after the 1926 merger. He assumed leadership of the new company in 1928. As outlined above, the technological transformation from labor-intensive vegetable ivory to capital-intensive plastics technologies followed.

Not a Simple Notion

This research project began more than twenty years ago with an invitation from the Rochester Museum and Science Center to conduct background research for and create an exhibit on button making in Rochester (funded by the New York State Council on the Arts). Although all buttons manufactured by Rochester Button Company in the 1980s were from plastic materials, there were still individuals working for the company, and retirees living in the city who had worked as vegetable ivory button makers. Through interviews and historical research I was able to establish the outlines of button manufacture presented earlier in this paper. The technology and the button men who developed and transformed the industry were the focus of the exhibit. Describing the change from labor intensive to capital intensive was a first step in explaining it. As an historically oriented anthropologist I have been uncomfortable with the limitations of the cultural materialist research strategy as noted earlier. Brian Ferguson's critique and Paul Magnarella's revision in the form of human materialism have provided incentive and a model for thinking anew about these data.

The approach described by Magnarella (1993) has been recast in terms of general systems by Maria Palov (1993: Appendix). As she notes, "A basic tenet of the systems approach is that the whole is greater than the sum of its parts." The whole that I have attempted to define provides insight into changes in American culture in the early twentieth century. At no time between 1925 and 1945 did Neil Broderson, or others with whom he was in contact, make an analysis of change such as I have attempted here. (Broderson's letters through fifty years as president are available among the papers of the Rochester Button Company.) Further, the model has allowed me to explore the role of individual actors, such as Neil Broderson and Henry Noyes, as well as a class of people, immigrants, in conjunction with structural components (cf. Magnarella 1993: 148). In this way I have been able to preserve the textures of normal historical analysis and achieve materialist insights about transformation in technical and economic systems.

In colloquial usage a notion is a small article such as a button, also an ingenious device (Webster's Third International Dictionary). Although relegated to the subconscious in daily habitual activity, the button as material culture is affixed to garments worn by human actors engaged in social and cultural life. These actors, here the immigrants of early-twentieth-century America, were themselves subject to economic, political, and ideological forces of the time. Button men such as Neil Broderson responded to declining markets through strategies available to them, a process of intensification based on cost/benefit analysis. Their response to perturbations in ideology, society, and economy in America produced a revolution in button making. Throughout this process the button was never just a simple notion.

Acknowledgments

Dodworth Rowe (deceased), button designer for Rochester Button Company, provided invaluable assistance in preparing the research for the exhibit at the Rochester Museum and Science Center and in making it possible to preserve the business papers of the company. In addition many thanks to my colleague in Sociology, Vincent Serravallo, for his thoughtful and detailed comments on an earlier draft of this paper. I returned to this project in the summer of 2006 while on retreat in the Adirondacks, Osgood Pond, near Paul Smiths. On the eastern shore of the pond is White Pine Camp, Calvin Coolidge's summer Whitehouse in 1926. Local guides reported that "silent" Cal fished but did not discuss politics or much else, for that matter. His comment on the Quota Law of 1924 (referred to in this article) was testament to his political views. It is those views and that law on which this story of change turns. I doubt that Coolidge gave much thought to the implications as he paddled these waters. It has been left to me, eighty years later, to reflect upon them.

Exercise

For most Americans material objects take on a life of their own. They are valued, purchased, used, and discarded as items disconnected from their sources, processes of manufacture, and systems of distribution, discard, and recycling. Anthropologists are trained to think about all human behavior holistically; that is, everything humans do and use has an inclusive cultural context. Examine the life of the modern button, or a similar "simple notion"—Where did the raw material come from? What technology was employed to transform the raw material into the item you see today, and how did it come to be a part of your life? In asking such questions you expand your view of American culture and its reach beyond the borders of society. You become an explorer in intracultural space.

References

Albes, Edward. 1913. Tagua-vegetable ivory. *Bulletin of the Pan American Union* XXXVII, no. 2: 192–208.

Anonymous. n.d. *Casein and plastic buttons*. Rochester Button Company Papers. Rochester Museum and Science Center.

Boorstin, Daniel J., 1973. *The Americans: the democratic experience*. New York: Random House.

Clune, Henry. 1936. *Who's got the button?* Rochester Button Company Papers. Rochester Museum and Science Center.

Ferguson, R. Brian. 1995. Infrastructural determinism. In Martin F. Murphy and Maxine L. Margolis, eds, *Science, materialism, and the study of culture*. Gainesville, Fl: University Press of Florida.

Harris, Marvin. 1999. *Theories of culture in postmodern times*. London: Altamira Press.

———. 2001. *Cultural materialism: the struggle for a science of culture*. Updated edition. New York: Altamira Press.

Harris, Marvin, and Eric B., Ross. 1987. *Death, sex, and fertility: population in preindustrial and developing societies*. New York: Columbia University Press.

Hockett, C. F., and Ascher, R. 1964. The human revolution. *Current anthropology* 5: 135–146.

Magnarella, Paul J. 1993. *Human materialism: a model of sociocultural systems and a strategy for analysis*. Gainesville, Fl: University Press of Florida.

Masson, Don, comp. 1959. *Plastics: the story of an industry*. 8th rev. edition. Society of the Plastics Industry.

Palov, Maria Z. 1993. A systems analysis of human materialism. Appendix in Paul J. Magnarella, *Human materialism: a model of sociocultural systems and a strategy for analysis*. Gainesville, Fl: University Press of Florida.

Rochester Button Company Papers. Rochester Museum and Science Center.

Ross, Eric B. 1980. Patterns of diet and forces of production: an economic and ecological history of the ascendancy of beef in the United States diet. In Eric B. Ross, ed., *Beyond the myths of culture: essays in cultural materialism*. New York: Academic Press.

Schaeffer, Richard T. 1984. *Racial and ethnic groups*. 2nd edition. Boston: Little, Brown, and Company.

Simon, Arthur James. 1949. *The distribution of buttons*. M.B.A. thesis, Wharton School, University of Pennsylvania

U.S. Bureau of the Census. 1975. *Historical statistics of the United States: colonial times to 1970*. Prepared by William Lerner. Washington, D.C.

Weiner, Lewis. 1983. The slide fastener. *Scientific American 248,* no. 6: 132–144.

9

Consuming New Hampshire's Nature: Changing Views of the White Mountains

John W. Burton
Connecticut College

As a preface for this article, John Burton writes, "I believe strongly that for a young anthropologist, the effort to become fluent in the language and behavior of a non–western society (even though this is increasingly difficult) is a fundamental demand of anthropological understanding. Given this experience, when returning 'home,' one will always interpret and experience one's original culture in dramatically different ways. Anthropologists become marginal individuals, never willing or able to accept a particular way of being human as the only natural choice. The anthropological quest is ever to stand outside the box, to see and understand accepted custom in some way different from those who profess it. No condition is permanent, and no culture has proven to be an ideal solution. We are always marginal natives."

John W. Burton, Professor of Anthropology at Connecticut College in New London, Connecticut, has carried out fieldwork in the Caribbean and in the southern Sudan and has written numerous articles and a number of monographs based on this research. He has also published a book on culture and the human body as well as an intellectual portrait of the late British anthropologist Sir Edward Evan Evans-Pritchard. He is currently writing a book on the interface between culture and evolutionary biology.

> *Mountains were invented in the nineteenth-century. (Howe 2001: 1)*

> *A lot, after all, rests on how we think about and what we make of nature. (Lancaster 2003: 21)*

I offer these brief remarks on the commodification of "nature" with a number of prefatory comments. First, I am an anthropologist and am thus accustomed to participating in varieties of social experience and simultaneously feeling distant from them. Second, I am an avid mountain climber, or in the local parlance of New Hampshire, a "tramper," ever seeking the sublime solitude of the world above tree line. Third, I have been engaged in fieldwork on the general topic of "nature" for a period of three years as a part-time sales associate at a local Eastern Mountain Sports (EMS) store. This is one of seventy-four in the retail chain, which markets a wide variety of outdoor gear items to those who want to "experience nature," and to countless others who seek to adorn their bodies with artifacts that announce their concerns for physical fitness, their environmental consciousness, and their passion for "nature." Ironically, by purchasing the goods offered, consumers often see themselves as escaping the materialism of contemporary American culture. A final note: these comments and observations are intended for a general public rather than an academic audience, and hence what I have to say is not cloaked in cryptic jargon.

Nature, Part 1

As a species, fairly recent on the scene in geologic time, humans are part of the global environment as we understand this concept in the twenty-first century. Yet for some time, in the so-called western tradition of thinking, we have depicted and conceived of ourselves as unique, somehow transcending the "natural" world. In a certain sense this is true, since our life experience is enacted through cultural and thus artificial constructions. However, this view of ourselves is clearly the product of a particular (and in some ways peculiar) intellectual genealogy.

"Nature," according to McKibben, refers to "a certain set of human ideas about the world around us and our place in it" (1989: 8). This observation points up the fact that the idea of nature is culturally constructed and thus has no universal consistency or point of reference. Nature is not an objective, disembodied, or self-evident phenomenon. Rather, nature is simultaneously a product of particular historical experiences and cultural dispositions. A vast literature in the western tradition, spanning many centuries, reveals the fluid and impermanent conceptualization of nature (see Lancaster 2003, Oelschlaeger 1991, Woody 1998, cf. Rudwick 2005). By way of comparison, in the languages and cosmologies of many indigenous societies, there is an absence of abstract conceptualizations of nature or culture—people are conceived as part of the world, rather than apart from it. Perhaps the classic illustration of this point comes from those whose primary social and individual experience is enacted on the basis of "totemic" categories, where the "natural" world of plants and animals provides the conceptual basis of social structure (see, e.g., Levi-Strauss 1962). As Lancaster has recently written:

> not every culture asserts a continuous line of demarcation between nature and culture, mind and body, and the other familiar dualisms. Indeed, not every culture gives place to a singular and unitary concept of "nature." And even in modern, Western cultures, nature's place is by no means stationary or unchanging. (2003: 36; see also MacCormack and Strathern 1980, Lienhardt 1961)

In an African language I know well, spoken by the Atuot of the southern Sudan, there is indeed no term that can be translated in a singular way as either "nature" or "culture." Here, instead, the world is conceived of as a seamless whole, where things that are "wild" (*waath*) overlap with those that are predictable or "tame" (*te cieng*). Further, in this view of things, what is wild may become tame and vice versa (see, e.g., Burton 1981).

In other words, one may suggest, the western tradition of depicting nature as a distinct and discernible entity set apart from the human realm must be understood as a product of a particular historical genealogy—one that now manifests itself as a product or commodity— generated by a world view based on capitalism.

Nature, Part 2

For the first generations of European colonists in the northeastern region of the United States, the "natural" environment they encountered was distinctively strange and different from the one they left on the other side of the Atlantic Ocean. By the seventeenth century much of western Europe had been denuded of natural vegetation. In contrast, the "new world" appeared to be dark, dangerous, and foreboding, inhabited by predatory animals and semi-human savages as well as dense forest. As envisioned so clearly in the recent film *The New World,* this provided a stunning contrast to their native experience of manicured gardens, of village greens, of an environment that was in a sense, fully domesticated by human use and design. Cronan observes:

> Once European visitors had arrived, their preconceptions and expectations led them to empha-size some elements of the landscape and to filter out others. Most of the early explorers sought to discover . . . merchantable commodities. . . . These were natural products which could be shipped to Europe and sold at profit . . . fish for salting, furs for clothing, timber for ships. (1983: 20)

As is well known, the first sparsely populated European settlements were possible only as a consequence of the initial goodwill and cultural knowledge of indigenous peoples, whose own modes of livelihood and production had long before transformed the "natural" environ-ment in accord with their own cultural plans (Cronan 1983). From the European perspective, "nature"—the dense woods, the frigid winters, the short growing season, and the intrusive savages—was a perpetual enemy to civilization, a host of demons that had to be controlled or exterminated. The first to go were native peoples, who either succumbed to newly introduced diseases (see Diamond 1997) or to repulsive and barbaric policies of genocide (see, e.g., Cave 1996). This was followed by the transformation of local environments via the process men-tioned above, namely the capture of "merchantable" commodities, from fish to fur to timber. To the European, New England was, of course, a "place" to live one's life, but it was also a product to consume. During the early colonial period, few souls took to the hills for pleasure, entertainment, or enlightenment. The notable exception to this generalization is the first recorded trek of a European into the White Mountains (as they would come to be known) by a man known as Darby Field (see Bennett 2003: 27–28, Burt 1960). In 1642, in hopes of find-ing precious stones and metals, Field enlisted two Native American guides to lead him to the summit of Agiockochook, later renamed Mt. Washington. His guides were initially adverse to this undertaking since they regarded high mountains as the home of a powerful spiritual being. Field failed to find his hoped-for El Dorado, and for the next two hundred years there is no surviving record of any European who sought a mountain summit. As Howe notes, "It takes security from physical and economic threat before people feel they can take time off; that is to say, it takes vacations to turn daunting high places into something to be enjoyed, into mountains" (2001: 3). Such luxuries were unthinkable for Europeans of the time.

In New Hampshire vast tracts of native forests were leveled to provide wood for fuel, building, and export, and to create open spaces for farming as well as pasturage for sheep and cattle. Although indigenous peoples had earlier played a part in transforming a pristine environment (Cronan 1983), the pace and scale of the European commodification of the landscape was unprecedented in this part of the world. By the early 1800s indigenous peoples had been virtually exterminated, enslaved, or exiled to reservations in the western United States. A host of new animal species were introduced, perhaps most importantly dairy cattle, which were raised for meat, milk, and the market. The human care for domesticated animals gave rise to the virtual extinction of local predatory animals, particularly wolves, puma, and bears. Stone walls rose yearly as frost heaves gave birth to boulders buried by glaciers. It is estimated that by the end of the nineteenth century, 80 percent of New Hampshire forests—its "nature"—had been leveled by lumber companies. Timber loss by clearcutting was only one factor in the transformation of the environment. Countless acres of native or "virgin" growth were also destroyed by random fires kindled from the burning ashes of locomotives that snaked their way through river valleys and up mountain slopes (see, e.g., Robertson 1996). Pike describes a typical occurrence in northern New Hampshire in 1912:

> A cloud of thick smoke hovered over the conflagration and large tributary curls could be seen twisting up from dozens of places. . . . The smoldering logs and charred trees, even then, when fanned by the wind, glowed and smoked. . . . In the great Maine fire of 1825, flames roared like thunder and could be heard a dozen miles away. . . . Contemporaries tell of sparks as big as bushel baskets being carried for miles, of great pitch-filled pines, exploding like fire-crackers, of deer and their hooves burned off, of the blackened bodies of women and children, of streams dried up, of dead fish and oxen. (1967: 186)

In short, the European conceptions and uses of "nature" were starkly different from those of native peoples, who thought of themselves as part of nature. For all intents and purposes, the Europeans essentially destroyed everything that was "natural," in the process devastating the indigenous people and denuding the land. Cronan puts the matter this way:

> Ultimately, English property systems encouraged colonists to regard the products of the land—not to mention the land itself—as commodities. . . . The dynamics which led colonists to accumulate wealth and capital were the most dramatic point of contrast between the New England economy of 1600 and that of 1800. The economic transformation paralleled the ecological one. . . . New England ecology was transformed as the region became integrated into the emerging capitalist economy of the North Atlantic. Capitalism and environmental degradation went hand in hand. (1983: 161)

On the matter of environmental degradation Cronan remarks at some length:

> Deforestation had in general affected the region by making local temperatures more erratic, soils drier, and drainage patterns less constant. A number of smaller streams and springs no

longer flowed year-round, and some larger rivers were dammed and no longer accessible to the fish which had once spawned in them. Water and wind erosion were taking place with varying severity, and flooding had become more common. Soil exhaustion was occurring in many areas as a result of poor husbandry, and the first of many European pests and crop diseases had already begun to appear. These changes had taken place primarily in the settled areas, and it was still possible to find extensive regions in the north where they did not apply. Nevertheless, they heralded the future. (1983: 160)

Nature, Part 3

By the turn of the twentieth century the woodlands of the White Mountains had been thoroughly scoured of their resources. Slowly there emerged a groundswell of concern for preserving the remaining "wilderness" and bringing an end to the utterly destructive process of clearcutting forests. The decisive moment in this trend was marked by the creation of the Weeks Act in 1911. This legislation was specifically enacted as a means to protect and preserve inland waterways, many of which had been poisoned by the residues of logging companies. For those whose emergent interests were focusing on the "preservation" of nature, this act had the unintended consequence of bringing the logging industries to a virtual halt. As the Watermans write:

> In 1901, as the White Mountains were being cruelly logged and burned, the Society for the Protection of New Hampshire Forests was formed. . . . On March 1, 1911, Congress passed the Weeks Act . . . by June 1912, the wheels were in motion to set aside more than 70,000 acres as the White Mountain National Forest. (1989: 310)

Specifically this action authorized federal purchases of forest lands to protect valuable watersheds (see also Smith 2001, Bennett 2003: 129).

The notion that an environment had to be protected from human use was one that emerged earlier in the nineteenth century through the writings and travelogues of such people as John Muir, Henry David Thoreau, and Ralph Waldo Emerson. Indeed, Emerson visited the White Mountains during the summer of 1832, as did Thoreau in 1839. In Washington, D.C., in the early twentieth century, President Roosevelt was a key spokesperson for this early environmental movement.

Earlier still, in the first half of the nineteenth century, a very significant cultural and economic transformation was under way in the White Mountains. The northern regions of the state became less a natural resource to consume and more of a cultural center to escape from the burgeoning cities of the northeastern United States. One can think of this consumption of "nature," now with a radically different meaning, as a means to escape culture. The primary railways laid down by logging companies along river valleys and on mountain slopes were slowly becoming highways for an emergent tourist industry. This social and economic phenomenon coincided with the growth of a larger middle class in industrializing America, a group of people that had not only greater wealth, but also that very scarce resource of earlier days, namely "leisure" time. Beginning in the 1830s, and continuing well into the 1920s, local enterprising residents began erecting large guest inns to house and entertain an emergent leisure class. In 1823, a stagecoach trip from Boston to Crawford Notch took a full four hours, but as the rail lines expanded the journey was cut down considerably. As one inn and then another was built, so too was a novel conception of nature. Entrepreneur Abel Crawford sensed early on that the White Mountains would attract casual visitors, and his own homestead eventually grew into one of the larger inns in the Notch that bears his name. In the 1820s Crawford blazed the first trail to the summit of Mt. Washington, along its southwestern ridge. Eventually, by the 1840s, the trail had been widened into a bridal path. The three small stone shelters he built on the summit in 1823 presaged the erection of two larger shelters in 1853; the Mount Washington Summit House was built in 1873 and could house and feed a hundred people. Crawford's early intuition certainly proved to be insightful. Widespread news of a tragic mudslide in Crawford Notch during the summer of 1826 drew a growing throng of visitors to the region over the next decades.

As Bennett (2003: 83) observes, the arrival of railroads into the region in the 1850s dramatically increased the tourist trade. In 1876, the Boston, Concord, and Montreal Railroad was extended to the base of the Cog Railway (first opened in 1869), so it was then possible to board a train in almost any east coast city and ride the rails to the summit of Mt. Washington. The increased rail service likewise fueled the growth of the upscale "grand inn." The mountains offered clean air, inspiring views, and simple escape from increasingly dirty and increasingly dangerous industrializing cities. By the middle of the nineteenth century it was possible for those with sufficient means to make annual summer pilgrimages to these massive hotels and dine from exotic menus served on imported china. The Profile House in Franconia Notch even offered enticements such as bowling alleys, a music room, boat excursions on Echo Lake as well as guided tours of tourist destinations such as the Flume Gorge, The Pool, The Basin, and the Old Man of the Mountain (see Bennett 2003: 95). By 1890, there were some two hundred inns and hotels in the White Mountains. In the span of less than one hundred years, the dreaded and dangerous forests and wilderness of northern New Hampshire had been domesticated, captured, and controlled. The growing desire to escape the consequences of industrialization had paradoxically produced the very technologies that created "pristine nature" as a commodity for consumption. The White Mountains provided, in fact, a very domesticated wilderness and one that was, after the logging decades, as far from pristine as one could imagine. By the turn of the twentieth century all but a handful of the grand hotels had burned to the ground, effectively ending what many historians of the region have termed "the golden era" of the White Mountains (see Bennett 2003: 83–118).

Nature, Part 4

At the same time the logging industries were creating a "condition of extreme desolation" (Bennett 2003: 120) in the White Mountains, an unprecedented number of people were arriving to enjoy the region's natural beauty. Among these was a growing community that wanted to experience the mountains on foot rather than on horseback, from a rail car, or from an automobile. The small village of Randolph, for example, became a summer hub for Boston intellectuals and nascent environmentalists, who took to the mountains to blaze one and then another "path," as they called them (in order to disassociate them from "trails," a term that connoted Indian-ness). The Randolph Mountain Club was born of such sentiments.

By the 1920s such voluntary organizations included the Wonalancet Out Door Club, Chocoma Mountain Club, the Waterville Athletic and Improvement Association, and the North Woodstock Improvement Association (Bennett 2003: 123). And as Smith notes, "The years from about 1915 to the mid-1930s brought the expansion and unification of the White Mountain trail system and the development of the Appalachian Mountain Association huts" (2001: xxiv). Bennett writes that by this time, "a vigorous new generation of recreational walkers and climbers . . . now poured into the highlands to trek up all the major peaks" (2003: 120). He continues:

> These late Victorian mountain lovers fervently believed in walking as the best way of experiencing the great outdoors . . . choosing as their base of operations smaller inns or boarding houses that were more affordable and, like the much beloved Ravine House in Randolph, removed from the grandiosity of hotel life. (2003: 121)

Moses Sweetser, author of the 1876 book *The White Mountains: A Handbook for Travellers,* had earlier on waxed philosophically about this more "intimate" nature experience:

> When the bust citizen has grown weary under the pressure of business or study, and loses his ability to eat or sleep, or to take pleasure either in present or anticipated comforts, let him visit the mountains and inhale their electric air, forgetting for a month he has home cares. . . . The sojourn in a summer hotel is well and beneficial, but the journey on foot is better, since it gives incessant variety and ever-changing throes of diversion. After a few days of marching, he will cease to complain of sleepless nights or zestless meals. . . . The pedestrian tour is of high value to men of sedentary habits, giving them a valuable and needed change of habit, expanding their shrunken lungs, and teaching their limbs pliancy and strength. (cited in Bennett 2003: 124–125)

While initially regarded as a curiosity when they were first produced, automobiles soon became an American passion and, as Bennett (2003: 133) observes, "The advent of auto touring, like the coming of the railroads 50 years earlier, transformed the region in dramatic ways to the dismay of many who viewed such fast-paced rambles as an intrusion into the exclusive world of the grand hotels" (2003: 133). Following the end of World War I, and increasingly after World War II, the automobile afforded growing numbers of opportunity to take to the hills on their own. Rail transportation to the White Mountains ceased to have any further significance since the era of massive logging had passed and since the automobile allowed for greater freedom of movement. Soon after Word War II there emerged an increasing attraction to "family camping" as an affordable means to experience the White Mountains. The government surplus jeep, the government surplus tent, and a vast inventory of related military gear oozed into the American marketplace. Middle-class Americans were experiencing greater material comfort in their lives and took to the hills via an ever-expanding highway system. My own youth was firmly located in the "see the USA in your Chevrolet" era, and my parents (both originally from New Hampshire) led the family up smaller peaks as well as to State Parks, National Parks, and campgrounds throughout the country. Family camping thrived, I sense, because it was significantly less expensive than eating at restaurants and sleeping in motels. For middle-class Americans in the 1950s, a summer vacation became virtually a necessity, or in starker terms, camping had become a product that growing numbers of people of modest means could consume. By this time, the few remaining grand inns had become an emblem of an era, when consuming the wilderness was an option primarily for those of affluence. Since this time the number of publicly and privately owned and managed campgrounds in the White Mountains has soared. Many families reserve campsites for two weeks or more, living in the woods on the cheap. For better or worse more and more of these sites are occupied by large, energy-inefficient recreational vehicles and mobile homes. Indeed, many owners of these vehicles book a campsite for the entire summer season. One can note in passing that recreational downhill skiing, cross-country skiing, and snowshoeing have grown in tandem with the popularity of camping, so that the consumption of nature is now a year-round rather than seasonal practice. For those averse to winter camping, a vast array of winter ski lodges and condominiums now litter the valleys of Conway, Lincoln, and Crawford Notch.

Nature in the 1970s

Yet another sea change in the American conception and consumption of nature emerged amidst other social and cultural phenomena of the late 1960s and early 1970s. Indeed, there is a long shopping list of novel events of the era. With specific reference to a concept of "nature," perhaps the most important of these was the 1959 publication of Rachael Carson's book *Silent Spring,* which shocked the reading public into an awareness of how DDT and industrial pollutants were harming the "natural" environment. The new environmentalism of the period emerged in a social environment of general protest and alarm—about the undeclared war in Vietnam, about racism and sexism in the social fabric, and about virtually any policy advanced and promoted by "the Establishment." Such concerns were also made evident in the nature-consumption industry.

This era witnessed the large-scale emergence of backpacking culture, and with it a host of new consumer products as well as a new nature ethic. As noted earlier, in American history there have always been number of individuals who took to the hills to experience nature "in the raw." But the culture of backpacking was part of an emergent *industry* intended to provide hundreds of thousands of consumers an inventory of high-end outdoor gear, much of which was first produced for the military. It focused on a "wilderness experience" based on self-sufficiency as the really authentic way to consume nature. Then as now, there are those tourists who prefer to pay ($100, currently) for a ride in the cog railway to the summit of Mt. Washington. However, from the 1970s to the present, the number of hikers on the Appalachian Trail and hundreds of paths in the White Mountains has trebled. The outdoor gear industry has grown in proportion. For example, in 1967, Eastern Mountain Sports comprised a single retail store. As previously mentioned, the company now consists of seventy-four stores (of varying size), with an estimated gross income of more than $160 million last year. The industry promotes a double-edged fantasy: that nature is to be consumed "in the raw," but only with a backpack full of high-end, technical gear. The nineteenth-century notion was to experience the mountains but in a way that one was protected from them. For example, people made their way to summits such as Mooselauke, LaFayette, or Washington either on horseback or sitting in a horse-drawn carriage, to return home at the end of the day, or to overnight in a mountain-top hotel, to dine and sleep in plush comfort. Armed now with geographical positioning systems, water-filter kits, ultra-light tents and down sleeping bags, the peaks are swarming with hikers conquering the hills with their gear. Indeed, I recently saw a hiker on the summit of Mt. Monadnock in southwestern New Hampshire, a modest peak requiring less than two hours to scale, toting enough gear to assure his survival at base camp on Mt. Everest! And again, tramping is a year-round rather than seasonal undertaking. Howe reflects on some of these matters in these terms:

> Useful winter seasons really arrived after World War II, when the civilian market was flooded with cold-weather equipment developed for the military. Since then, winter equipment has advanced with exponential strides and now there are stores near the Presidential range where an enthusiast can walk out with $4,000.00 worth of clothing in addition to a wealth of hardware. (2001: 258)

The "need" to own/consume such gear and goods continues to make this a growth industry. Howe continues:

> On New Year's Day of 1998 I drove "around the mountains"—up through Pinkham Notch, around the north end of the range through Randolph, down the west side to Twin Mountain, around the south and through Crawford Notch, and back up to Pinkham. I stopped at every parking lot that served trails giving access to 4,000 foot peaks and counted cars. The weather had been brutal. . . . A generation earlier I would have been surprised to find any cars at all in these parking lots, but on this day I counted 231 vehicles. . . . I did it again in 1999. . . . I made the same stops and counted 289 cars. (2001: 258)

Some Reflections

Just as a physical environment is constantly in the process of change, so too are our perceptions and sentiments about the physical world. I spent almost every summer of my youth on my maternal grandmother's small dairy farm in central western New Hampshire. The bold western shoulder of Mt. Mooselauke rose in the near distance, beyond a small brook that babbled outside my bedroom window. I never climbed that peak in my youth; it seemed just too big and imposing, even threatening. My more constant playground was Black Mountain, not quite 3000 feet high, south of the small town of Haverhill. It is a handsome little peak, in many ways like Mt. Monadnock. On each peak, for the last quarter-mile or so, trails scramble up open ledge to treeless summits. In those days my "gear" consisted of a white cotton T-shirt, a pair of denim shorts, sneakers, and cotton socks. I never carried a backpack (I don't recall that they existed at the time) and I didn't see the need to carry anything with me to the summit. I'd speculate that most hikers in those hills were similarly dressed.

Something of the tramping experience has remained the same. Most people one encounters on these usually friendly trails are white, middle-class, and by some majority, male. Reflecting now on some forty years of hiking in New Hampshire, I can really only remember encountering a handful of people not essentially like myself—these are indeed very white mountains. What has changed most, however, are the artifacts that are toted to the top.

But a number of other factors have changed. The trailhead parking lots are increasingly occupied by vehicles that look like they could be driven halfway up a mountain, and advertisements for such modes of transportation suggest that this is indeed their primary function. Second, for a growing number of hikers, it appears that the aim of the exercise is less a matter of experiencing "nature" in these protected settings, and more an effort to "bag the peaks," reaching the summits on a checklist, consuming them like so many berries on a bush. As a recent issue of the magazine *AMC Outdoors* notes:

> In 2005, 29-year-old Andrew Thompson set the current standard for the Appalachian Trail, completing [it] in 47 days, 13 hours and 31 minutes—an average of more than 45 miles a day. For Vermont's 270-mile Long Trail, the record is 4 days, 13 hours and 15 minutes. The current mark for summiting all 48 White Mountain 4,000 footers is 3 days, 15 hours and 51 minutes. (2006: 13)

The advertising angle on this is that without the high-end gear such goals are more elusive.

There is no questioning the fact that contemporary outdoor gear products help protect the body from weather extremes far better than in the past. The common adage "cotton kills" is patently true. Dressed the way I was years ago, perhaps I can only say I was lucky I never experienced serious hypothermia, a life-threatening condition when core body temperature can plunge to 80 degrees. Cold, rain-soaked clothing rapidly fuels this process. Indeed, in the past, hypothermia has been a consistent cause of death in these mountains (see, e.g., Howe 2001, Allen 1998). I confess that countless times at the local EMS, I reviewed a mental text about the "need" to wear synthetic materials to be well-prepared for changing weather. The company line is that clothing is a type of thermostat.

The majority of customers I worked with were white men and women, at least on the surface, well to do. It is, after all, an expensive place to shop. (Some call it Expensive Mountain Shit.) Mostly in their forties and fifties, the men were typically, though to varying degrees, overweight. During my three-year stint in the store, I made something like the following sale at least one hundred times:

Waterproof "breathable" rain jacket	$99.00
Synthetic "wicking" base layer shirt	$25.00
Soft-shell wind jacket	$125.00
Fleece jacket	$100.00
Nylon pants/shorts	$79.00
Wool socks	$18.00
Waterproof hiking boots	$200.00
Backpack	$150.00
Light-weight tent	$300.00
Sleeping bag	$179.00
Sleeping mat	$79.00
Freeze-dried food	$25.00
Total	**$1379.00**

This figure simply covers the "bare essentials." For the four-season hiker/camper, there are additional costs such as a down jacket (around $200.00), snowshoes (around $150.00), ice crampons (around $120.00), a winter tent (around $500.00), and a long list of other items including gloves, hats, headlamps, stoves, and water filtration systems, to name but a few. Thus, for an initial outlay of approximately $2349.00, consumers can take to the hills feeling confident that they will successfully survive, conquer the elements, and have a deep experience of nature. I surmise that the "typical" EMS customer whom I came to know (this does not include hard-core gear heads) would use such gear three or four times a year, but would return to the store month after month—and year after year—to check out and often buy the new product line: a different-colored fleece jacket, additional wicking shirts, the latest soft-shell jacket, a second pair of boots.

As noted, contemporary gear is better designed than what was once available. But it became my clear conviction (after what I would claim was serious participant/observer fieldwork in the store) that *what was really selling*—and hence, obviously what people wanted to buy—was an image: products, and very expensive name-brand items at that, which publicized customers' passion for nature and their own self-image. In the course of three years I worked with only two customers who were planning a trip up Mt. Kilimanjaro in Tanzania. However, some customers imagine Everest base camp even though they will never climb above 6000 feet. Indeed, most customers wear their fleece jackets to keep warm while walking their dogs. The gear is more an emblem of how they would like the world to perceive them and how they would like to think of themselves.

In his remarkably insightful, ironic, and humorous book *Bobos in Paradise,* David Brooks (2000) has reflected on these and related matters at length. In his view, conquering nature isn't really about conquering nature at all; it's more about bragging rights and building a currency of "achievements" that testify to high social class and the status this confers. In his words, the high-end trekker turns nature into an adventure course, an amusement park in the raw, where the participants encounter "a series of ordeals and obstacles they can conquer" (2000: 209). His recollections of a trip to an REI store in Seattle, Washington, amply repay multiple readings (2000: 211–217). For example:

> The thing that got me was the load of requirements. If you are going to spend any leisure time with members of the educated class, you have to prove you are serious. "Serious" is the biggest compliment Bobos [i.e., bourgeois Bohemians] use to describe their leisure activities. . . . The most accomplished are so serious they never have any fun at all. . . . But the real reason for the REI store is upstairs on the mezzanine level, where the clothing department is. Because while not a lot of people actually go climb glaciers, there are millions who want to dress like they do. (2000: 213)

In short, the proper dress, the proper gear, the proper currency of knowledge, combine to make the experience of nature that much more authentic, even while, in many instances, what is bought and paraded in public is authentic fantasy (see Lears 1994) and is similar to so many other experiences within the capitalist system.

A recent *New York Times* article fetishizes these mountain experiences as a means of "finding philosophy on the side of a cliff" (Hurt 2006: B5). For a mere $225 a day the enthusiastic consumer can now spend a day with a guide (gear is included with the fee), climbing an elevation of (a scant) forty feet in the Shawangunk "mountains" in New York. According to this article, some fifty thousand people visit the site annually. Is this pilgrimage about *nature*? Apparently not, I think, to most. Rather, it is about identity, fashion, consumption, and achievement—the bragging rights to which Brooks refers. As one participant cited in the article states, "I've done lots of other sports, but nothing comes close to the all-encompassing way climbing challenges you mentally, physically, even emotionally." (Of course, one should note in passing, any true challenge to the human being is a complex combination of mental, physical, and emotional dispositions!) There is no mention here, however, of the splendor of nature or the discovery of one's small place in this seemingly vast world. Rather, this is just another example of consumption.

It wasn't like this when the first passionate adventurers took to the hills at the end of the nineteenth century. Indeed, as early as 1784, the reverend and early White Mountains wanderer Jeremy Belknap observed:

> Almost everything in nature, which can be supposed capable of inspiring ideas of the sublime and beautiful is here realized. Aged mountains, stupendous elevations, rolling clouds, impending rocks, verdant woods, crystal streams, the gentle rill, and the roaring torrents, all conspire to amaze, to soothe and to enrapture.

Surely this experience and perception of nature is radically different from the one I recently observed on a White Mountain peak. A white man, probably in his middle twenties, came running up the trail to a summit where I sat. On arriving at the top, he slapped the summit marker, exclaiming "Got this one!" and headed back down the trail, never breaking his stride. It could have been a fast-food stop at McDonald's. Actually, in a way, it was.

Questions For Further Discussion

In many respects the term "wild" in American English designates the Other—that which is ordinarily Not Us, although we may claim to be wild ourselves if we wish to appear rebellious. To whom and to what do we apply the word "wild"? Is "wild" dangerous, or alluring, or both? For Americans, what does "wild" say about nature, gender, the proper way to behave?

References

Allen, D. H. 1998. *Don't die on the mountain*. New London, NH: Diapensia Press.

AMC (Appalachian Mountain Club). Outdoors. 2006. October.

Bennett, R. 2003. *The White Mountains*. Charleston, NC: Arcadea Press.

Brooks, D. 2000. *Bobos in paradise*. New York: Simon and Schuster.

Burt, Frank Allen. 1960. *The story of Mount Washington*. Hanover, NH: Dartmouth Publications.

Burton, J. W. 1981. *God's ants: a study of Atuot religion*. Wein: Studia Institute Anthropos.

Cave, A. 1996. *The Pequot War*. Amherst: University of Massachusetts Press.

Cronan, W. 1983. *Changes in the land*. New Haven: Yale University Press.

Diamond, J. 1997. *Guns, germs and steel*. New York: W. W. Norton.

Howe, N. 2001. *Not without peril: one hundred and fifty years of misadventure on the Presidential Range of New Hampshire*. Boston: AMC Books.

Hurt, H. 2006. Finding philosophy on the side of a cliff. *The New York Times,* September 9.

Lancaster, R. 2003. *The trouble with nature*. Berkeley: University of California Press.

Lears, J. 1994. *Fables of abundance: a cultural history of advertising in America*. New York: Basic Books.

Levi-Strauss, C. 1962. *Totemism*. Chicago: University of Chicago Press.

Lienhardt, G. 1961. *Divinity and experience: the religion of the Dinka*. Oxford: Clarendon Press.

MacCormack, C. and M. Strathern, eds. 1980. *Nature, culture and gender*. Cambridge: Cambridge University Press.

McKibban, B. 1989. *The end of nature*. New York: Random House.

Oelschlaeger, M. 1991. *The idea of wilderness*. New Haven: Yale University Press.

Pike, R. 1967. *Tall trees, tough men*. New York: W. W. Norton.

Robertson, E. 1996. *A century of railroading in Crawford Notch*. Private publication.

Rudwick, M. 2005. Picturing nature in the age of the enlightenment. *Proceedings of the American Philosophical Society* 149: 279–303.

Smith, S. 2001. *The 4,000-footers of the White Mountains*. Littleton, NH: Bondcliff.

Waterman, L. and G. Waterman. 1989. *Forest and crag: a history of hiking, trail blazing and adventure in the northeast mountains*. Boston: AMC.

Woody, J. M. 1998. *Freedom's embrace*. University Park: University of Pennsylvania Press.

10

The Female World of Cards and Holidays: Women, Families, and the Work of Kinship

Micaela di Leonardo

Northwestern University

Americans profess to value family, but we frequently fail to recognize the amount of effort involved in maintaining its emotional vitality. It is generally women who tend the family in this way, and not only do they receive no remuneration for what they accomplish in this area, but it is seldom even graced with the designation of "work." Micaela di Leonardo rectifies this injustice in the following classic article, which first appeared in print in 1987.

Micaela di Leonardo, who received her Ph.D. from the University of California at Berkeley in 1981, is Professor of Anthropology and Performance Studies at Northwestern University. She is a cultural anthropologist with broad interests in the social and economic inequality arising from differences in class, race, gender, and sexuality, as well as the public-cultural representations and misrepresentations of that inequality. Her primary geographic focus is American urban life, but she also works in and teaches on global political economy. She has written the books Varieties of Ethnic Experience *(Cornell, 1984) and* Exotics at Home *(Chicago, 1998), and edited or co-edited* Gender at the Crossroads of Knowledge *(California, 1991) and* The Gender/Sexuality Reader *(Routledge, 1997). Her co-edited* New Landscapes of Global Inequality *is under review for publication, and she is finishing her ethnography on political economy and public culture in New Haven, Connecticut.*

> *Why is it that the married women of America are supposed to write all the letters and send all the cards to their husbands' families? My old man is a much better writer than I am, yet he expects me to correspond with his whole family. If I asked him to correspond with mine, he would blow a gasket.*
>
> —Letter to Ann Landers

di Leonardo, Micaela. "The Female World of Cards and Holidays: Women, Families, and the Work of Kinship." *Signs* 12.3 (Spring 1987): 440–453. © 1987 the University of Chicago Press. Reprinted by permission.

> *Women's place in man's life cycle has been that of nurturer, caretaker, and
> helpmate, the weaver of those networks of relationships on which she in turn
> relies.*
>
> —Carol Gilligan, *In a Different Voice*[1]

Feminist scholars in the past fifteen years have made great strides in formulating new
understandings of the relations among gender, kinship, and the larger economy. As a result
of this pioneering research, women are newly visible and audible, no longer submerged
within their families. We see households as loci of political struggle, inseparable parts of
the larger society and economy, rather than as havens from the heartless world of industrial
capitalism.[2] And historical and cultural variations in kinship and family forms have become
clearer with the maturation of feminist historical and social-scientific scholarship.

Two theoretical trends have been key to this reinterpretation of women's work and
family domain. The first is the elevation to visibility of women's nonmarket activities—
housework, child care, the servicing of men, and the care of the elderly—and the definition
of all these activities as *labor,* to be enumerated alongside and counted as part of overall
social reproduction. The second theoretical trend is the nonpejorative focus on women's
domestic or kin-centered networks. We now see them as the products of conscious strategy,
as crucial to the functioning of kinship systems, as sources of women's autonomous power
and possible primary sites of emotional fulfillment, and, at times, as the vehicles for actual
survival and/or political resistance.[3]

Recently, however, a division has developed between feminist interpreters of the
"labor" and the "network" perspectives on women's lives. Those who focus on women's
work tend to envision women as sentient, goal-oriented actors, while those who concern
themselves with women's ties to others tend to perceive women primarily in terms of nurturance, other-orientation—altruism. The most celebrated recent example of this division is the
opposing testimony of historians Alice Kessler-Harris and Rosalind Rosenberg in the Equal
Employment Opportunity Commission's sex discrimination case against Sears Roebuck and
Company. Kessler-Harris argued that American women historically have actively sought
higher-paying jobs and have been prevented from gaining them because of sex discrimination
by employers. Rosenberg argued that American women in the nineteenth century created
among themselves, through their domestic networks, a "women's culture" that emphasized
the nurturance of children and others and the maintenance of family life and that discouraged women from competition over or heavy emotional investment in demanding high-
paid employment.[4]

I shall not here address this specific debate but, instead, shall consider its theoretical
background and implications. I shall argue that we need to fuse, rather than to oppose, the
domestic network and labor perspectives. In what follows, I introduce a new concept, the
work of kinship, both to aid empirical feminist research on women, work, and family and to
help advance feminist theory in this arena. I believe that the boundary-crossing nature of the
concept helps to confound the self-interest/altruism dichotomy, forcing us from an either–or
stance to a position that includes both perspectives. I hope in this way to contribute to a more
critical feminist vision of women's lives and the meaning of family in the industrial West.

In my recent field research among Italian-Americans in Northern California, I found
myself considering the relations between women's kinship and economic lives. As an

anthropologist, I was concerned with people's kin lives beyond conventional American nuclear family or household boundaries. To this end, I collected individual and family life histories, asking about all kin and close friends and their activities. I was also very interested in women's labor. As I sat with women and listened to their accounts of their past and present lives, I began to realize that they were involved in three types of work: housework and child care, work in the labor market, and the work of kinship.[5]

By kin work I refer to the conception, maintenance, and ritual celebration of cross-household kin ties, including visits, letters, telephone calls, presents, and cards to kin; the organization of holiday gatherings; the creation and maintenance of quasi-kin relations; decisions to neglect or to intensify particular ties; the mental work of reflection about all these activities; and the creation and communication of altering images of family and kin vis-à-vis the images of others, both folk and mass media. Kin work is a key element that has been missing in the synthesis of the "household labor" and "domestic network" perspectives. In our emphasis on individual women's responsibilities within households and on the job, we reflect the common picture of households as nuclear units, tied perhaps to the larger social and economic system, but not to *each other*. We miss the point of telephone and soft drink advertising, of women's magazines' holiday issues, of commentators' confused nostalgia for the mythical American extended family: it is kinship contact *across households,* as much as women's work within them, that fulfills our cultural expectation of satisfying family life.

Maintaining these contacts, this sense of family, takes time, intention, and skill. We tend to think of human social and kin networks as the epiphenomena of production and reproduction: the social traces created by our material lives. Or, in the neoclassical tradition, we see them as part of leisure activities, outside an economic purview except insofar as they involve consumption behavior. But the creation and maintenance of kin and quasi-kin networks in advanced industrial societies is *work*; and, moreover, it is largely women's work.

The kin-work lens brought into focus new perspectives on my informants' family lives. First, life histories revealed that often the very existence of kin contact and holiday celebration depended on the presence of an adult woman in the household. When couples divorced or mothers died, the work of kinship was left undone; when women entered into sanctioned sexual or marital relationships with men in these situations, they reconstituted the men's kinship networks and organized gatherings and holiday celebrations. Middle-aged businessman Al Bertini, for example, recalled the death of his mother in his early adolescence: "I think that's probably one of the biggest losses in losing a family—yeah, I remember as a child when my Mom was alive . . . the holidays were treated with enthusiasm and love . . . after she died the attempt was there but it just didn't materialize." Later in life, when Al Bertini and his wife separated, his own and his son Jim's participation in extended-family contact decreased rapidly. But when Jim began a relationship with Jane Bateman, she and he moved in with Al, and Jim and Jane began to invite his kin over for holidays. Jane single-handedly planned and cooked the holiday feasts.

Kin work, then, is like housework and child care: men in the aggregate do not do it. It differs from these forms of labor in that it is harder for men to substitute hired labor to accomplish these tasks in the absence of kinswomen. Second, I found that women, as the workers in this arena, generally had much greater kin knowledge than did their husbands, often including more accurate and extensive knowledge of their husbands' families. This was true both of middle-aged and younger couples and surfaced as a phenomenon in my interviews in the form of humorous arguments and in wives' detailed additions to husbands' narratives. Nick Meraviglia, a middle-aged professional, discussed his Italian antecedents in the presence of his wife, Pina:

> *Nick:* My grandfather was a very outspoken man, and it was reported he took off for the hills when he found out that Mussolini was in power.
>
> *Pina:* And he was a very tall man; he used to have to bow his head to get inside doors.
>
> *Nick:* No, that was my uncle.
>
> *Pina:* Your grandfather too, I've heard your mother say.
>
> *Nick:* My mother has a sister and a brother.
>
> *Pina:* *Two* sisters!
>
> *Nick:* You're right!
>
> *Pina:* Maria and Angelina.

Women were also much more willing to discuss family feuds and crises and their own roles in them; men tended to repeat formulaic statements asserting family unity and respectability. (This was much less true for younger men.) Joe and Cetta Longhinotti's statements illustrate these tendencies. Joe responded to my question about kin relations: "We all get along. As a rule, relatives, you got nothing but trouble." Cetta, instead, discussed her relations with each of her grown children, their wives, her in-laws, and her own blood kin in detail. She did not hide the fact that relations were strained in several cases; she was eager to discuss the evolution of problems and to seek my opinions of her actions. Similarly, Pina Meraviglia told the following story of her fight with one of her brothers with hysterical laughter: "There was some biting and hair pulling and choking . . . it was terrible! I shouldn't even tell you. . . ." Nick, meanwhile, was concerned about maintaining an image of family unity and respectability.

Also, men waxed fluent while women were quite inarticulate in discussing their past and present occupations. When asked about their work lives, Joe Longhinotti and Nick Meraviglia, union baker and professional, respectively, gave detailed narratives of their work careers. Cetta Longhinotti and Pina Meraviglia, clerical and former clerical, respectively, offered only short descriptions focusing on factors of ambience, such as the "lovely things" sold by Cetta's firm.

These patterns are not repeated in the younger generation, especially among younger women, such as Jane Bateman, who have managed to acquire training and jobs with some prospect of mobility. These younger women, though, have *added* a professional and detailed interest in their jobs to a felt responsibility for the work of kinship.[6]

Although men rarely took on any kin-work tasks, family histories and accounts of contemporary life revealed that kinswomen often negotiated among themselves, alternating hosting, food-preparation, and gift-buying responsibilities—or sometimes ceding entire task clusters to one woman. Taking on or ceding tasks was clearly related to acquiring or divesting oneself of power within kin networks, but women varied in their interpretation of the meaning of this power. Cetta Longhinotti, for example, relied on the "family Christmas dinner" as a symbol of her central kinship role and was involved in painful negotiations with her daughter-in-law over the issue: "Last year she insisted—this is touchy. She doesn't want to spend the holiday dinner together. So last year we went there. But I still had my dinner the next day . . . I made a big dinner on Christmas Day, regardless of who's coming—candles on the table, the whole routine. I decorate the house myself too . . . well, I just feel that the time will come when maybe I won't feel like cooking a big dinner—she should take advantage of the fact that I feel like doing it now." Pina Meraviglia, in contrast, was saddened by the centripetal force of the developmental cycle but was unworried about the power dynamics involved in her negotiations with daughters- and mother-in-law over holiday celebrations.

Kin work is not just a matter of power among women but also of the mediation of power represented by household units.[7] Women often choose to minimize status claims in their kin work and to include numbers of households under the rubric of family. Cetta Longhinotti's sister Anna, for example, is married to a professional man whose parents have considerable economic resources, while Joe and Cetta have low incomes and no other well-off kin. Cetta and Anna remain close, talk on the phone several times a week, and assist their adult children, divided by distance and economic status, in remaining united as cousins.

Finally, women perceived housework, child care, market labor, the care of the elderly, and the work of kinship as competing responsibilities. Kin work was a unique category, however, because it was unlabeled and because women felt they could either cede some tasks to kinswomen and/or could cut them back severely. Women variously cited the pressures of market labor, the needs of the elderly, and their own desires for freedom and job enrichment as reasons for cutting back Christmas card lists, organized holiday gatherings, multifamily dinners, letters, visits, and phone calls. They expressed guilt and defensiveness about this cutback process and, particularly, about their failures to keep families close through constant contact and about their failures to create perfect holiday celebrations. Cetta Longhinotti, during the period when she was visiting her elderly mother every weekend in addition to working a full-time job, said of her grown children, "I'd have the whole gang here once a month, but I've been so busy that I haven't done that for about six months." And Pina Meraviglia lamented her insufficient work on family Christmases, "I wish I had really made it traditional . . . like my sister-in-law has special stories."

Kin work, then, takes place in an arena characterized simultaneously by cooperation and competition, by guilt and gratification. Like housework and child care, it is women's work, with the same lack of clear-cut agreement concerning its proper components: How often should sheets be changed? When should children be toilet trained? Should an aunt send a niece a birthday present? Unlike housework and child care, however, kin work, taking place across the boundaries of normative households, is as yet unlabeled and has no retinue of experts prescribing its correct forms. Neither home economists nor child psychologists have much to say about nieces' birthday presents. Kin work is thus more easily cut back without social interference. On the other hand, the results of kin work—frequent kin contact and feelings of intimacy—are the subject of considerable cultural manipulation as indicators of family happiness. Thus, women in general are subject to the guilt my informants expressed over cutting back kin-work activities.

Although many of my informants referred to the results of women's kin work—cross-household kin contacts and attendant ritual gatherings—as particularly Italian-American, I suggest that in fact this phenomenon is broadly characteristic of American kinship. We think of kin-work tasks such as the preparation of ritual feasts, responsibility for holiday card lists, and gift buying as extensions of women's domestic responsibilities for cooking, consumption, and nurturance. American men in general do not take on these tasks any more than they do housework and child care—and probably less, as these tasks have not yet been the subject of intense public debate. And my informants' gender breakdown in relative articulateness on kinship and workplace themes reflects the still prevalent occupational segregation—most women cannot find jobs that provide enough pay, status, or promotion possibilities to make them worth focusing on—as well as women's perceived power within kinship networks. The common recognition of that power is reflected in Selma Greenberg's book on nonsexist child rearing. Greenberg calls mothers "press agents" who sponsor relations between their own children and other relatives; she advises a mother whose relatives treat her disrespectfully to deny those kin access to her children.[8]

Kin work is a salient concept in other parts of the developed world as well. Larissa Adler Lomnitz and Marisol Perez Lizaur have found that "centralizing women" are responsible for these tasks and for communicating "family ideology" among upper-class families in Mexico City. Matthews Hamabata, in his study of upper-class families in Japan, has found that women's kin work involves key financial transactions. Sylvia Junko Yanagisako discovered that, among rural Japanese migrants to the United States, the maintenance of kin networks was assigned to women as the migrants adopted the American ideology of the independent nuclear family household. Maila Stivens notes that urban Australian housewives' kin ties and kin ideology "transcend women's isolation in domestic units."[9]

This is not to say that cultural conceptions of appropriate kin work do not vary, even within the United States. Carol B. Stack documents institutionalized fictive kinship and concomitant reciprocity networks among impoverished black American women. Women in populations characterized by intense feelings of ethnic identity may feel bound to emphasize particular occasions—Saint Patrick's or Columbus Day—with organized family feasts. These constructs may be mediated by religious affiliation, as in the differing emphases on Friday or Sunday family dinners among Jews and Christians. Thus the personnel involved and the amount and kind of labor considered necessary for the satisfactory performance of particular kin work tasks are likely to be culturally constructed.[10] But while the kin and quasi-kin universes and the ritual calendar may vary among women according to race or ethnicity, their general responsibility for maintaining kin links and ritual observances does not.

As kin work is not an ethnic or racial phenomenon, neither is it linked only to one social class. Some commentators on American family life still reflect the influence of work done in England in the 1950s and 1960s (by Elizabeth Bott and by Peter Willmott and Michael Young) in their assumption that working-class families are close and extended, while the middle class substitutes friends (or anomie) for family. Others reflect the prevalent family pessimism in their presumption that neither working-class nor middle-class families have extended kin contact.[11] Insofar as kin contact depends on residential proximity, the larger economy's shifts will influence particular groups' experiences. Factory workers, close to kin or not, are likely to disperse when plants shut down or relocate. Small businesspeople or independent professionals may, however, remain resident in particular areas—and thus maintain proximity to kin—for generations, while professional employees of large firms relocate at their firms' behest. This pattern obtained among my informants.

In any event, cross-household kin contact can be and is effected at long distance through letters, cards, phone calls, and holiday and vacation visits. The form and functions of contact, however, vary according to economic resources. Stack and Brett Williams offer rich accounts of kin networks among poor blacks and migrant Chicano farmworkers functioning to provide emotional support, labor, commodity, and cash exchange—a funeral visit, help with laundry, the gift of a dress or piece of furniture.[12] Far different in degree are exchanges such as the loan of a vacation home, a multifamily boating trip, or the provision of free professional services—examples from the kin networks of my wealthier informants. The point is that households, as labor- and income-pooling units, whatever their relative wealth, are somewhat porous in relation to others with whose members they share kin or quasi-kin ties. We do not really know how class differences operate in this realm; it is possible that they do so largely in terms of ideology. It may be, as David Schneider and Raymond T. Smith suggest, that the affluent and the very poor are more open in recognizing necessary economic ties to kin than are those who identify themselves as middle class.[13]

Recognizing that kin work is gender-based rather than class-based allows us to see women's kin networks among all groups, not just among working-class and impoverished women in industrialized societies. This recognition in turn clarifies our understanding of the privileges and limits of women's varying access to economic resources. Affluent women can "buy out" of housework, child care—and even some kin-work responsibilities. But they, like all women, are ultimately responsible, and subject to both guilt and blame, as the administrators of home, children, and kin network. Even the wealthiest women must negotiate the timing and venue of holidays and other family rituals with their kinswomen. It may be that kin work is the core women's work category in which all women cooperate, while women's perceptions of the appropriateness of cooperation for housework, child care, and the care of the elderly varies by race, class, region, and generation.

But kin work is not necessarily an appropriate category of labor, much less gendered labor, in all societies. In many small-scale societies, kinship is the major organizing principle of all social life, and all contacts are by definition kin contacts.[14] One cannot, therefore, speak of labor that does not involve kin. In the United States, kin work as a separable category of gendered labor perhaps arose historically in concert with the ideological and material constructs of the moral mother/cult of domesticity and the privatized family during the course of industrialization in the eighteenth and nineteenth centuries. These phenomena are connected to the increase in the ubiquity of productive occupations *for men* that are not organized through kinship. This includes the demise of the family farm with the capitalization of agriculture and rural–urban migration; the decline of family recruitment in factories as firms grew ended child labor and began to assert bureaucratized forms of control; the decline of artisanal labor and of small entrepreneurial enterprises as large firms took greater and greater shares of the commodity market; the decline of the family firm as corporations—and their managerial work forces—grew beyond the capacities of individual families to provision them; and, finally, the rise of civil service bureaucracies and public pressure against nepotism.[15]

As men increasingly worked alongside of nonkin, and as the ideology of separate spheres was increasingly accepted, perhaps the responsibility for kin maintenance, like that for child rearing, became gender focused. Ryan points out that "built into the updated family economy . . . was a new measure of voluntarism." This voluntarism, though, "perceived as the shift from patriarchal authority to domestic affection," also signaled the rise of women's moral responsibility for family life. Just as the "idea of fatherhood itself seemed almost to wither away," so did male involvement in the responsibility for kindred lapse.

With postbellum economic growth and geographic movement, women's new kin burden involved increasing amounts of time and labor. The ubiquity of lengthy visits and of frequent letter-writing among nineteenth-century women attests to this. And for visitors and for those who were residentially proximate, the continuing commonalities of women's domestic labor allowed for kinds of work sharing—nursing, child-keeping, cooking, cleaning—that men, with their increasingly differentiated and controlled activities, probably could not maintain. This is not to say that some kin-related male productive work did not continue; my own data, for instance, show kin involvement among small businessmen in the present. It is, instead, to suggest a general trend in material life and a cultural shift that influenced even those whose productive and kin lives remained commingled. Yanagisako has distinguished between the realms of domestic and public kinship in order to draw attention to anthropology's relatively "thin descriptions" of the domestic (female) domain. Using her typology, we might say that kin work as gendered labor comes into existence within the domestic domain with the relative erasure of the domain of public, male kinship.

Whether or not this proposed historical model bears up under further research, the question remains, Why do women do kin work? However material factors may shape activities, they do not determine how individuals may perceive them. And in considering issues of motivation, of intention, of the cultural construction of kin work, we return to the altruism versus self-interest dichotomy in recent feminist theory. Consider the epigraphs to this article. Are women kin workers the nurturant weavers of the Gilligan quotation, or victims, like the fed-up woman who writes to complain to Ann Landers? That is, are we to see kin work as yet another example of "women's culture" that takes care of others as its primary desideratum? Or are we to see kin work as another way in which men, the economy, and the state extract labor from women without a fair return? And how do women themselves see their kin work and its place in their lives?

As I have indicated above, I believe that it is the creation of the self-interest/altruism dichotomy that is itself the problem here. My women informants, like most American women, accepted their primary responsibility for housework and the care of dependent children. Despite two major waves of feminist activism in this century, the gendering of certain categories of unpaid labor is still largely unaltered. These work responsibilities clearly interfere with some women's labor force commitments at certain life-cycle stages; but, more important, women are simply discriminated against in the labor market and rarely are able to achieve wage and status parity with men of the same age, race, class, and educational background.[18]

Thus for my women informants, as for most American women, the domestic domain is not only an arena in which much unpaid labor must be undertaken but also a realm in which one may attempt to gain human satisfactions—and power—not available in the labor market. Anthropologists Jane Collier and Louise Lamphere have written compellingly on the ways in which varying kinship and economic structures may shape women's competition or cooperation with one another in domestic domains.[19] Feminists considering Western women and families have looked at the issue of power primarily in terms of husband–wife relations or psychological relations between parents and children. If we adopt Collier and

Lamphere's broader canvas, though, we see that kin work is not only women's labor from which men and children benefit but also labor that women undertake in order to create obligations in men and children and to gain power over one another. Thus Cetta Longhinotti's struggle with her daughter-in-law over the venue of Christmas dinner is not just about a competition over altruism, it is also about the creation of future obligations. And thus Cetta's and Anna's sponsorship of their children's friendship with each other is both an act of nurturance and a cooperative means of gaining power over those children.

Although this was not a clear-cut distinction, those of my informants who were more explicitly antifeminist tended to be most invested in kin work. Given the overwhelming historical shift toward greater autonomy for younger generations and the withering of children's financial and labor obligations to their parents, this investment was in most cases tragically doomed. Cetta Longhinotti, for example, had repaid her own mother's devotion with extensive home nursing during the mother's last years. Given Cetta's general failure to direct her adult children in work, marital choice, religious worship, or even frequency of visits, she is unlikely to receive such care from them when she is older.

The kin-work lens thus reveals the close relations between altruism and self-interest in women's actions. As economists Nancy Folbre and Heidi Hartmann point out, we have inherited a Western intellectual tradition that both dichotomizes the domestic and public domains and associates them on exclusive axes such that we find it difficult to see self-interest in the home and altruism in the workplace.[20] But why, in fact, have women fought for better jobs if not, in part, to support their children? These dichotomies are Procrustean beds that warp our understanding of women's lives both at home and at work. "Altruism" and "self-interest" are cultural constructions that are not necessarily mutually exclusive, and we forget this to our peril.

The concept of kin work helps to bring into focus a heretofore unacknowledged array of tasks that is culturally assigned to women in industrialized societies. At the same time, this concept, embodying notions of both love and work and crossing the boundaries of households, helps us to reflect on current feminist debates on women's work, family, and community. We newly see both the interrelations of these phenomena and women's roles in creating and maintaining those interrelations. Revealing the actual labor embodied in what we culturally conceive as love and considering the political uses of this labor helps to deconstruct the self-interest/altruism dichotomy and to connect more closely women's domestic and labor-force lives.

The true value of the concept, however, remains to be tested through further historical and contemporary research on gender, kinship, and labor. We need to assess the suggestion that gendered kin work emerges in concert with the capitalist development process; to probe the historical record for women's and men's varying and changing conceptions of it; and to research the current range of its cultural constructions and material realities. We know that household boundaries are more porous than we had thought—but they are undoubtedly differentially porous, and this is what we need to specify. We need, in particular, to assess the relations of changing labor processes, residential patterns, and the use of technology to changing kin work.

Altering the values attached to this particular set of women's tasks will be as difficult as are the housework, child-care, and occupational-segregation struggles. But just as feminist research in these latter areas is complementary and cumulative, so researching kin work should help us to piece together the home, work, and public-life landscape—to see the female world of cards and holidays as it is constructed and lived within the changing political economy. How female that world is to remain and what it would look like if it were not sex-segregated are questions we cannot yet answer.

Acknowledgments

Many thanks to Cynthia Costello, Rayna Rapp, Roberta Spalter-Roth, John Willoughby, and Barbara Gelpi, Susan Johnson, and Sylvia Yanagisako of *Signs* for their help with this article. I wish in particular to acknowledge the influence of Rayna Rapp's work on my ideas.

Questions For Further Discussion

1. Who does kin work in your own kin networks? Are any males involved? Is it recognized as labor?

2. How does kin work function in your life? Do goods and services flow through the kin or fictive kin ties encouraged by the kin-workers in your family?

3. How does your experience chime with or differ from those of your classmates? Why?

Notes

1. Ann Landers' letter printed in *Washington Post* (April 15, 1983); Carol Gilligan, *In a Different Voice* (Cambridge, Mass.: Harvard University Press, 1982), 17.

2. Heidi I. Hartmann, "The Family as the Locus of Gender, Class, and Political Struggle: The Example of Housework," *Signs* 6, no. 3 (Spring 1981): 366–94; and Christopher Lasch, *Haven in a Heartless World: The Family Besieged* (New York: Basic Books, 1977).

3. Representative examples of the first trend include Joann Vanek, "Time Spent on Housework," *Scientific American* 231 (November 1974): 116–20; Ruth Schwartz Cowan, "A Case Study of Technological and Social Change: The Washing Machine and the Working Wife," in *Clio's Consciousness Raised,* ed. Mary Hartmann and Lois Banner (New York: Harper & Row, 1974), 245–53; Ann Oakley, *Women's Work: The Housewife, Past and Present* (New York: Vintage, 1974); and Susan Strasser, *Never Done: A History of American Housework* (New York: Pantheon Books, 1982). Key contributions to the second trend include Louise Lamphere, "Strategies, Cooperation and Conflict among Women in Domestic Groups," in *Women, Culture and Society,* ed. Michelle Zimbalist Rosaldo and Louise Lamphere (Stanford, California: Stanford University Press, 1974), 97–112; Mina Davis Caulfield, "Imperialism, the Family and the Cultures of Resistance," *Socialist Revolution* 20 (October 1974): 67–85; Carroll Smith-Rosenberg; "The Female World of Love and Ritual: Relations between Women in Nineteenth-Century America," *Signs: Journal of Women in Culture and Society* 1, no. 1 (Autumn 1975): 1–29. Sylvia Junko Yanagisako, "Women-centered Kin Networks and Urban Bilateral Kinship," *American Ethnologist* 4, no. 2 (1977): 207–26; Jane Humphries, "The Working Class Family, Women's Liberation and Class Struggle: The Case of Nineteenth Century British History," *Review of Radical Political Economics* 9 (Fall 1977): 25–41; Blanche Weisen Cook, "Female Support Networks and Political Activism: Lillian Wald, Crystal Eastman, Emma Goldman," in *A Heritage of Her Own,* ed. Nancy F. Cott and Elizabeth H. Pleck (New York: Simon & Schuster, 1979); Temma Kaplan, "Female Consciousness and Collective Action: The Case of Barcelona, 1910–1918," *Signs 7,* no. 3 (Spring 1982): 545–66.

4. On this debate, see Jon Weiner, "Women's History on Trial," *Nation* 241, no. 6 (September 7, 1985): 161, 176, 178–80; Karen J. Winkler, "Two Scholars' Conflict in Sears Sex-Bias Case Sets Off War in Women's History," *Chronicle of Higher Education* (February 5, 1986), 1, 8; Rosalind Rosenberg, "What

Harms Women in the Workplace," *New York Times* (February 27, 1986); Alice Kessler-Harris, "Equal Employment Opportunity Commission vs. Sears Roebuck and Company: A Personal Account," *Radical History Review* 35 (April 1986): 57–79.

5. Portions of the following analysis are reported in Micaela di Leonardo, *The Varieties of Ethnic Experience: Kinship, Class and Gender among California Italian-Americans* (Ithaca, N.Y.: Cornell University Press, 1984), chap. 6.

6. Clearly, many women do, in fact, discuss their paid labor with willingness and clarity. The point here is that there are opposing gender tendencies in an identical interview situation, tendencies that are explicable in terms of both the material realities and current cultural constructions of gender.

7. Papanek has rightly focused on women's unacknowledged family status production, but what is conceived of as "family" shifts and varies (Hanna Papanek, "Family Status Production: The 'Work' and 'Non-Work' of Women," *Signs* 4, no. 4 [Summer 1979]: 775–81).

8. Selma Greenberg, *Right from the Start: A Guide to Nonsexist Child Rearing* (Boston: Houghton Mifflin Co., 1978), 147. Another example of indirect support for kin work's gendered existence is a recent study of university math students, which found that a major reason for women's failure to pursue careers in mathematics was the pressure of family involvement. Compare David Maines et al., *Social Processes of Sex Differentiation in Mathematics* (Washington, D.C.: National Institute of Education, 1981).

9. Larissa Adler Lomnitz and Marisol Perez Lizaur, "The History of a Mexican Urban Family," *Journal of Family History* 3, no. 4 (1978): 392–409, esp. 398; Matthews Hamabata, *Crested Kimono: Power and Love in the Japanese Business Family* (Ithaca: Cornell University Press, 1990); Sylvia Junko Yanagisako, "Two Processes of Change in Japanese-American Kinship," *Journal of Anthropological Research* 31 (1975): 196–224; Maila Stivens, "Women and Their Kin: Kin, Class and Solidarity in a Middle-Class Suburb of Sydney, Australia," in *Women United, Women Divided,* ed. Patricia Caplan and Janet M. Bujra (Bloomington: Indiana University Press, 1979), 157–84.

10. Carol B. Stack, *All Our Kin: Strategies for Survival in a Black Community* (New York: Harper & Row, 1974). These cultural constructions may, however, vary within ethnic/racial populations as well.

11. Elizabeth Bott, *Family and Social Network,* 2nd ed. (New York: Free Press, 1971); Michael Young and Peter Willmott, *Family and Kinship in East London* (London: Routledge & Kegan Paul, 1957), and *Family and Class in a London Suburb* (London: Routledge & Kegan Paul, 1960). Classic studies that presume this class difference are Herbert Gans, *The Urban Villagers: Group and Class in the Life of Italian-Americans* (New York: Free Press, 1962); and Mirra Komarovsky, *Blue-Collar Marriage* (New York: Random House, 1962). A recent example is Ilene Philipson, "Heterosexual Antagonisms and the Politics of Mothering," *Socialist Review* 12, no. 6 (November–December 1982): 55–77. Edward Shorter, *The Making of the Modern Family* (New York: Basic Books, 1975), epitomizes the pessimism of the "family sentiments" school. See also Mary Lyndon Shanley, "The History of the Family in Modern England: Review Essay," *Signs* 4, no. 4 (Summer 1979): 740–50.

12. Stack; and Brett Williams, "The Trip Takes Us: Chicano Migrants to the Prairie" (Ph.D. dissertation, University of Illinois at Urbana–Champaign, 1975).

13. David Schneider and Raymond T. Smith, *Class Differences and Sex Roles in American Kinship and Family Structure* (Englewood Cliffs, N.J.: Prentice-Hall, Inc., 1973), esp. 27.

14. See Nelson Graburn, ed., *Readings in Kinship and Social Structure* (New York: Harper & Row, 1971), esp. 3–4.

15. The moral mother/cult of domesticity is analyzed in Barbara Welter, "The Cult of True Womanhood, 1820–1860," *American Quarterly* 18, no. 2 (Summer 1966): 151–74; Nancy Cott, *The Bonds of Womanhood: "Women's Sphere" in New England, 1780–1835* (New Haven, Conn.: Yale University Press, 1977); and Ruth Bloch, "American Feminine Ideals in Transition: The Rise of the Moral Mother, 1785–1815," *Feminist Studies* 4, no. 2 (June 1978): 101–26. The description of the general political-economic shift in the United States is based on Harry Braverman, *Labor and Monopoly Capital: The Degradation of Work in the Twentieth Century* (New York: Monthly Review Press, 1974); Peter Dobkin Hall, "Family Structure and Economic Organization: Massachusetts Merchants, 1700–1850," in *Family and Kin in Urban Communities, 1700–1950,* ed. Tamara K. Hareven (New York: New Viewpoints, 1977), 38–61; Michael Anderson, "Family, Household and the Industrial Revolution," in *The American Family in Social-Historical Perspective,* ed. Michael Gordon (New York: St. Martin's Press, 1978), 38–50;

Tamara K. Hareven, *Amoskeag: Life and Work in an American Factory City* (New York: Pantheon Books, 1978); Richard Edwards, *Contested Terrain: The Transformation of the Workplace in the Twentieth Century* (New York: Basic Books, 1979); Mary Ryan, *The Cradle of the Middle Class: The Family in Oneida County, New York, 1790–1865* (Cambridge: Cambridge University Press, 1981); Alice Kessler-Harris, *Out to Work: A History of Wage-Earning Women in the United States* (New York: Oxford University Press, 1982).

16. Ryan, 231–32.
17. Sylvia Junko Yanagisako, "Family and Household: The Analysis of Domestic Groups," *Annual Review of Anthropology* 8 (1979): 161–205.
18. See Donald J. Treiman and Heidi I. Hartmann, eds, *Women, Work and Wages: Equal Pay for Jobs of Equal Value* (Washington, D.C.: National Academy Press, 1981).
19. Lamphere (n. 4 above); Jane Fishburne Collier, "Women in Politics," in Rosaldo and Lamphere, eds (n. 4 above), 89–96.
20. Nancy Folbre and Heidi I. Hartmann, "The Rhetoric of Self-interest: Selfishness, Altruism, and Gender in Economic Theory," in *The Consequences of Economic Rhetoric,* eds. Arjo Klamer, Donald McCloskey, and Robert M. Solow (New York: Cambridge University Press, 1988).

11

Fort Bragg on the Verge of a New Century: Military Restructuring, Civilian Camouflage, and Hot Peace

Catherine Lutz

Brown University

In the book Homefront: A Military City and the American Twentieth Century *(Beacon 2001), Catherine Lutz recounts her six years of historical and ethnographic research carried out at Fort Bragg in Fayetteville, NC. The guiding questions of her project were "How did it come to be that we live in a society made by war and preparations for war? How has our social world been shaped by the violence our nation has made and threatened . . .?" (2001: 9). This article is an excerpt drawn from her closing reflections, as, unbeknownst to her at the time, another war was looming on the horizon.*

    Catherine Lutz is a professor of anthropology at Brown University. In addition to Homefront, *she has written* Reading National Geographic *(with Jane Collins, Chicago 1993) and* Unnatural Emotions: Everyday Sentiments on a Micronesian Atoll and Their Challenge to Western Theory *(Chicago 1988), as well as a forthcoming volume,* Local Democracy under Siege: Activism, Public Interests and Private Politics *(New York University Press, in press). She is immediate past president of the American Ethnological Society and recipient of the Leeds Prize, the Victor Turner Prize, and the Sterling Award. Dr. Lutz has conducted some of her research in collaboration with activist organizations, including the American Friends Service Committee, indigenous rights groups, and organizations aligned against domestic violence.*

The U.S. military restructured itself in important ways as the Soviet empire was collapsing. Externally, it applied itself more vigorously to the new forms of what can be called Hot Peace:

training other people's armies and police, drug interdiction, hurricane relief, hostage rescue, the quelling of civil disorder, and what it called nation-building assistance. Internally, it reorganized itself in the manner of American business: it downsized, outsourced, and privatized.

Both of these kinds of restructuring—new modes of warfare and institutional renovation—heated and reshaped civil-military politics. On the one hand, there was intense renegotiation over the moral status of soldiers versus civilians, with the Army generally emerging with a widely perceived higher status than before. On the other, civilians became more central than ever before to the prosecution of war, not only as replacement labor for soldiers, but as spectators of military adventure. For Fayetteville, this has meant the Army and the city are both more united and more divided than ever before.

Civilian Camouflage: The New Military Politics

On a moist summer morning, the gas fumes leave visual ripples as two men pump gas into their cars at the Amoco on Bragg Boulevard. One has lots of visible scalp under a red beret, starched desert camouflage, and several pounds of black boots. The other has gel-styled hair and wears lightly pressed Docksiders and a Tommy Hilfiger shirt. Americans have been taught to view this pair through the freighted distinction between *soldier* and *civilian,* categories that have been changing with the emergence of Hot Peace and military restructuring.

Of long standing are these contrasts: A civilian is protected, a soldier the protector. A civilian enjoys peace and safety, the soldier faces danger and war. No matter his or her gender, a civilian is feminized, a soldier masculinized. The status that a warrior accrues is obvious from the frequent mention of veteran status on job résumés and in political campaigns: Valor gives value, virility virtue (Lincoln 1991: 40). In stronger terms, the soldier is emotionally disciplined, self-sacrificing, vigorous, and hardworking. By definition, then, the civilian is weak, cowardly, materialistic and wealthy, and self-centered. The civilian is soft, lacking experience with both the physical discipline that hardens muscles and with the hard facts of death and evil that the soldier faces down. The soldier has a calling, most civilians only a job—the exceptions in religion and medicine reveal the assumption that the work is sacred (see, e.g., Huntington 1957). One ex-soldier driving through Fort Bragg with me pointed out off-duty soldiers jogging in the suffocating Southern summer heat, one toting a full pack on his back. "It's a monastic order," the driver observed.

The distinction has gotten a sharper edge over the last twenty years. "In times of protracted peace, citizens grow fat and lazy and careless," reads one recently popular book on the military that supports the stereotype described above (Gutmann 2000: 24–25). Another widely read, celebratory book on Marine Corps boot camp, *Making the Corps* by *Wall Street Journal* Pentagon reporter Thomas Ricks, is called by one reviewer "a powerful indictment of many other institutions in American society—especially public schools and parents. In an age of moral relativism, and a narcissistic American society steeped in victimization, individualism, and materialism, what other institutions are as unequivocal about their own ethos and hierarchy of values?" Ricks paraphrases a sergeant who says of his recruits, "'Parris Island is the first place many of them encounter absolute and impersonal standards of right and wrong, of success and failure'" (Ricks 1997: 51). And in a recent cyberdiscussion on soldiers' tax breaks in Fayetteville, several veterans struck themes of civilian whiney immaturity and overindulgence: "If you want the privileges [of the] military, join! Just remember, you can't quit like a civilian job when things get tough." Said another: "Very few other careers have a global responsibility for protecting and promulgating the objectives of the greatest and freest society that the world has ever known. Local jurisdictions should not look to service as another group to fatten the tax coffers."

But the evaluation is also reversible, though done much less often and less publicly. When it is, the soldier is a slacker, playing cards and drinking, while the civilian supports him. In a society in which productive and free labor historically represented a pinnacle republican value, the soldier could easily become a pariah (Foner 1995). For he is defined by waiting, not activity, and destroying, not producing. And his freedom to come and go is severely restricted. When post-World War II abundance increasingly defined the American Dream in terms of ever higher levels of leisure and consumption, the soldier's spartan life could be seen as a self-indictment. Although the enhanced army pay after 1973 gave some reprieve from this cultural judgment, the prejudices of class and race could continue to stick to a military identity when soldiers so often came from more impoverished or nonwhite backgrounds.

As the word itself suggests, the *civilian* is assumed more civilized or civil, that is, peace loving, polite, or well bred, while the soldier is a barbarian with a club, witlessly pursuing war. Said one soldier with whom I spoke, "I came here in 1947 for two weeks' training. And there were signs on the streets downtown: 'Soldiers and Dogs Not Allowed.' . . . The civilian folks who don't deal with the military don't understand at all. We're human beings. We raise our kids like they raise their kids. . . . [But the people in town see us as] martinets versus real people. . . . The killers were at Fort Bragg, and the real people were downtown." The soldier's "blood sacrifice" (killing others and risk of being killed) while heroic, even Christlike, in one reading of the dualism, is tainted with deviance or sin in another (see, e.g., Ehrenreich 1997, Marvin 1999). Around the world and through time, societies have paid attention to the blood on warriors' hands and have explicitly and often ritually worked at "cleansing" and reintegrating them into the social home they left for war (Ehrenreich 1997: 12).

The relationship between those who have killed and seen killing in battle and those who have not is always fraught with tension, taboo, and unrecognized effects. Studies of World War II soldiers' attitudes toward civilians showed a contradictory mix of desires: to protect people back home from knowledge of the horrors they sometimes saw and made, the wish to have the people understand their experience, and despair for their ability to do so. Civilians, for their part, often wanted simply to believe there was a simple moral clarity to the war (Hynes 1997, Linderman 1997). So, too, might there be fear that the soldier's dehumanizing of the enemy (and of himself, at times) might easily spill over to the civilian at home (Lincoln 1991). Little communication would come of such a stew.

Some of the negative judgment of soldiering comes from three aspects of its cultural context. First in the contradiction between the imperative to be free and autonomous—seen as the birthright of each American, but especially of men—and the hierarchy and compulsion of military life. One woman told me about an argument she watched between her husband, a Fort Bragg soldier, and a Marine. In a classic style of interservice rivalry, the Marine said every other branch of service was "full of faggots." To this standard putdown of homosexuality and claim about which service "real men" choose, the soldier retorted that the Marines are "dummies and machines." When she chimed in with the rejoinder, "You're *all* slaves!" she was body-slammed—a playful response, she thought.

Moreover, military work is called *service* because people see soldiers as giving the country something larger than what they take home in their paychecks. It is a never completely reciprocal exchange because life is sacred, no less so for American troops than for those they take in battle. But for this reason, soldiering can have a weak if noble cultural reputation, as do nurses, day care providers, sanitation workers, and others. Even weaker might be the reputation of those who serve the servers, as Fayetteville's citizens do.

Finally, there is the related issue of how to interpret soldiers' dependency on a government wage. Because they receive cash payments from the government and many services in kind, soldiers live in something that bears a strong family resemblance to a social welfare state. This is a potential problem in a nation that does not generally acknowledge a universal right to work or to health care. One solution to the stigma that might otherwise attach to this is to make a sharp cultural distinction between earned and unearned social benefits. The acrimony that goes with the debate over individual military benefits often centers on the dangerous work soldiers do to earn them or the idea of a promise of such made to the soldier in his or her contract.

People define the kind of society they want when they characterize soldiers and civilians. Over the course of American history, some have defined military values as the antidote to the sickness they see in their era, such as materialism, corruption, or selfishness. In Fayetteville, some people use the soldier to identify how their city should change. When they celebrate the military's cosmopolitan experience and racial integration, they at least implicitly criticize the town's parochialism and segregation. Many—though more soldiers than civilians, according to a 1999 survey—believe that civilian society would improve if it adopted more military values and customs. In doing this, though, as Michael Sherry has noticed, Americans have "tried to extract the virtues of war from war itself" (Sherry 1995: 3). They set the killing aside and celebrate instead war participants' values of idealism, discipline, courage, strenuous effort, self-sacrifice, and love of country. And, like former President Clinton in an address delivered to the North Carolina General Assembly in 1997, they select the values to emphasize: the democratizing effect of standing among a mass of equally endangered soldiers, for example, rather than the authoritarian and coercive character that an institution based in automatic obedience and violence encourages. This view also obscures how some of the same values celebrated as military also or even better characterize civilian service work, from teaching and nursing to building bridges. And it can entail the confusion of economics and culture, with the wealth of army resources conflated with the character of those who use them to maintain their surroundings.

The identities of soldier and civilian are more complicated than this cultural ideology suggests, however. How they affect the so-called crisis in civil–military relations was brought home to me when I met Michael Trimble at a Cross Creek Mall restaurant. At 35 years of age, he has spent most of his life in the city, brought there when his father was stationed at Fort Bragg. He is a construction worker who makes a reasonable wage, but he dislikes Fayetteville so much that he plans to move someday. He has experiences the city's crime rate personally, having twice been mugged. When he said, "Fayetteville is like a little New York now," he was not being complimentary.

When I asked if he had friends in the military, he glanced around the room, lowered his voice, and said no. In explanation, he pointed to some buzz-cut men at another table and said, sounding angrily perplexed, "I've had a soldier say to me, 'I protect *your* country.'" The implication, Michael suggested, was that he was negligent for not doing the work himself and obligated to soldiers for their labors. Michael wondered at the soldier's choice of possessive pronoun, and I shared with him a sense that something was amiss. While it may suggest that the volunteer soldier easily sees himself as somewhat mercenary, it can also be heard as a reversal and a rebuke. The civilian world lacks patriotism, so much so that the soldier removes himself from membership in the "imagined community" of the nation, as historian Benedict Anderson (1991) calls it. The exchange between these two men might have been an anxious rendering of the contemporary relationship between soldiers and civilians, a relationship journalists and others have increasingly identified as problematic, even explosive.

This man defies the categories of that punditry, however. He should be Army-knowledgeable and sympathetic, having lived in a military family and city and doing a job that depends on military spending. His resentments of the military are not based in a broader politics or in a misunderstanding of what the military is about, but in the Army's undercutting of his economic and social interests as he sees them. He resents the economic advantages soldiers have that he does not (despite the fact that some members of the lower ranks with children have incomes that qualify them for food stamps). When he goes to bars to meet women in his hometown, he finds many soldiers standing in his way. And, in a more overtly political vein, he is unhappy with the erosion of a former egalitarianism of citizenship between soldiers and civilians.

Despite the monolithic image outsiders often have of it, the Army, too, like the civilian world, contains multitudes. The historian Richard Kohn has called it a "pernicious myth . . . that there was, or is, any such thing as the American soldier—a prototypical American in uniform—or that our military forces, either as institutions or as collections of individuals, reflect our true character as a people and as a nation" (Kohn 1987: 53). Some of those in uniform are about to leave the service disgusted; others are enthusiasts of Army custom and discipline or ardent nationalists or true believers in the power of violence to get things done; yet others, pragmatists doing time to get college tuition (the number-one reason given for enlisting). Some love the idea of American empire, others hate it with libertarian or democratic fervor. Some are part-timers, others lifers. They get socialized into units with different "personalities" like the Airborne, Quartermasters, or Seabees. If many think of the Army as monolithic, however, it may be because military propaganda suggests as much, with its images of soldiers all facing their flag, families, and enhanced future in united enthusiasm. Such images can also motivate soldiers to present themselves as conforming to a single, uniform model of why they join, what they do, and what they value.

A tension exists between the impulse to distinguish clearly between two cultures of the military and civilian worlds (often to either celebrate or criticize one of them) and the desire to see a single set of military and civilian values, and a single America. So it was when the Army chief of staff, in 1998, settled on an official set of "seven Army Values and their definitions": loyalty, duty, respect, selfless service, honor, integrity, and personal courage. A Fort Bragg Webmaster tried to satisfy both desires by heading the list, "Soldier/Civilian Values."

There are advantages to the military to having it both ways. Democratic values and local citizens can be harmed, however, either with a sharpened distinction (hostility or subordination can be produced, and civilians' responsibility for, and social and cultural connections to, soldiers' actions lost) *or* a blurred one (the genuine differences of interest between the two groups are mystified).

Just as the soldier's identity is more complicated than popular stereotype, so is the civilian's. Many people walking around Fayetteville in blue jeans or business suits are in what can be called "civilian camouflage." They include all the people who are getting military pensions or benefits, paying war taxes, selling things to GIs, watching war on TV as the twelfth man on the team, or people who are war refugees or war brides. In each of these ways, individuals become less clearly or simply civilians, even when some of them see themselves as having nothing to do with the military or are unsympathetic to it.

Moreover, *civilian* has been a category rarely discussed explicitly in America. This is because it has the quality linguists have discovered in many antonyms. Not simply two sides of a coin, one is "unmarked"—or the dominant, normalized, or culturally unproblematic term—and the other "marked"—the one that more often comes up for explicit discussion because it is seen as presenting some kind of "problem." So, in ordinary conversation, an "unhealthy" state is more often discussed than a "healthy" one. "How deep is the water?" we ask, not, "How shallow?" Throughout American history, black has been marked as a race, white remaining invisible. Female has been a gender, male a kind of prototype human being, without gender. The identity of a civilian is clearly the unmarked of the soldier–civilian pair. Despite the power of the military physically and economically, civilian is the majority, dominant category, and so is less recognizable as such.

Civilian identity has been sharpened, however, by the All Volunteer Force. The punditry has generally agreed to see this as a problem of growing ignorance and hostility toward the military as fewer civilians have enlisted. Instead we might say the civilian has become more visible as many begin to hypervalue the soldier. A kind of "supercitizenship" (Donald Nonini, personal communication) is offered by military recruiters whose ads promise elevated character to those who join. Their overheated advertising rhetoric is blown forcefully across the country with each year's recruiting budget, which was over $2 billion in 2001. Beyond these ads' influence, civilians are motivated to value soldiers in this way in exchange for not being required to kill or die. Such barter was not so urgent when the draft meant more families had already given their own children to the Army. Some civilians, of course, reject the very idea of this burden or that it should be so constantly and widely created by the drive for American global dominance. Or they see the professional army as simply one occupation among many, duly compensated and requiring no cultural premium. But all civilians become, through this process, "subcitizens." And as first-class citizenship is militarized, those who are excluded explicitly or implicitly, including gays and lesbians and straight women, can see further erosions in their social status (Enloe 2000).

The civilian has also become more visible as the volunteer Army's politics have become more distinct—and more conservative—than civilians' and than the drafted army's. While American voters now are about equally likely to identify themselves as Republicans or Democrats, a recent survey showed 64 percent of elite officers were Republican and only 8 percent Democrats. Among retirees, reservists, and ROTC students, conservatism also dominates. This has given Fayetteville's Republican Party, once a minuscule and forlorn band, a tremendous boost, particularly when veterans retire, register, and become politically active. On the national level, too, veterans are a potent political force, well organized to press for benefits, recognition, and a stronger military, through the Association of the United States Army (AUSA; with one hundred thousand members), the Veterans of Foreign Wars, and others. Such groups lobby Congress, send literature into veterans' homes, and help organize informal networks in local communities. The AUSA's position is that the Army is "underpaid, overcommitted and underresourced" (Moore 1999), but the source of its enthusiasm for higher budgets comes as much from its corporate partners to whom it offers "face to face meetings with Army decision-makers and government officials" (Silverstein 2000: 201–202).

One soldier for whom AUSA might claim to speak is Eric Fisher. After spending many unhappy years in the city—a favorite phrase being "yogurt has more culture than Fayetteville"—his disgust at local politicians finally brought him out to work on the successful campaign of a Republican elected to the state Senate. He also took a lively interest in a local taxpayer revolt group, which was vigorously attacking city government's spending habits. In the regular and reserve Army for twenty-four years, his attraction to being a soldier came from its code of high principle. It is, he said, a job that can sometimes require falling on "the grenade of honor," if that is good for the organization, or sacrificing oneself for the greater good. "The Army is like the Church to me," he said, because it is where he talks with others about things of ultimate value, like God and country. And he stayed with the military because he "bonded" with other soldiers over these values and over shared hardships. He contrasted the Army with the civilian world by pointing to a recent story he had heard on National Public Radio about a furniture factory closing elsewhere in North Carolina. When it and the rest of corporate American downsized, he said, the owners simply discarded their people. When the Army cut personnel in the early 1990s, by contrast, the soldier got "a ticket home, his goods moved, and help with the transition." The civilian world, he was saying, has no heart and no soul compared to the Army "family."

Such alienation from civilian society indexes erosion of the principle of civilian control of the military that some commentators see as a sign of a coming "crisis in civil–military relations" (Kohn 1994: 3; see also Dunlap 1992–1993). If people in the military see themselves as sole custodians of authentic American values, their cultural and political leadership might be required to save the country. But while there are overt attempts to expand the military's authority globally, nationally, and locally, the more basic and pressing problem is that civilian camouflage and the widespread acceptance of a military definition of the situation leaves few to ask questions when soldiers settle into high schools in Fayetteville and around the country to sell the military.

When the question of civil–military relations is raised, people almost invariably talk about the relationship between the Army, the president, and Congress. But Fayetteville's history shows that local relations between post personnel and city governments, soldiers and local women, or soldiers and merchants, are where the quotidian struggle occurs to define what a soldier and a civilian are, what cultural and economic capital they ought to have, and what authority each ought to have over the other.

I learned some of this from William Reeves, who worked in the schools for decades. "One of the day-to-day most obvious relations people may think of at the end of the month," he said, "[is] payroll and merchants and what not, but [school] was a day-to-day relation—sometimes good, sometimes bad." His students' parents who were soldiers often complained about their children's schools because they had just emerged from the relatively lushly funded Department of Defense system before they came to the financially more limited city schools. Soldiers, on the other hand, also

> Felt that they had a right, because they were defending the nation . . . to be looked after. Somebody needs to take care of us and make sure that our children are safe and happy and well educated. . . . Friends who live at Fort Bragg and work at Fort Bragg, they would wash my face over and over: "You wouldn't be having these [Federal Impact Aid] dollars if it were not for us. So, attend to our wishes." . . . Never mind the fact that we wouldn't need the money it if were not for your children. But you don't tell them that, you see. You have a little bit more diplomacy than that.

He bristled at the domineering attitude officers sometimes brought when they came to school to complain. He noticed that they often came to parent conferences carrying a briefcase, which he saw as a status symbol meant to put him in his place.

> Sometimes he'd open the attaché case [and I would see] two pencils and a pack of cigarettes or something. But they looked the part. . . . And I guess it's good that the military calls people to feel superior because if you want to go in battle with the enemy, you need to feel superior, but not necessarily when you go to the school. [Well, did you ever feel like they were coming in to battle?] Oh, yeah, they'd be prepared and the attaché case was just like, just like the mortar. . . . So I can understand that if I had lived all of my last twenty-some days not having dealt with any civilians, and everybody around me, under me . . . shows they respect [me]. It's hard for a person to just take off that personality, simply because they come into the civilian community.

And he saw the domineering approach in officers' relationships with their children as well.

> I used to feel sorry for some of the children and I said I will not send for this parent again because first sergeant, drill sergeant mentality would come in and sit and say . . ." If you do that again, boy, if I hear of you doing that, I'll knock your head through that cinder block wall" and I couldn't do that. . . . [In] the city you'll have signs on the bus that says, "please do not smoke," [but] people get on the bus on the post and the sign on the bus is saying, "you *will* not smoke." It's just that different. And that kind of attitude and framework on the part of the adults. . . . There was just no debating, you don't, you don't, you don't. Well, we had to say "please don't."

As military and civilian institutions face each other each day in Fayetteville, their contrasting styles, political differences, and variously funded interests are usually negotiated peacefully. But the changing political landscape in America includes a growing number who believe the nation is sick and that the cure is the return of a disciplined traditional race and gender order. A small but also growing number believe violence will achieve it. While violent white supremacism is found both in and outside of the military, the death of two people at neo-Nazi hands in Fayetteville in 1995 had much to do with the consequences of the American century of war and war preparation.

The end of the Cold War brought no peace to Fayetteville. The Army and its missions were restructured but the goal was more to rearrange budget categories than priorities. As was the case throughout the century, however, the conditions of life for Fayetteville's people were subtly reshaped. They became drawn, even more than previously, into a collaborative role, though the full extent of their job remained camouflaged. Commentators sounded alarms that civilians had veered dangerously away from the Army, or vice versa. But many decades of a national security culture and state have obscured the reality that the distinction between the civilian and the military has worn down rather than intensified. For the post–Cold War era has seen the rise of the ideas that the sofa spectator is a linchpin of military success and that soldiers shopping at the mall, teaching Junior ROTC to high-school students, and getting educated through Montgomery GI Bill benefits are key to the health and wealth of civil society. And as at the century's beginning, war and racism were intertwined. The city's white supremacist murders were one illustration of the complex process whereby the formation of a military welfare state in lieu of a broader sense of public welfare continues to contribute to the poverty and scapegoating of large segments of the black community.

Despite the massive military buildup of the 1980s and continued heavy military spending in the 1990s, Fayetteville today watches the rest of urban North Carolina pass it by in wealth and status. As it does, Fayetteville's people have struggled to imagine another future beyond the base. The millennium opened with a behemoth military museum honoring the Army's Airborne and Special Operations units as the city's major investment in new development. But one local politician dared to imagine, at least in private, the whole base turned back to the city. Its golf courses and basketball courts and residences would house families now in deteriorated mill housing, and businesses would turn to modern ploughshares and the work of social and environmental repair.

Fayetteville's people have enjoyed a unique and cosmopolitan history, but they have also suffered a history only partly of their own making. Like people across America, choices made in Washington about war and war preparation have deeply shaped their lives. Those choices have wreaked havoc on soldiers' bodies and psyches, cost people their sons and daughters, lowered the wages and raised the taxes of most, intensified social inequalities, and yoked the progress of their democracy and egalitarian hopes to war's secrecies, redefined citizenship, and political and racial hatreds. The sacrifice and suffering war exacts from the homefront has often been denied by official narratives, even as the costs abroad have been. But however permanent the present may seem, other histories—both of the past and of the future—can still be made from the insights of all the people who have lived under war's shadow and nursed its hidden injuries.

Questions for Further Discussion

The United States is and has been a military superpower—how does this fact affect your life as an American? What are the economic, political, and social ramifications of American militarism? How does it influence how you speak, how you present yourself, what you think about your country, what you think about the world?

References

Anderson, Benedict R. O'G. 1991. *Imagined communities: reflections on the origin and spread of nationalism.* London: Verso.

Dunlap, Col. Charles, J., Jr. 1992–1993. The origins of the American military coup of 2012. *Parameters* 22, 4: 2–20.

Ehrenreich, Barbara. 1997. *Blood rites: origins and history of the passions of war*. New York: Metropolitan Books.

Enloe, Cynthia. 2000. *Maneuvers: the international politics of militarizing women's lives*. Berkeley: University of California Press.

Foner, Eric. 1985. *Free soil, free labor, free men: the ideology of the Republican Party before the Civil War*. New York: Oxford University Press.

Gutmann, Stephanie. 2000. *The kinder, gentler military: can America's gender-neutral fighting force still win wars?* New York: Scribner.

Huntington, Samuel. 1957. *The solider and the state*. Cambridge: Harvard University Press.

Hynes, Samuel Lynn. 1997. *The soldiers' tale: bearing witness to modern war*. New York: Allen Lane/ Penguin Press.

Kohn, Richard. 1987. The American soldier: myths in need of history. In Garry D. Ryan and Timothy K. Nenninger, eds, *Soldiers and civilians: the U.S. Army and the American People*. Washington, D.C.: National Archives and Records Administration.

———. 1994. Out of control: the crisis in civil–military relations. *The National Interest* Spring 35: 3.

Lincoln, Bruce. 1991. *Death, war, and sacrifice: studies in ideology and practice*. Chicago: University of Chicago Press.

Linderman, Gerald F. 1997. *The world within war: America's combat experience in World War II*. New York: Free Press.

Marvin, Carolyn. 1999. *Blood sacrifice and the nation: totem rituals and the American flag*. Cambridge: Cambridge University Press.

Moore, J. Frank III. 1999. The CEO's report. *Army* (November): 43–48.

Ricks, Thomas E. 1997. *Making the corps*. New York: Scribner.

Sherry, Michael S. 1995. *In the shadow of war: the United States since the 1930s*. New Haven: Yale University Press.

Silverstein, Ken. 2000. *Private warriors*. New York: Verso.

12

Explorations of Class and Consciousness in the United States

E. Paul Durrenberger

Pennsylvania State University

Americans are uncomfortable about class. Many of us believe, simultaneously that (1) class is a European phenomenon that did not make the journey across the Atlantic with the first colonists, (2) today we are all essentially middle-class [whatever that is], (3) every American, regardless of class, has an equal opportunity to succeed, and (4) politicians who broach the subject of class are just instigating "class warfare" for their own nefarious ends. In this article, Paul Durrenberger identifies class and class attitudes as far more complex phenomena than received American wisdom would suggest. Nonetheless, the ethnographer is well placed to "see" class, not just in what people say but in what they do.

E. Paul Durrenberger is Professor of Anthropology at The Pennsylvania State University. His extraordinarily varied career has included ethnographic work on rice and opium production in Thailand, industrial fishing and farming in Iceland, commercial fishing in Alabama and Mississippi, industrial swine production in Iowa, and labor unions in Chicago and Pennsylvania. Not only has he written a number of books and published prodigiously in professional journals, but he has also provided commentary for such venues as National Public Radio so as to enlighten both his colleagues and the public on the everyday relevance of anthropological work. His most recent book, co-written with his wife Suzan Erem, is an affordable and accessible introductory textbook, Anthropology Unbound: A Field Guide to the 21st Century *(Paradigm Publishers 2006). He and Erem also collaborated on* Class Acts: An Anthropology of Urban Service Workers and Their Union *(Paradigm Publishers 2005).*

Durrenberger, Paul. Excerpt of "Explorations of Class and Conciousness in the U.S." *Journal of Anthropological Research* 57.1 (2001): 41–60. © 2001 University of New Mexico. Reprinted by permission.

The paradox of studying class in America is the denial of classes—our folk models tell us that the thing we want to understand does not exist. "Social mobility based on character and hard work is written into our institutions as well as our Constitution, our popular sayings and our myths," writes Goldschmidt (1998: 62). Pre-industrial stratified social orders coded the system of stratification into their cultures as surely as ours denies it (Goldschmidt 1950, 1955).

In her studies of downward mobility, Katherine Newman (1988, 1993) outlines a folk model of "meritocratic individualism" that characterizes the managerial middle class who are in positions of command or authority. "Their job," Barbara Ehrenreich (1990: 133) tells us, "is to conceptualize . . . what others must do. The job of the worker, blue or pink collar, is to get it done." She continues that

> the fact that this is a relationship of domination—and grudging submission—is usually invisible to the middle class but painfully apparent to the working class.

I use ethnographic data to explore the folk model of meritocratic individualism among such unquestionably middle-class folks as lawyers and such clearly working-class people as union stewards in the service sector.

A lawyer with the Legal Assistance Foundation of Chicago (LAFC) told me:

> A literary tradition is to use a crazy man like Don Quixote to reflect normalcy and in the end reality is crazy. People who work here aren't normative. Reflect society against us and see if it makes any sense.
>
> It's not the same for paralegals and secretaries. Attorneys have schooling. In a manufacturing job, of importance is working conditions, benefits, salary. People who work here have these three things in common. People have an agenda and are crazy enough to try to implement it. We're here to provide equal justice and we actually believe in it. Most jobs, after a while, you're just pushing it through. Here the final outcome is alive and fresh and now.

A few days before, I had been in the 10×10 waiting room of a tall, dark, urban building in Chicago's Loop. The lowered ceiling and wall, cutting the transom above the door in half, suggested that this ante room had once been larger. There were six chairs, one man in his thirties, and a woman in her twenties with a year-old baby on her shoulder. Across the space, in a 5×8 compartment separated from us by a glass window, were two women incessantly answering their telephones with "Legal Assistance." The travel magazines on the tables seemed out of place. A sign announced in Spanish that the minimum wage was $4.75 per hour. Another in English was about food stamps. I was waiting to talk to paralegals, support staff, and attorneys on the other side of the door, but fortunately, not about the legal problems with which they are accustomed to dealing.

United Auto Workers Local 2320 (UAW Local 2320) organizes legal aid workers who work for legal aid foundations providing legal assistance to poor people, especially those who run afoul of the myriad of bureaucracies that govern their lives—from social services to child and family services to landlords. UAW Local 2320 represents the attorneys, paralegals, and support staff of the LAFC. What made this unit especially interesting to me is that they had united two bargaining units (support staff and paralegals, on the one hand, and attorneys on the other) into one unit. The rationale of the union local was that employees all had the same interests relative to management.

One of the union organizers at Local 2320, himself an attorney, explained to me that during the 1950s the Supreme Court had ruled that some workers are professional while others are not and that while professionals can vote to be in the same bargaining unit with non-professionals, the non-professionals cannot on their own volition include professionals. When the LAFC was first organized twenty years earlier, the National Labor Review Board ruled in favor of the employer's petition that there need not be a single bargaining unit, so there was one unit for attorneys and one for others. There was one union with two halves with a unified executive board and equal representation and joint bargaining. Each unit had the right to vote on its own contract separately—there were two parallel documents. The problem arose if one unit adopted its contract and the other did not.

The support staff tended to ratify contracts, and lawyers tended not to. In 1994 or 1995, when the current contract was being negotiated, there were funding cuts and a proposal from management to postpone raises for attorneys so management would not have to lay off seven of them. Attorneys thought the support staff would agree to postpone raises to save the jobs of seven fellow-members.

> That was the worst day in the history of this unit. People brought to a head all of their differences and stresses between them. Everyone was outraged. Support staff for contradictory reasons. Attorneys were doing something THEY were not being asked to do. Attorneys had control of their destiny. Support staff were equally outraged but for contradictory reasons. It wasn't logical. . . . We saved the seven jobs; it was unifying for attorneys. We made a sacrifice and called on management to sacrifice and they did. Support staff thought it was a betrayal.
>
> As a footnote: we were going to set up a committee to explore the laws and become a single unit. I have favored it since 1991, but it was not favored by anyone else. But we did it this year. So now we are one unit.
>
> The victory of the last campaign here is that we got the units unified. The vote was overwhelming to unify. It was higher from attorneys than from support staff. [Some] attorneys felt they couldn't get their special interests if they were in with support staff and the fact that the staff went into epileptic fits over the saving of jobs didn't help. But we pulled it off in spite of that.

When I discussed Newman's findings with him, he said:

> This would be a good place to test the meritocracy versus structural distinction. But some lawyers are ideologically motivated. It might not show up.

Class?

Fifty years ago, Goldschmidt stated what he called the enigma of American social structure thus: "despite great differentials in wealth, prestige and power, there are no clearly marked social classes" (1950: 483). He reviewed the anthropological, sociological, and psychological literature on class in America up to then. Since he did a thorough job of it, I refer readers to that article rather than repeat it here. Anthropological and sociological work failed to raise the question of whether informants were representing social realities or whether the methods select "that pattern of thought which coincides with the predilection of the investigator" (487).

He concluded that because the differences in wealth, economic conditions, prestige, and power are as great in America as in any stratified society, and because of minimal mobility as well as differences of life ways, systems of values, and attitudes, there is a class system in America. He also pointed out that it is a tenet of American culture that all have equal opportunity, and, reported evidence of that time that "over half of the working class and two-thirds of the middle class believe ability is an essential element to mobility" (492).

Goldschmidt went on to describe four classes: an elite, a middle class whose power is derivative from the elite and which acts as a local pseudo-elite, a working class that rejects the middle-class ideal of economic advancement through individual achievement and attempts collective action for social gains, and a fourth sector of laboring people who are so hopeless that they do not expect to advance individually or collectively—an underclass (494–495).

As anthropologists return to the challenge of understanding class in the United States, one of our continuing problems is to be able to see the phenomenon in a land where the very notion, much less the discussion, of class and class privilege is anathema because of incessant proclamations of the equality of opportunity if not achievement. Race, ethnicity, personal initiative or failure—but not class—explain privilege, power, poverty, and impotence (Ortner 1998).

In the United States, the ideology of the individual and experience of diversity mask the realities of class (Sacks 1988). This is easy to see in a small, less diverse land devoted to egalitarian ideology such as Iceland (Durrenberger and Pálsson 1989, Pálsson and Durrenberger 1983). It is more difficult to see in a large diverse land that actively promotes such an obfuscation as official ideology (Ehrenreich 1990). Kingsolver (1998) reviews recent anthropological literature on the ways people claim and assert power in workplaces based on gender, ethnicity, age, regional identity, and ownership of capital. She also discusses anthropologists such as those whose work is collected in Lamphere, Stepick, and Greiner (1994), who consider the impact of gender and ethnicity in the experience of workers both on and off the job. Here I focus more explicitly on the folk model of meritocratic individualism.

In my work on shrimpers in Mississippi and Alabama (Durrenberger 1992a; 1996) I found a similar folk model of individualism. All agreed that shrimpers were so independent that they could not engage in collective action. This folk model is counter-factual. The history of the rise and fall of the Mississippi shrimpers' union illustrates the changes in the political and economic system that made a union impossible in one configuration, made it possible in another, and impossible again in a third. As long as packers controlled access to schooners for shrimping, fishermen were unable to organize unions, though they tried and carried out several long strikes (Durrenberger 1994). When fishermen began to own their own power boats and trawlers, packers could not produce sufficient shrimp to satisfy their needs without the independent shrimpers, and shrimpers successfully banded together in unions. Their organizations were effective because of the favorable legal climate of the New Deal and federal-level recognition of their legitimacy and because, even organized, they provided processors a more favorable alternative than owning their own fleets. When alternative sources of shrimp became available to processors through imports, shrimpers could no longer control the flow of raw materials to processors. Shrimpers borrowed heavily to invest in large gulf boats and needed the processors more than processors needed them. Finally, the union was outlawed under antitrust law (Durrenberger 1992b; 1995).

Anthropology is accustomed to showing that folk models do not fit realities and explaining why and how the folk models gained salience. Kottak (1998: 65), for instance, says, "By 1965 I recognized that the opinions held by some of these groups were misconceptions that interfered with their understanding of what actually determined fishing success. I had also come to realize that such confusion and misunderstanding were essential." Gìsli Pálsson and I (Pálsson and Durrenberger 1983; 1990; 1992a; 1992b, Durrenberger and Pálsson 1983) have analyzed how Icelandic folk models of fishing success are misleading and explained them in terms of their evolving relationships with economic systems.

Anthropologists can turn to a critique of sociological practice to help us avoid familiar pitfalls. Sociologists call the official invisibility of class "American Exceptionalism." This is the idea that while other industrial countries such as Britain and Poland have well-developed class structures that are visible in their union movements and political organization, the United States is the exception to the rule. Sociologists and others have offered explanations for American Exceptionalism. One is that Americans are exceptional in even talking about equality, while the more general pattern is to accept and expect inequality based on class position (Goldschmidt 1998, Lewis 1993). The exception to American Exceptionalism in Sociology is those Marxists represented in the collections edited by McNall, Levine, and Fantasia (1991), Burawoy and Skocpol (1982), and Bonanno, Busch, Friedland, Gouveia, and Mingione (1994).

The Middle Class?

The folk model of meritocratic individualism that Newman (1988) describes includes the following tenets:

- REWARDS GO TO THOSE WHO ARE REALLY DESERVING
- OCCUPATION IS A MEASURE OF MORAL WORTH
- PEOPLE ARE MASTERS OF THEIR OWN DESTINIES
- THOSE WHO SUCCEED ARE MORALLY BETTER
- YOU WOULDN'T BE IN THIS MESS IF SOMETHING WEREN'T WRONG WITH YOU
- SOLUTIONS ARE MOSTLY UP TO INDIVIDUALS
- INDIVIDUALS CAN ALTER THEIR FUTURES VS. IDEA THAT INDIVIDUALS ARE SUBORDINATE TO LARGER FORCES
- SUCCESS IS A RESULT OF DETERMINATION AND TALENT
- PEOPLE WHO DON'T HAVE JOBS HAVEN'T BEEN TRYING HARD ENOUGH
- HIERARCHY IS MERIT BASED
- PEOPLE GET WHAT THEY DESERVE
- MARKET FORCES ARE MORE IMPORTANT THAN MORALITY—THE MARKET *DEFINES* MORALITY
- INEQUALITY IS NATURAL

Newman documents how this folk model serves middle-class individuals while they have jobs but destroys them when they lose their jobs and the self-reifying daily practice and context for this folk model that explains their success or failure.

In her discussion of a factory closing she indicates that workers did not hold themselves responsible for being out of work but blamed remote authorities. This perspective, she argues, is grounded in working-class experience. There was nothing personal when Singer would hire and lay off hundreds of people at a time (1988: 199). She concludes that such experience bolsters a structural outlook among working-class people in contrast to the meritocratic individualism of middle-class people.

Because these ideas of class-based differences in folk models of success and failure seemed ethnographically grounded and valid to me, I wanted to test them more systematically. The legal workers of LAFC seemed to be an ideal site.

I hypothesized, on the basis of Newman's ethnographic accounts, that attorneys would be more personalistic and less structural and that support staff and paralegals would be more structural and less personalistic in outlook. I interviewed support staff, paralegals, and attorneys at the various offices LAFC maintains, informally talked with employees and their union representatives, observed meetings, and observed the union representatives in negotiations with other units. To collect quantitative data to test the hypothesis formally, I administered a questionnaire based on Newman's articulation of meritocratic individualism.

I asked people how much they agreed with each of the following statements on a scale of 1 (not at all) to 5 (very much):

- People's success or failure depends on factors beyond their control
- The people who are in positions of authority are there because of their merit
- People make their own luck
- Hard work is not the main thing that explains the success of people in higher positions
- People in higher positions are more talented or able than others
- People who make bad decisions deserve to get into trouble
- People should respect the market and economic facts more than ideas of morality
- People who get rewards such as higher salaries and higher positions deserve them
- Solutions to peoples' problems are up to them
- People in higher positions owe their success mainly to their own good decisions
- Social inequality is natural

Cultural status of ideas suggests some degree of consensus (Romney 1999). I used *Anthropac,* the consensus procedure of the set of computer programs Borgatti (1996) compiled, to test for consensus, and found none among any of the three subgroups, by gender or by ethnicity. Furthermore, I could show no statistical difference between or among the responses by group, ethnicity (Hispanic, African American, and White), or by gender. Most attorneys and staff agreed that people make their own luck (in agreement with the folk model), disagreed that people should respect the market and economic facts more than ideas of morality (not in agreement with the folk model), agreed that solutions to people's problems are up to them (in agreement), and disagreed that social inequality is natural (not in agreement). The results are equally in agreement and not in agreement with the folk model.

To further explore Newman's formulation, I asked whether respondents thought most people deserve the salary they get. If respondents answered positively, I asked a series of further questions using paired comparisons. These ask people to select between two items which is "more" according to some criterion. In tabulations, the selected response gets one point and the alternative gets none. The number of times an item is selected is its rank order (Weller and Romney 1988). For instance, if we wanted to know about the conceptual size rankings of elephants, goats, and mice, we could make a paired comparison test with all combinations of the three. If we asked which of each pair is larger, people would probably select elephant twice (in the pairs elephant–goat and elephant–mouse), goat once (in the pair goat–mouse) and mouse never. This would make a ranking of elephant (2), goat (1), and mouse (0). One advantage of the paired comparison method is that while it can show a ranking if there is one, it does not assume there is a ranking by asking respondents either to rank items or to score them on a scale. Thus the paired comparison test can show whether there is a scale. In this example, if the results were different from our expectations, we would want to check the ethnography and our understanding of the language.

I asked people who said that people deserve their salaries whether it is because they have connections, have talent, have good luck, have a good education, or work hard. I also asked what is more important in determining a person's chances in life—race, gender, innate ability, or how hard they work.

Thirty-one percent of attorneys, 67 percent of paralegals, and 89 percent of support staff thought that people deserve the salaries they receive and there was consensus on the reasons. That less than one-third of attorneys, more than two-thirds of paralegals, and most of support staff think people deserve the salaries they get suggests that the attorneys are thinking differently from staff and are less inclined to the meritocratic individualism model. Figure 1 shows that attorneys who agreed that people do deserve their salaries also agreed that networks were most important followed by education, work, talent, and luck. Paralegals thought work was most important followed by talent, education, luck, and networks. Support staff thought work was most important followed by education, talent, networks, and luck. Even the attorneys who agree with the premise of connecting merit and salary stress structural features (networks) over personal ones (talent, work) while paralegals and support staff stress personal characteristics (work, talent) over structural ones (networks). None of these findings confirmed my hypothesis that attorneys would represent the middle-class folk model of success that Newman outlined. They did raise two further questions: (1) what kind of lawyers are these? and (2) do other kinds of workers share the meritocratic individualism folk model of success with LAFC staff?

What Kind of Lawyers are These?

These findings may say more about these attorneys than about lawyers in general. One union representative of the local cautioned me as I began this study that many of the attorneys were ideologically driven, that they could make much more money in other kinds of practice than in this work, but they did work that paid half what they could expect elsewhere for ideological reasons.

One attorney said:

> I like fighting for what seems right to me. To try to balance power. To try to promote justice. I like working with clients—individual contact—getting to know the person and the problems. If I hadn't gone into law I would have gone into some other social service work. One thing that Legal Services as opposed to public defender is that I feel we're almost always on the right side of the case.

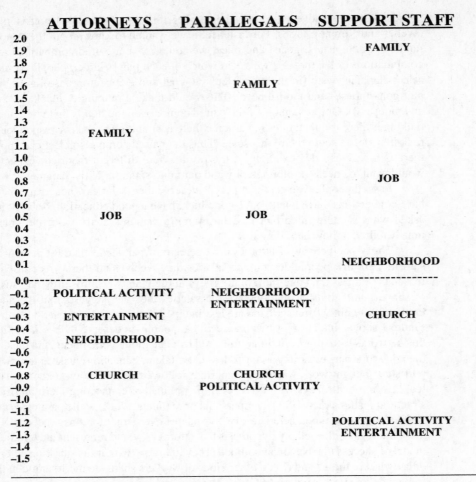

FIGURE 1 Most important institutions/activities.

Another attorney said:

There are differences among people in the bargaining unit, but it isn't clear. Attorneys are one way and staff another. Nearly all attorneys are here as part of a mission—not just a job. All of us here make less than the market, but attorneys make a lot less than the private sector. To come here represents more of a sacrifice for attorneys than support staff. Staff see it as more of a job. Some attorneys work nine to five. . . . There are paralegals and secretaries that work more than nine to five.

"I wouldn't do private practice" she continued.

"Private practice isn't an avenue to justice?" I asked.

"I did some good work. And other work I thought was despicable. I don't hold it against people in private practice. They represent clients. But it's not what I want to do with my life. I hated it. It's not that I'm sacrificing something I'd rather do."

Later, discussing a recent strike the unit had participated in and the union, I asked why attorneys stay in the union.

"That's an interesting issue for someone like an anthropologist. Part of why attorneys stay in the union is because it does protect our jobs. It allows me to feel I won't get fired for politics—office politics, not outside politics. If I think [the director] is a jerk, I can say that. You'd always have to be kissing butt without a union. The same reasons all people stay in unions—job protection. But it's part of the same reason we work at Legal Assistance Foundation."

"Being?" I asked,

"Doing justice. Our having a union here permits economic justice for support staff that would be paid less—they're paid shit, but if [the director] had his way, he'd pay less. . . . Attorneys went on strike to our detriment so support staff [would benefit]."

These views were not unique to the attorneys. A receptionist in one of the neighborhood offices said:

"[The attorneys] are concerned to represent people—to get out to see those people who are out here. . . . Landlords are totally slumlords making people pay to stay in unsafe places. Unscrupulous people tell people they'll get them a job with an education program and leave them with debts. A utility monopoly. It's death defying to people who are slow. THEY're the ones that give us the impact to stay here and fight. There but for the grace of God go I."

"Do you like your job?" I asked.

"I love it."

"Why," I continued.

"There are times you see people come through your office and they have tears in their eyes and the pressure is great and that burden is lifted and they can go back to normal lives and smile. That's a beautiful thing when someone cared enough to help and make this bad guy get up off their back."

A Hispanic paralegal working at a neighborhood office said this:

Someone told me about this job and I applied. When they told me the salary, I said, forget it. I'll stay two months and go on vacation and not come back. Then I saw what they were doing here. Helping people for free. I came from another country—there they don't do those things for anybody. I decided not to go on vacation. I was going to leave because of the salary. Half the salary I was making in a factory at General Electric. But when I saw what they were doing, I liked it. Helping people for free. They've offered me other positions as I am an interpreter from Spanish to English and English to Spanish and I have good skills as an interpreter. Some attorneys who worked here offered me a job, but I like the idea of helping people. I could make more money as a secretary for a law firm or interpreting. It is a nice feeling to help other people, especially people who don't have any money.

I have no quantitative data on ideological motivations except the summation of such interviews, but lest it be concluded that because there was little consensus on the answers to these questionnaire questions there was no consensus among these people, I want to emphasize again Fantasia's (1988) caveat about the difference between abstract questions and practice. In the summer of 1997 when I was doing this study, this unit had recently come through a thirty-four day strike against their management. My interviews indicated there was no unanimous judgment about the strike—whether it had been useful, necessary, successful or well handled. All agreed it had been stressful. And they had won their bargaining point. The important observation is that they had participated in the strike. This is not to say that strikes are the be-all and end-all of negotiation or the labor movement. Current legislation and policy make it certain that is not true (see Durrenberger and Erem 1997). In spite of differing opinions these units merged into one by their own decision to consider the needs of other components in their negotiation and practice and to remain a coherent bargaining unit. On those points there was unanimity.

When I discussed these questions with a partner in a private law firm in a large Midwestern city, she said:

> They are completely impractical. I'm paid by the hour. These people don't care. It doesn't matter to them. Let me see if I can say it better. I have to deliver a product to a client at a rate they can pay. I have to tailor it to what a client is willing to pay. These guys don't have that constraint. They can pursue stuff forever. They don't care if they're paid or not. They spend more time and money than we would. They are unwilling to enter into any compromise.
>
> Lawyers are governed by codes of professional conduct. [Her spouse, also an attorney] finds—he is a member of a bargaining unit—he isn't sure what he'd do if the bargaining unit struck. He's not sure he'd strike, he feels conflicts with his obligation to represent a client.
>
> [Her spouse] characterizes [her] firm from outside—the overwhelming motivation is greed.
>
> We like what we do and also want to get paid for it.

Six of her colleagues (20 percent), all attorneys, completed the same survey I used for LAFC. Of these, 66 percent said that most people deserve the salary they get. The two who disagreed commented, "The pay scales are dictated more by politics than merit, both in the case of under-compensated and over-compensated," and "Many people get comfortable in their job to the point of not working very hard and doing the minimum to get by." The first might be a structural response, but the second is individual. As Figure 3 shows, those who agreed that people deserve the salaries they get also agreed on the reasons—principally hard work and talent followed by education, luck, and networks. This is quite a different configuration than Figure 2 shows for the LAFC attorneys.

On the scales, five of the six agree that people make their own luck, all agree (5 at 4 and 1 at 5) that solutions to people's problems are up to them; but five of six disagree that people should respect the market and economic facts more than ideas of morality while one is neutral. On the other items there is no consensus.

To the question on reasons for success, these attorneys agree that work is the most important element followed by ability and that race and gender are less important. Neither attorneys, paralegals nor support staff of LAFC showed any consensus on this question.

This small exercise would lend credence to the conclusion of the interviews that LAFC workers may be different in outlook from other legal workers.

The Working Class?

To get a more clear representation of working-class views, I administered a survey to the 1998 annual meeting of stewards of Service Employees International Union (SEIU) Local 1 in Chicago. One hundred and forty-eight people returned their surveys. Of these, 51 percent

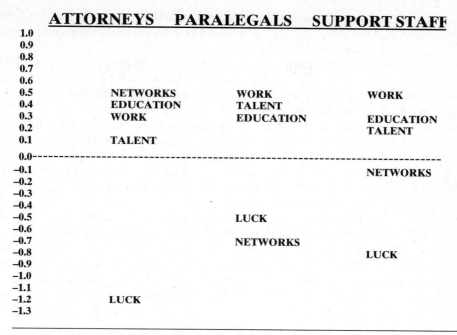

FIGURE 2   The reason people deserve their salary.

were female, 46 percent male, and 3 percent unreported gender. They were 35 percent Black (the term used 2.6 times more frequently than the alternative "African American"), 16 percent Hispanic, 22 percent White, 15 percent Polish, and 12 percent unidentified. The mean age was 47 with a mean of 11.2 years at the current job. At that time, this local represented workers in three sectors—Industrial and Allied including school-bus drivers working for contractors, factory workers, cemetery workers and others; Public Sector including workers in schools and other municipal functions such as public works departments and fire departments; and Building Services including downtown and suburban janitors in office and apartment buildings.

I asked a series of questions I derived from Newman's work, similar to the ones I asked of the LAFC workers. They included the same five point–scale judgments of agreement with the following statements:

- People's success or failure is pretty much beyond their control
- People make their own luck
- Hard work is *not* the main thing that explains the success of people in higher positions
- People in higher positions are more talented or able than others
- People who make bad decisions deserve to get into trouble
- Solutions to people's problems are up to them.

The judgments showed no consensus for any category of respondents. Whether I grouped respondents by sector, race, or gender, there was no consensus. There was substantial agreement (at 4 or 5) that people make their own luck, disagreement (at 1 or 2) that people in higher positions are more talented, and disagreement (at 1 or 2) that people who make decisions deserve to get into trouble. These findings are similar to the result of similar questions I asked of the LAFC workers.

To further examine the salience of structural-versus-personal factors, I included this paired comparison item: "Please circle the thing in each line that is more important in determining a person's chances in life," followed by all combinations of race, ability, gender, and how hard they work.

There was a strong consensus among all stewards (together and by sectors) that ability is most important, followed by work, gender, and race least important. Figure 3 shows these relationships. There was also consensus by ethnicity and gender. While there is some variation, as Figure 4 shows, all agreed that personal factors are more important than structural ones. Thus, by this measure, these union stewards are using the meritocratic individualist folk model that Newman outlined.

In 1999 I administered the same survey to a sample of twenty-eight stewards of Chicago's SEIU Local 4, a much smaller local whose membership is focused on residential care facilities Of these 14 percent identified themselves as White, 78 percent as Black or African American (72 and 27 percent, respectively, of the 78 percent), 4 percent as Hispanic, and 4 percent did not identify themselves (Figure 5). Seventy-eight percent were female, 18 percent male, and 4 percent unidentified. The mean age was 49 with a mean of 13 years working in the same place.

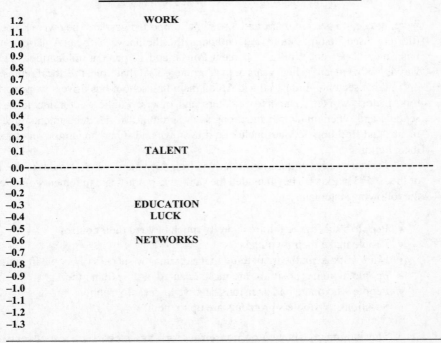

PRIVATE PRACTICE ATTORNEYS

```
1.2                    WORK
1.1
1.0
0.9
0.8
0.7
0.6
0.5
0.4
0.3
0.2
0.1                    TALENT

0.0-------------------------------------------------------------------------
−0.1
−0.2
−0.3               EDUCATION
−0.4                 LUCK
−0.5
−0.6               NETWORKS
−0.7
−0.8
−0.9
−1.0
−1.1
−1.2
−1.3
```

FIGURE 3   The reason people deserve their salary.

	ALL	INDST	PUBLIC	BUILDING
1.5				
1.4				
1.3				
1.2				
1.1				
1.0				
0.9		ABILITY		
0.8				
0.7	ABILITY		ABILITY	ABILITY
0.6		WORK		
0.5	WORK			WORK
0.4				
0.3			WORK	
0.2				
0.1				
0.0	----	----	----	----
−0.1				
−0.2				
−0.3				
−0.4				
−0.5	GENDER	GENDER	RACE/GENDER	GENDER
−0.6				
−0.7	RACE			RACE
−0.8				
−0.9				
−1.0		RACE		
−1.1				
−1.2				
−1.3				
−1.4				
−1.5				

FIGURE 4 What is important in determining a person's chances in life by sector.

On the dimensions of meritocratic individualism there was strong consensus that people make their own luck, but none on the others. There is also consensus about the reasons for success—work, talent, race, gender in that order in virtually identical pattern to the stewards of Local 4 taken as a whole.

Conclusions

The union stewards think ability and work are more important in achieving success than structural factors such as race and gender. Attorneys, paralegals, and support staff of the Legal Assistance Foundation show no consensus in the matter of the relative importance of personal and structural features in achieving success but are clearly capable of sustained action to achieve collective goals. The attorneys think more structurally than other members of the bargaining unit. Other attorneys do not necessarily follow the same pattern. The test of degree of agreement with archetypal middle-class values does not differentiate the three groups at LAFC, nor is there widespread consensus among stewards about these elements of meritocratic individualism. Other evidence shows that an individualistic folk

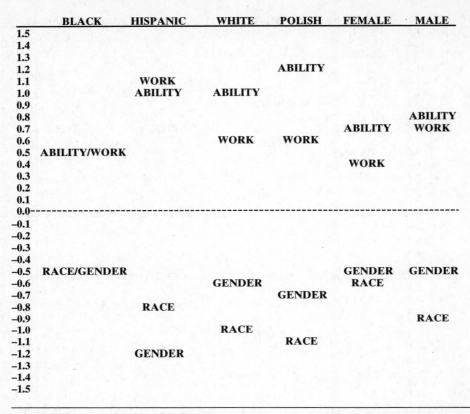

FIGURE 5   What is important in determining a person's chances in life by ethnicity and gender.

model is a cultural construct for stewards of two union locals, support staff of LAFC, and some lawyers in private practice but not LAFC attorneys.

Matters of class in America are fraught with symbolism, much of it misleading. The folk model of equality is so powerful and pervasive that it disguises the realities of class and the daily practice and practices of inequality. We have to ask how such a model can be perpetuated in the face of such overwhelming experiential evidence of daily life to the contrary.

Goldschmidt (1950, 1955) is right to say that to understand why people do what they do we must comprehend the cultural categories that inform their actions and explanations. But to grasp why those cultural categories take those forms is a different question, one of the relations among cultural categories, realities, and historical dynamics. It is to step outside the structure and ask questions about the structure itself and how it came to be, as Wolf (1999: 62) says, to understand symbols in relation to economics and politics. People make and unmake cultures as they "engage each other in diverse social, economic, and political arenas," and culture is constructed through the exercise of power (Wolf 1999: 274–275).

Even in the "exceptional" United States there was a union movement, and working people began to see themselves as members of a working class as Goldschmidt defined it in 1950. But owners found common interests, and the conflict between "labor and capital became open and often bloody" (Goldschmidt 1998: 64). Goldschmidt attributes the dissipation of the confrontation to the unity inspired by World War II and the era of prosperity that followed, during which all began to see themselves as middle-class, and class dissolved as a meaningful cultural category in America. The result is unquestionable; the mechanisms were more complex.

Bronfenbrenner, Friedman, Hurd, Oswald, and Seeber (1998) provide an accessible summary of the current state of the American labor movement. It is weak not because of worker disinterest, individualism, or some inscrutable difference between the United States and European countries that makes it an exception to the rule, but because of well-organized, massive, and often violent opposition (Vanneman and Cannon 1987, Durrenberger 1992b, 1995). The organized share of the workforce peaked in 1946, the year before the Taft–Hartley amendments to the Wagner Act limited union organizing and mutual aid tactics and empowered employers with new means of opposing unions. The chief factors in labor's decline are structural, such as the flight of capital to low-wage countries and unorganized areas, the shift to a service economy, and the changes of law and administration that have moved unions toward being bureaucracies for handling quasi-legal cases (Durrenberger and Erem 1997a, b).

Written by corporate lawyers to benefit corporations, the Taft–Hartley Act of 1947 outlawed the forms of class solidarity—from strikes to a strong system of shop stewards—that had proven effective means for workers to organize to deal with employers in the past (Fantasia 1988: 56). Union bureaucracy replaced labor solidarity, and sociologists could not find classes in the United States. If they did find a working class, it was peopled with authoritarian, narrow-minded, intolerant people with no talent for democracy (Ehrenreich 1990: 110).

Vanneman and Cannon (1987) chronicle the governmental repression of radical working-class movements that left workers a choice between a defeated radical movement and a conservative American Federation of Labor (AFL) that was less promising but was permitted to exist. They argue this re-alignment behind the AFL reflects rationality in the face of historical alternatives rather than lack of class consciousness. They review sociological literature that indicates Americans ascribe wealth and power to personal qualities and argue that such concepts keep Americans docile and make the case that it is vulnerability to coercion rather than concepts that keeps the poor unsuccessful.

Fantasia (1988) agrees and adds that legislation effectively works against class-based organizing. Even though "the world may be a paradoxical and contradictory place to those negotiating it" (5), survey research overlooks paradoxes and records responses as fixed and static. Survey research is so narrow that it neglects the most important and interesting dimensions of class relations because it abstracts attitudes and ideas from the "world of class practices in which they are embedded" (8). Patterns of thought are generated and changed by social action. By only looking at verbal responses about attitudes, sociologists have "been generally blinded to class sentiments expressed in the collective activities of workers" (10) that create and express class consciousness. In the parlance of anthropologists, sociologists of class have not attended to the ethnography of class. As Fantasia says:

> The point is that analyses of class consciousness should be based on actions, organizational capabilities, institutional arrangements, and the values that arise within them, rather than on attitudes abstracted from the context of social action.

Vanneman and Cannon (1987) argue that class consciousness is the cultural expression of the experience of class and is a broad set of practices and repertories that are available for empirical investigation (see Rubin 1992) rather than disembodied mental attitudes. Culture, Fantasia (1988: 33) argues, is not an integrated system that patterns life to minimize discontinuity, as Malinowski, Benedict, and Kroeber argued, but complex, contradictory, and changing with situations and contexts in the organization and reproduction of daily life. Previous work on union stewards in Chicago indicates the changing relationships between everyday practice and cultural conceptualization (Durrenberger 1997, Durrenberger and Erem 1997a, Durrenberger and Erem 1999)

Why are the realities of class hidden in the United States? If Goldschmidt could so accurately and lucidly outline the realities of class in America half a century ago, why are we still discussing it in anthropology as though we had no clue about class or class dynamics? Everyday structures and structural relationships produce the daily realities that people code as cultural. Law and management practice determine the everyday realities of workplaces. In these realities the practice and conception of class-based or union relationships meet great resistance.

Ehrenreich (1990) details the class bias and ideological co-optation of sociologists. Vanneman and Cannon (1987) agree and elaborate "Restraining Myths" following Richard Hamilton. These are reality-defining paradigmatic assumptions that limit the sociological imagination, including the conventional sociological wisdom such as American exceptionalism. They argue that selective citation and ignoring of disconfirming work reinforces this view. Echoing the prevailing wisdom, the organizations that claim to represent working people themselves deny the relevance of class. Finally, sociologists misrepresent data to confirm the conventional wisdom. Anthropologists are not immune from these processes (Durrenberger 1995).

Universities, the institutions that replicate the managerial middle class (Ehrenreich 1990), encode meritocratic individualism in the ideology, if not the practice of merit pay raises for instructors, promotion criteria for professors, grading individual students in classes, and taking seriously various exam scores as measures of merit, if not virtue. University folk experience an incessant inundation in this fallacious folk model as daily practice. There is little wonder that anthropologists participate in the perpetuation of an appropriate folk model of and for the middle class and the institutions we serve. The wonder of it is that so many anthropologists have provided alternative views.

Given the role of universities as purveyors of meritocratic individualism, we have to return to Goldschmidt's (1950: 492) methodological question and ask whether our methods are not simply projecting the predilections of anthropologists. When we see such attention devoted to issues of identity and cultural definitions of the middle class, when groups of experts are empanelled to discuss their high school–class reunions and the symbolism of the middle class, we can wonder why we are not more busily investigating the realities of historical dynamics, power, and control of resources that determine the nature of structural relationships rather than reproducing them or the structures of daily workplace experience that create cultures. I think we need to do what Wolf (1999) suggested and stand outside our structures to better understand the relationships between them and our thought, to explain the relationships between our folk models of class and the realities of power.

Acknowledgments

I gratefully thank the many individuals of the two locals I discuss here for their help with this project. UAW Local 2320 organizers Robert T. (Tim) Yeager and John Bowman made the LAFC study possible. Pasquale Lombardo made possible my interviews with LAFC attorneys and Daniel Romero helped with the surveys. SEIU Local 1 president Douglas L. Hart, Vice-Presidents Nancy Cross and Rod Bashir, and Jay Cannon as well as the other officers, staff, reps, stewards, and members of Local 1 made the work with that Local possible. I thank them all for their assistance with this study. I thank Suzan Erem for her help and support.

Questions for Further Discussion

1. According to the American myth, people deserve what they get and get what they deserve. Discuss your experience and that of your family—does this seem to be true? Do you know people who have lost their jobs? Did they lose their jobs because they did something wrong? Why did they deserve the job when they got it, but then, some time later, no longer deserve it?

2. In the United States, we believe people get ahead through hard work. Do you think that chief executive officers and other successful people work harder than you and your family members? How much harder do you think they work to deserve millions of dollars a year? Is there something else that makes them more deserving of success than you and your family? How do you explain the difference?

References

Bernard, H. Russell. 1988. *Research methods in cultural anthropology.* Newbury Park: Sage.

Bonanno, Alessandro, Lawrence Busch, William, H. Friedland, Lourdes Gouveia, and Enzo Mingione. 1994. *From Columbus to ConAgra: the globalization of agriculture and food.* Lawrence: University Press of Kansas.

Borgatti, Stephen P. 1996. *Anthropac 4.0 methods guide.* Natick, MA: Analytic Technologies.

Bronfenbrenner, Kate, Sheldon Friedman, Richard W. Hurd, Rudolph A. Oswald, and Ronald L. Seeber. 1998. Introduction. In Kate Bronfenbrenner et al., eds., *Organizing to win: new research on union strategies,* 1–15. Ithaca: Cornell University Press.

Burawoy, Michael, and Theda Skocpol. 1982. *Marxist inquiries: studies of labor, class, and states.* Chicago: University of Chicago Press.

Durrenberger, E. Paul. 1990. Policy, power, and science: the implementation of turtle excluder device regulations in the U.S. Gulf of Mexico shrimp fishery. *Maritime Anthropological Studies* 3, 1: 69–86.

———. 1992a. *It's all politics: South Alabama's seafood industry.* University of Illinois Press.

———. 1992b. Psychology, unions, and the law: folk models and the history of shrimpers unions in Mississippi. *Human organization* 51: 151–154.

———. 1996. *Gulf Coast soundings: people and policy in the Mississippi shrimp industry.* Lawrence: University Press of Kansas.

———. 1995. Mississippi unions again: facts, figures, and misrepresentations. *Human organization* 54, 4: 474–477.

———. 1994c. The history of shrimpers' unions in Mississippi, 1915–1955. *Labor's heritage* 5, 3: 66–76.

———. 1997. That'll teach you: cognition and practice in a Chicago union local. *Human organization* 56, 4: 388–392.

Durrenberger, E. Paul, and Suzan Erem. 1999. The weak suffer what they must: a natural experiment in thought and science. *American anthropologist* 101, 4: 783–793.

———. 1997a. Getting a raise: organizing workers in an industrializing hospital. *Journal of anthropological research* 53, 1: 31–46.

———. 1997b. The dance of power: ritual and agency among unionized American health care workers. *American anthropologist* 99, 3: 489–495.

Durrenberger, E. Paul and Gìsli Pálsson. 1983. Riddles of herring and rhetorics of success. *Journal of anthropological research* 39: 323–335.

———. 1989. *The anthropology of Iceland.* Iowa City: University of Iowa Press.

Ehrenreich, Barbara. 1990. *Fear of falling: the inner life of the middle class.* New York: Harper Perennial.

Fantasia, Rick. 1988. *Cultures of solidarity: consciousness, action, and contemporary American workers.* Berkeley: University of California Press.

Goldschmidt, Walter. 1950. Social class in America—a critical review. *American anthropologist* 52: 483–498.

———. 1955. Social class and the dynamics of status in America. *American anthropologist* 57: 1209–1217.

———. 1998. The dynamics of status in America. *Anthropology Newsletter* 40, 5: 64.

King, Thomas D., and E. Paul Durrenberger. 2000. Introduction. In E. Paul Durrenberger and Thomas D. King, eds., *State and community in fisheries management: power, policy, and practice.* Westport, CT. Greenwood.

Kingsolver, Ann E. 1998. *More than class: studying power in U.S. workplaces.* Albany: State University of New York Press.

Kottak, Conrad Phillip. 1998. *Assault on paradise: social change in a Brazilian village.* 3rd ed. Boston: McGraw-Hill.

Lamphere, Louise, Alex Stepick, and Guillermo Greiner. 1994. *Newcomers in the workplace: immigrants and the restructuring of the U.S. economy.* Philadelphia: Temple University Press.

Lewis, Michael. 1993. *The culture of inequality.* 2nd ed. Amherst: University of Massachusetts Press.

McNall, Scott G., Rhoda F. Levine, and Rick Fantasia. 1991. *Bringing class back in contemporary and historical perspectives.* Boulder, Westview Press.

Newman, Katherine S. 1988. *Falling from grace: the experience of downward mobility in the American middle class.* New York: The Free Press.

———. 1993. *Declining fortunes: the withering of the American Dream.* New York: Basic Books.

Ortner, Sherry. 1998. Identities: the hidden life of class. *Journal of anthropological research* 54, 1: 1–17.

Pálsson, Gìsli, and E. Paul Durrenberger. 1983. Icelandic foremen and skippers: the structure and evolution of a folk model. *American ethnologist* 10: 511–528.

———. 1990. Systems of production and social discourse: the Skipper Effect revisited. *American anthropologist* 92, 1: 130–141.

———. 1992a. Icelandic dialogues: individual differences in indigenous discourse. *Journal of anthropological research* 48, 4: 301–316.

———. 1992b. Rhetorics of skill and skillful rhetorics. *American anthropologist* 92, 2: 452–454.

———. 1997. *Images of contemporary Iceland: everyday lives and global contexts.* Iowa City: University of Iowa Press.

Romney, A. Kimball. 1999. Culture consensus as a statistical model. *Current anthropology* 40 (Supplement): 103–115.

Romney, A. Kimball, Susan C. Weller, and William H. Batchelder. 1986. Culture as consensus: a theory of culture and informant accuracy. *American anthropologist* 88, 2: 313–338.

Romney, A. Kimball, Carmella Moore, and Craig D. Rush. 1994. Cultural universals: measuring the semantic structure of emotion terms in English and Japanese. *Proceedings of the National Academy of Sciences* 94: 5489–5494.

Romney, A. Kimball, and Carmella Moore. 1998. Toward a theory of culture as shared cognitive structures. *Ethos* 26, 3: 314–337.

Rubin, Lillian B. 1992. *Worlds of pain: life in the working-class family.* New York: Basic Books.

Sacks, Karen B. 1988. Toward a unified theory of class, race, and gender. *American ethnologist* 16, 3: 534–550.

Vanneman, Reeve, and Lynn Weber Cannon, 1987. *The American perception of class*. Philadelphia, PA: Temple University Press.

Weller, Susan C., and A. Kimball Romney. 1988. *Systematic data collection*. Newbury Park: Sage.

Wolf, Eric R. 1999. *Envisioning power: ideologies of dominance and crisis*. Berkeley: University of California Press.

13

Welcome to an East Harlem Shooting Gallery

Philippe Bourgois

University of Pennsylvania

Are drug addicts Americans? Some of us might like to think they are not; many of us would prefer not to know that places like shooting galleries even exist. Although he has also conducted research in Central America, Philippe Bourgois has perhaps carried out his most challenging ethnographic work in his hometown, New York City. He moved with his family to East Harlem for five years, and became part of a social network of crack dealers and heroin addicts, whom he came to know as human beings and as friends. In this article, he elaborates on the view that the people involved in illicit trade and activities in East Harlem are far more American than most of us suspect or, more to the point, are willing to admit.

Philippe Bourgois is Richard Perry University Professor of Anthropology in the Departments of Anthropology and Family Medicine and Community Practice at the University of Pennsylvania. As a medical anthropologist, he recognizes that such subjects as disease and treatment must be understood in context—factors like poverty, danger, and discrimination create and exacerbate threats to human health. Throughout his anthropological career, he has never chosen the safe path—in addition to the East Harlem research [on which he published an important book, In Search of Respect: Selling Crack in El Barrio *(Cambridge 1995 {new edition 2003})], he elected to undertake fieldwork in El Salvador at the height of its civil war in the 1980s. Dr. Bourgois has assumed these risks because, like so many of the anthropologists who have contributed articles in this volume, he believes that anthropology should be actively directed toward improving the human condition.*

We passed through a gaping hole smashed out of the rear brick wall of the only abandoned tenement still standing in the middle of an East Harlem rubble field. My friend did not even pause to allow his eyes to adjust to the late-night darkness, and I had to scramble behind

Bourgois, Philippe. "Just Another Night in a Shooting Gallery." *Theory Culture & Society* 15.2 (1998): 37–66. © 1998 Sage Publications. Reprinted by permission.

him through the entrails of the burnt building pretending everything was perfectly normal. We paused by a large slab of plywood that blocked yet another fractured brick wall, and he knocked: "It's me, Mikey—white Mikey . . . with a friend. He's white too, but don't worry; he's cool." Shivering wet from the drizzle of a New York City December night, we waited to be invited into the shooting gallery. Fidgeting anxiously, I stepped out of the way of a persistent trail of drops that somehow were making their way through five floors of charred rafters directly onto my baseball cap. I noticed that my mouth tasted of metal and wondered if perhaps I was overstepping my limits as an anthropologist. I also thought of the warning the Puerto Rican crack dealers, operating out of the video arcade next to the tenement building where I lived with my family, had given me when I told them I wanted to visit a shooting gallery: "Stay away from dopefiends. Especially *morenos*. They're bad, all of them. And you're a *blanquito!* Don't be stupid!" But when Mikey invited me to come along with him on his way to buy heroin, I could not resist the opportunity.

Before I knew it, I was ducking sideways through yet another overhanging slab of broken bricks into what had apparently once been a ground floor apartment. Blinking in what seemed like bright candlelight, I felt a vague warmth emanating from a sputtering fire to my right. Striving to compose myself, I smiled eagerly at Doc, the manager of the shooting gallery who was introducing himself with a loud, "Welcome to my place." To my surprise he graciously shooed me into one of the four dilapidated chairs ringing a grimy table cluttered with drug debris.

Mikey was not needing or paying attention to any awkward introductions. He no longer needed to prove or justify his identity to anyone as he was instantly recognizable to everyone to be a heroin addict. Intent on his upcoming shot of relief—and possibly of ecstatic pleasure if the quality was as good as everyone waiting on line in the park had claimed—Mikey hardly nodded hello before eagerly dumping the entire contents of both of his two $10 packets of heroin into a charred spoon that he picked up off of the detritus in the middle of the table. He did, however, clearly turn down Doc's offer to "rent" him the "house needle" as that would have cost him an extra $2. I vaguely heard him mumble something to Doc about his "buddy" having "change" for the "house fee."

Not yet fully aware that he was hustling me for his share of the $2 admission fee, I somewhat overeagerly pulled out two crumpled single-dollar bills I had purposely left easily accessible in my outside coat pocket. To my consternation, Doc suddenly tensed up. Mikey, meanwhile, skidded his chair to the far end of the table and ducked his head even closer to his spoon of heroin. My primary concern was to prevent any ambiguity arising from my not being a drug injector—or even a drug user—and nervously I began explaining, in what I feared was a hopelessly lame tone of voice, that I would not be shooting up as I was just drinking tonight and simply wanted to "hang with my buddy Mikey" in order to "learn about the street." In my bubbling confusion, I even heard myself stammering something to the effect of my being a cultural anthropologist and a college professor who was thinking of writing a book about "life on the street." Persuaded that Doc was now going to be completely convinced that I was an undercover police officer, I struggled to understand why he was ignoring my semi-coherent and highly dubious—even though perfectly true— explanation of self and was instead tapping his finger with irritation on top of the two single-dollar bills I had placed on the table. I stared at him blankly, prolonging the silence until he finally snarled, "Someone owes me two dollars more, whether you be shooting or not." Mikey was now hissing directly in my ear, "Come on, Phil, can't you cover for me? Just this one time? I don't got no change, brother."

With a flood of relief, I finally realized that all the tension in the room was being caused by Mikey's attempt to make me pay his $2 house fee. Assailing Mikey with what I hoped was an appropriately aggressive flood of curses over his stinginess, I quickly handed over his share of the house fee to Doc. I now finally understood why Mikey had insisted on single-dollar bills in change at the Yemeni grocery store, where I had bought a quart of malt liquor.

Doc immediately pocketed my money and broke out into a wide, friendly smile. To my surprise, he began to concentrate on making me feel comfortable. In retrospect, I realized that Doc's decision to befriend me followed the straightforward *lumpen* logic of the street economy. Having publicly proved myself to be ineffective at guarding my money and a little too friendly, gentle, and full of smiles, I represented an ideal victim. It was well worth investing the time and energy of building a long-term street hustle relationship with me. Furthermore, Doc was probably a bit bored and looked forward to the curiosity of "conversating" with a white boy who claimed—of all outlandish things—to be a college professor.

It had been difficult to buy heroin tonight because the city's "Tactical Narcotics" team was out in force and two "white boys" stand out like sore thumbs on East Harlem streets, especially after midnight. An emaciated "steerer" advertising that "Knockout"—a well-established local brand—was "open, workin', and pumpin', man!" had waved us toward the three-man Knockout team (composed of a "pitcher" who actually makes the hand-to-hand sale, and his two helper-bodyguards/touters) selling in the middle of the block. As we walked toward them, however, a hail of whistles pierced the air. I thought perhaps the lookouts at the end of the block had changed their minds and decided we were undercovers rather than heroin addicts, but the whistles switched to calm shouts in street code announcing the arrival of a police car. Despite all being second-generation, New York–born youths, the lookouts rolled their "r's" with the rural Puerto Rican *jibaro* accents of their immigrant parents and grandparents, "*carhrho feo* [ugly car], *bajando, bajando* [coming down] *carhrho feo!*"

We found ourselves squarely in view of the squad car; it was too late to turn back. The police were bearing down directly on us, flashing their lights but not using the siren. They slowed to a crawl as they passed us, and my pulse began to race. I anticipated we would be thrown roughly against the wall and searched from head to foot—this had happened to me several times before, when the police caught me out on the street after dark in East Harlem. Behind us we heard more whistles and "*bajando*" shouts as customers at the far corner were being turned back so that they would not have to make the dangerously conspicuous trek in front of the raiding officers. I wished we had arrived two minutes later.

Ironically, many of my closest calls with violence, during the almost five years I lived and worked among drug addicts and dealers in East Harlem, were with law enforcement (Bourgois 2003a). From the perspective of the police, I was an obnoxious provocation violating New York City's unwritten apartheid laws: the only reason for a "white boy" to be in the inner city, especially at night, is to buy drugs. My presence on the street made some officers incredibly angry. They cursed at me, berated me, and shoved me against the wall, no matter how polite and cooperative I tried to be. On this particular night, however, the police left us alone; perhaps the freezing drizzle dissuaded them from leaving their dry, warm squad car.

Around the corner a woman called out softly from behind a defaced pillar of the abandoned school building: "SunShine at 114th in the Park." We did not dare pause lest this self-appointed steerer also demand payment. In fact, both of us pretended not to hear the gentle voice, or notice the huddled, emaciated form. She was what they call a "toss-up" (Bourgois and Dunlap 1993), a woman who sold sex for crack. Toss-ups are the most vulnerable of all street-level prostitutes. In a mid-winter drizzle, after midnight, this toss-up seemed especially pathetic.

Arriving at the Park entrance six blocks away, we were both relieved to see three orderly single-file lines of heroin addicts buying from three separate teams, all selling the "SunShine" brand. We were greeted by the angry, barked orders of a steerer, instructing us to proceed to the back of the nearest line along the chain-link fence at the far end of the playground. He also warned us that this was strictly "a place of business," and since Mikey and I were together, only one of us needed to wait on line. Mikey stepped aside and walked a safe distance away into the shadows of some nearby trees, thereby manipulating me to pay for his two packets of heroin. He knew I did not want to call attention to us (the only two white faces in the crowd) by arguing with him and refusing to stand in line.

But nobody seemed to notice our whiteness. Presumably everyone assumed that only full-blown dopefiends could possibly tolerate being so cold and wet on such a miserable late night. I was further reassured when I was immediately included in the line's anxious discussion of the quality of the heroin being sold: "Have you tried it?" "Is it good? Does it work?"

Coincidentally, at this very moment, a legal street hawker, attracted to our huddle of exceptional buying power, walked up with half a dozen bright blue foldable umbrellas: "Only 2 dollahs; 2 dollahs. For the little lady at home. Take a look. These is 17 dollahs in the store." The lookouts and steerers immediately converged on him in a rage, perhaps suspecting the camouflaged activities of a well-organized stick-up crew: "If you ain't buyin', get goin'." Someone on the line was trying to buy an umbrella, but the hawker was forced to run away without completing the sale, because one of the lookouts had reached conspicuously into the groin area of his baggy jeans as if to draw a firearm. I chuckled at this all-American manifestation of determined, high-risk, cutthroat entrepreneurship in the inner city. Despite what politicians, social workers, or social scientists might claim, U.S. inner cities have emerged as the latest frontier for the descendants of immigrants and other marginalized citizens of color to scramble violently for a proverbial piece of the American pie. The multibillion-dollar drug economy is, sadly, an irrefutable testament to how alive and vital capitalism remains among the thousands of people who are dismissed by policy makers as the passive, demoralized "underclass" (see critique by Gans 1996). Rain, snow, or shine, in inner cities across the United States, fistfuls of money and drugs flow among tens of thousands of skinny, sick men and women, desperately seeking material sustenance and emotional meaning (see Bourgois and Schonberg, in press).

The pitcher ran out of heroin with only three customers ahead of me in the line, prompting a chorus of groans and curses. To our relief, however, we were not ordered to leave; the pitcher merely trotted fifty yards back into the darkness of the playground and huddled with a newly arrived "runner" and then trotted back with a fresh supply of product announcing, "This is it! This is the last bundle. After this there's no more. Get what you need now!" Those at the end of the line groaned anxiously and someone at the very end of the line begged, "Leave some for me! All's I need is two." Moments later, the pitcher was asking me, "How many?" and I was pushing two $10 bills through the chain-link fence. Without even looking up from his wad of tiny rectangular glassine packets, he handed me two crisp packets of heroin. Each packet was carefully stamped in pink ink, with the logo

"SunShine" covered by a strip of scotch tape to prevent unauthorized opening by addicted employees. I returned to Mikey and we proceeded to the ruined tenement where Doc ran his shooting gallery.

The table at the gallery was littered with a tangled mess of discarded glassine heroin envelopes, miniature ziplock coke packets, and crack vials. Doc was asking what we had purchased, telling us (without even waiting for an answer) the brand names of what was good that night—Rambo, 007, SunShine, Latin Power, O. J., Mandela—what was "open," and where the cops were patrolling. We added our bit of information to the street-savvy pool of knowledge to be imparted to the next customer: "Knockout's open on 117th but is crazy-hot, and SunShine in Jefferson Park just closed." I was sort of disappointed that everything of significance from our last two rain-drenched hours striving to buy heroin could be summed up in such a matter-of-fact sentence.

As my eyes continued to adjust to the flickering candlelight, I tried to discern what— or who—the two bundled shapes were on the far side of the room. My reconnoitering was interrupted by a loud knock on the plywood plank door. Two new clients, Slim and his friend Flex, walked through the hole in the wall, stamping their feet and shaking off melting snowflakes with the satisfied expressions of eager customers entering a welcoming place of business. Apparently, the rain outside had turned into snow flurries. Slim sat down next to me and to my surprise immediately addressed me in a relaxed, affable conversation about how the pitcher on the SunShine line had run out of heroin just when it was his turn to buy.

It took me a few seconds to realize that I had earned Slim's friendly familiarity by waiting at his side along the chain-link fence in the Jefferson Park playground. I was almost embarrassed not to have recognized him right away. He had been one of the more aggressive rasping voices that had complained threateningly each time someone at the front of the line had purchased more than a couple of packets, and/or took too long to count his money. Slim had been left stranded without his "cure," and had been forced to go three blocks further downtown to purchase "DOA," a less reputable brand. On the DOA line, he had met Flex, who was now sitting next to him, his brow knit in earnest concentration while he dumped his precious powder into the same kitchen spoon ("house cooker") that Mikey had just finished using.

Meanwhile, Doc was asking Mikey if he needed a "tie" for his arm. I had not even seen Mikey fill his syringe with water from out of the topless plastic jug that lay under the table; or watched him re-empty this same water into the little pile of white powder at the bottom of his spoon which was hanging over the edge of the table balanced under the weight of a wooden candle holder; or admired the steadiness of his hands as he lifted the spoon to heat it over the candle to make sure every last bit of precious heroin was fully dissolved; or noticed him drop a tiny ball of cigarette filter into the dissolved heroin to trap particles as he drew the cloudy liquefied narcotic back into his syringe. I kicked myself for my lapse in concentration; I had meant to document potential vectors for infectious diseases from the micro-practices of preparing injections in a shooting gallery. Ethnographic methods are important for improving public health messages and programs that do not address the everyday pragmatic realities of street-based injectors (Bourgois 2002, Bourgois and Bruneau 2000, Bourgois et al. 2006, Ciccarone 2003). On the run from law enforcement, addicts often find themselves injecting in filthy sites with no running water. They frequently clean out their bloodied syringes in the same containers from which they draw their water. They often share their cookers (usually bottle caps, old spoons, or the bottoms of crushed beer cans) in which heroin is dissolved, as well as their "cottons"—cigarette filters or pinches of real cotton swabs for trapping undissolved particles. At busy shooting galleries, clients sometimes inject water pink from the blood residues of the previous half-dozen injectors (Bourgois and Bruneau 2000, Koester and Wiebel 1990). We know that needle-sharing can transmit HIV, but it is not clear whether the sharing of other types of drug paraphernalia also spreads the virus. However, hepatitis C and abscesses, which are more highly infectious than HIV, are very likely spread through these "indirect sharing" practices (Bourgois et al. 2004, Ciccarone et al. 2001, Ciccarone and Bourgois 2003, Koester et al. 2003).

In my irritation, I was only vaguely aware that Doc's offer to hold Mikey's tie was impatiently refused. Mikey unrolled his shirt sleeve to expose a scrawny white forearm with a long line of red prick marks. It took Mikey less than 20 seconds to shoot up. He flexed his fist a few times to make his veins pop out and then hit a vein far up towards his wrist artery, just beyond where the last red pockmark had been left from his injection the morning before. Once the needle was a few millimeters below the skin he pulled back on the stopper with his thumb to make sure blood flooded the syringe's chamber. This is called "registering" and indicates that the needle tip is squarely inside the vein and has not pierced right through, or rolled off the casing of the vein into the surrounding tissue. Registering is a crucial part of shooting up because if an injector carelessly injects the heroin into the muscle or fatty tissue surrounding the vein, it balloons up into a painful bruise. More importantly, the expectant addict will miss the initial euphoric rush when a successful hit of heroin is released directly inside a racing blood vessel and pulses within seconds up the arm, through the heart, and into the brain for a bullseye of sedated warmth and relaxation.

Slim and Flex heated their heroin and loaded the house needle with the same swift, efficient hand motions that Mikey had used—as well as the same dirty water and the same dirty cooker spoon, and the same crumpled cigarette filter cotton. Mikey was already heading out the door with a barely audible "I'll-see-you-later," followed by further spasms from his hollow, racking cough. Perhaps he was concerned that Doc might demand another two dollars from him should he overstay his welcome; maybe he was irritated by my repeated injunctions to have his lungs checked out at the local hospital for pneumonia; or perhaps he was just being commonsensical about the real dangers of hanging out for longer than strictly necessary in an East Harlem shooting gallery well past midnight on a stormy winter night— especially when you are white. More to the point, he had already hustled—several times!— the only easy victim in this space. It was time to move on and scrounge up enough money for his next fix before his body once again started aching for heroin sometime around sunrise.

Doc, either to express companionship and solidarity with me or to create a moral hierarchy where he might seem more worthy of trust, converted my concern over Mikey's pneumonia-like cough into a forum where Mikey was berated for not taking care of himself. For a moment everyone injecting around the table sounded like wise, elderly matrons eager to impart their words of wisdom to an errant child wearing inadequate clothing on a cold day. Slim clucked something about how important it was to wear a warm hat, and he actually pulled a large red, yellow, and green wool Rastafarian cap out of his pocket and covered his overgrown afro. We were all clearly happy with ourselves to be able to share our righteous concern over the behavior of a wayward dopefiend.

As if following the cue of our common respectability, Doc stood up and began, somewhat precipitously, to clean off the table. Throughout the tidying process, in an effective attempt to welcome, reassure, and further evaluate me, Doc kept up a steady, happy chatter about "the decent place" that he tried to run, how he was "not gonna let things get dirty," how he "ran a classy joint," and so on. Indeed, within minutes, most traces of the past several hours of injecting had been wiped up. The table looked spotlessly clean and orderly. Pushing his offended housekeeper scenario to the limit, Doc reproached Flex, who was nodding heavily from the effects of his injection, for having carelessly left a fresh pack of litter scattered about him. In the same breath of righteousness, Doc picked up the open house hypodermic needle that Flex had also dropped on the table in front of him, and carefully capped it, laying it strategically in the center of the table, ready for the next customer. Doc did not bother rinsing the syringe to kill any trapped HIV; he simply shrugged when I suggested that maybe it should be cleaned.

Slim had not "hit" yet. He was carefully adding some powder cocaine into his spoon of already heated and dissolved heroin solution. Slim was preparing a "speedball," the contradictory combination of stimulant-cum-depressant that is highly appreciated by street addict connoisseurs. Speedballs became the rage among even the most down-and-out dopefiends when the Colombian cartels, in response to the 1980s' "War on Drugs" and its crackdown on bulky and less profitable marijuana shipments (Bourgois 2003a: 350n77) began flooding the U.S. market with low-volume, high-value, inexpensive cocaine. Once Slim had finally loaded his works, I expected him to take off his jacket and roll up his sleeve, or at worst take off his shoes, or roll up his jeans and search for a clean vein below the knees. Instead, Slim arched back his neck and called over to one of the dark forms huddled, under a mound of covers and plastic bags, on the old mattress against the far wall.

Pops, a true veteran heroin addict who was considerably older and even frailer than Doc, jumped eagerly to his feet. Perhaps he was anticipating a "taste," that is, a drug tip for the service he was about to render, or maybe he was just trying to be helpful. Nobody likes to be taken for granted, but in this instance there was a worse fate to be had—Pops might be thrown out of the gallery if he did not prove himself useful. Pops vigorously massaged Slim's jugular while holding the loaded syringe high above his head, well out of harm's way. The wavering silhouette thrown by the candlelight reminded me of the Statue of Liberty, although the hypodermic needle full of heroin, coke, and perhaps HIV, hepatitis C, and abscess bacteria from the traces of a previous customer's blood, was substituting for the torch of freedom.

I tried—and almost succeeded—to ignore this spectacle, acting as if it were totally normal for a shriveled old man to jab a syringe into a middle-aged man's neck. I was unable, however, to prevent myself from noticing how carefully Pops pulled back the hypodermic's plunger to make sure blood from the neck's vein spurted into the syringe before injecting its contents. His head cocked tensely to the side, Slim let out a steady stream of directions and feedback. Somehow he remained frozen motionless throughout the operation: "That's right; keep steady; you're in. Steady now; that's right; slowly; that's right. Go ahead! Come on! YEAH!"

Slim dropped back into his chair to allow the competing waves of cocaine and heroin to flush through his synapses. Moments later, he burst into urgent conversation as the initial coke rush from his speedball overwhelmed the heroin in the mixture. I forgot to notice if Slim paid Pops or gave him a taste.

In the meantime, Flex had become sufficiently roused from his nodding to pursue the same speedball high as Slim had, except that Flex "chased it" by "stemming," that is, smoking crack in a four-inch-long cylindrical glass pipe, or "stem," with crumpled wire mesh stuffed down one end. Crack is merely an alloy of cocaine and baking soda. Its psychoactive ingredient is the same as that of powder cocaine, except that unlike cocaine, crack releases the psychoactive agent efficiently when it is burned, resulting in a faster euphoric rush than injection or sniffing because the capillaries in the lungs pass the drug almost instantaneously into the brain's synapses.

Pops had dragged himself back out of the range of the candlelight to crumple onto a filthy mattress in the self-effacing manner of a hired helper. Desperate to trap as much of his body heat as possible and to deflect the occasional rain drops falling from the charred rafters high above us, he swathed himself in an amorphous pile of ragged blankets that he then wrapped with ripped sheets of plastic. When Pops realized that I was looking directly at him, he shyly nodded his head and propped himself up on his elbows. He gave me a faint smile, only to break eye contact moments later to collapse once again, exhausted and shivering under his ragged patchwork of covers.

After finishing my bottle of malt liquor, I stood up and stretched so as to obtain a clearer look into the back recesses of the room, where a second bundled shape had begun emitting, at unpredictable intervals, deep guttural moans of delight. This explicitly happy, relaxed form turned out to be an elderly woman. Her eyes lidded three-quarters shut as if to appreciate more fully the internal peace of her heroin nod, she also had a glass crack stem balanced delicately between her fingers as if it were an imported cigarette. With the phlegmy rasp that is the trademark of superannuated dopefiends, her almost obscene groans of pleasure seemed to burst forth involuntarily, from deep inside her blankets. Everyone seemed to think her choruses of bizarrely proto-erotic bliss were completely normal. It was as if she were the shooting gallery's speedball conductor—she effectively paced and punctuated the rise and fall of the various combinations of coke, crack, and heroin tides that were washing through the synapses of the patrons, some of whom were "conversating" in an animated way while others nodded deeply.

Every now and then the old woman would fumble with her crack pipe, light it up, and temporarily snap to a wide-awake consciousness. On these occasions, she contributed enthusiastic affirmations to whatever was being said in the nearest conversation audible to her. For example, she interrupted one of Doc's redundant tirades over "the good place" he ran with: "Yes that's a fact. And ain't it something! We been gettin' straight every day now for almost a year. I know it's hard to believe but it's the truth. Keepin' warm, and staying straight every day—mmm-hmmm." Slim and Flex, meanwhile, were rallying their energies around Flex's crack stem, which they were now earnestly passing back and forth—almost grabbing it from one another—reminding me of pre-teenage buddies huddled around a forbidden cigarette in a school yard. Somehow ferreting out additional stashes of crack from the recesses of their pockets, sleeves, and hems, they repeatedly lit up tiny chunks of the precious stuff. Each inhalation precipitated a burst of happy conversation. The advantage of the speedball high for crack smokers is that the heroin they inject, or sniff, provides an underlying stabilizing foundation for their coke-induced exaltation. This prevents them from losing control to the hyper-paranoid fantasies that massive, concentrated ingestion of cocaine often brings on—the sense that "coke bugs" are swarming over their skin, for example, or a panic that inspires them to sprint away from imaginary police officers or attack would-be assailants.

Only Doc and I clung to any vague pretense of sobriety, but Doc soon changed that by drawing water into his syringe from the filthy water jug under the table, and then dissolving in the house cooker the jumble of heroin shavings-cum-cocaine he had scraped from the sides of the empty packets cleaned off the table earlier. He also added the used cottons from the night's previous injections into the mix to eke out any residue (and viruses and bacteria) trapped in their fibers. Doc dropped his jeans, shuffled over closer to the fire, squatted in the flickering light, and shot himself up in one of the veins below his knee. The coke part of his makeshift speedball was the first part of his high to hit him. All of a sudden he was standing above me at full height, gesturing excitedly. Oblivious to whatever it was that he was telling me, I focused all my attention on the open needle that was clutched in his right hand as he began to pace the small space between me, the table, and the fire. To my dismay he began punctuating his more emphatic remarks by jabbing the open house needle at me.

Doc's cocaine-inspired needle-waving diatribe proved to be contagious; it galvanized the group back into a single, "conversating," coke-rushing unit. Following the unpredictable ebbs and flows of the group's contradictory chemical tides, the room's speedball roller-coaster dissolved a few minutes later into yet another ebb of heroin-induced relaxation. Eventually, Doc, too, became calmer. He sank into the front bucket seat of a long-gone car that he had dragged from out of the back of the shooting gallery closer to the fire.

Only moments later, however, he was shivering and announced aggressively that someone needed to break up a large hunk of nailed plywood boards that lay near the entrance to feed the fire. Flex, presumably still flush from the crack he had just finished smoking with Slim, jumped to his feet, seized the plywood boards, and began whacking at them with an oversized club of gnarled iron gas piping. His positioning of the plywood on an unstable marble step created the acoustics of an oversized drum. Soon the entire building was echoing with each bang. Our hands over our ears, we shouted at him to stop, but this merely encouraged him to swing faster and harder, sweat flying off of his contorted face. He started to look angry and I happened to be the person sitting closest to him, directly in the path of his metal club. Was he about to bug-out into cocaine paranoia and hallucinate me into an evil white enemy undercover cop?

Slim rose from his cot, cursing Flex for potentially attracting the attention of the police with this outrageous racket. Others in the gallery, quickly oscillating from their heroin highs to cocaine-induced anxiety, began shouting obscenities at Flex, but no one dared stop him physically because his gnarled iron pipe was swinging faster and faster. Slim's mention of the police flooded me with a new worry: being trapped for three days in an overcrowded New York City "bullpen," waiting to be arraigned by a Narcotics Circuit judge overwhelmed with cases due to the recent Tactical Narcotics Team crackdown. I flashed on the prison rape stories I had been tape-recording in the crackhouse where I normally spent my evenings. U.S. drug policies, along with the growing concentrations of unemployed populations in the inner city, have turned prisons and jails throughout the country into chaotic race-segregated cesspools. The United States has the highest per-capita incarceration rate of any industrialized nation in the world, and African Americans are approximately seven times more likely than whites to be in prison, primarily due to ethnic disparities in drug arrests since the escalation of the War on Drugs in the 1980s. This is exacerbated, of course, by the dramatic statistical rise in poverty rates during these same decades. Sociologist Loïc Wacquant identifies the explosion in the size of the incarcerated African American population as the government's new way of managing race and class relations since the time of the War on Poverty and the civil rights movement (Wacquant 2002, 2006). As factories move out of big cities and overseas in search of lower labor costs, ever larger proportions of the population in the United States have been pushed into generating incomes through crime and the underground economy (Duster 1987, Wilson 1996).

The planks finally gave in and Flex surveyed us proudly, panting and wiping his brow. I was surprised to find that everyone was instantly happy with him again. Both Slim and Doc praised him for his hard work, and Doc busily stacked the shredded wood into a neat pile by the fire. I realized that I—rather than my coke-pumped friends—had been the paranoid one during this incident. I had misjudged the aggressive street-tone of their shouts and curses. In fact, I was embarrassed at myself for my lapse in street-smart sensitivity. Despite having lived for almost four years in East Harlem at this point, and spending most of my nights among dealers and addicts on the street (Bourgois 2003a), I was still confused by the nuances of emphasis that distinguish genuinely volatile rage from normally stylized emphatic discourse.

In the ensuing calm, I began to appreciate my role as Doc's guest of honor. Treated to candy, popcorn, potato chips, and even a second quart of malt liquor that Doc sent Slim out to buy for me, it occurred to me that these tasty snacks paralleled the gallery's speedball pleasure principle of maximizing sensory input through contradictory unhealthy chemicals. The unhealthy substances in which I was indulging, however, were packaged legally by billion-dollar multinational corporations allowed by the government to pack huge quantities of sugars, salts, and nonmetabolized fats into our increasingly obese and diabetic bodies.

Settling into the preferential fireside seat Doc had given me, I remembered my initial "research aim": to place these most broken-down of heroin addicts in the historical and structural context of mainstream America (Bourgois 2004). I steered the conversation away from their constant references to the logistical particulars of their narcotized lifestyles onto the larger array of power constraints ripping apart their lives and destroying their communities. I wanted to explore their relationship to a society that has managed to turn them into the actual agents devastating themselves and everyone around them, while simultaneously suggesting they were "getting over" on the system in a lifelong sprint after narcotic euphoria. So I encouraged them to discuss their parents' migration experience from the rural South, the "chump change" jobs they had held in their youth, and, of course, their experience of racism as African Americans. Doc's mother, I soon learned, had been forced to flee her sharecropping community in "Carolina" when her uncle was lynched, "for lookin' at a white woman the wrong way."

But Doc most definitely did not consider himself to be a structural victim of a racist society. He was not interested in confirming a college professor's political-economy analysis of how the unemployed children of rural immigrants displaced by the closing of factories were victimized. He did not subscribe to dreams of hopeful struggle and liberation. His oppression was fully internalized. Like most poorly educated people in the United States, Doc takes full responsibility for his poverty, illiteracy, and homelessness, and fails to see the structural economic and political policy forces that dole out a disproportionate share of suffering, unemployment, poverty, and poor health to African Americans, Latinos, and native Americans.

It was 4:30 in the morning and my legs were shivering uncontrollably from the cold. I bid everyone goodbye and hurried home through the blizzard outside. Warm in my bed ten minutes later, like most employed and housed people in the United States, I tried not to think of how physically painful it was to be a homeless addict in the middle of the winter.

Conclusion: *Confronting Inner-City Apartheid*

The breakdown of both public-sector services and private market forces in the U.S. inner city is overwhelming. Miles and miles of abandoned buildings and rubble-strewn lots of vacant garbage, and the millions of drug-shattered lives all across the urban United States are testimony to a profound political and economic dysfunction in how resources are distributed to the socially vulnerable. Except for the massive investment in the counter-productive and ineffectual War on Drugs, the government has failed to intervene on behalf of desperately poor inner-city residents. The private sector has also failed to help anyone but the real-estate tycoons who come in to gentrify and exacerbate the problems of poverty and segregation by pricing out the poor from their former neighborhoods of refuge (Dávila 2004). The disproportionate ethnic and class-specific statistics on life expectancy, disease burden, infant mortality, homicide, suicide, childhood hunger, addiction, family income, and homelessness also clearly point to a profoundly racist political economy in the United States that punishes the poor by subjecting them to far more than their share of social suffering. The United States has the highest levels of income inequality and arguably the worst overall quality of life indices of any wealthy industrialized nation in the world.

U.S. common sense blames poverty on character flaws and moral fiber. Individual responsibility reigns supreme; public responsibility for protecting a citizenry's human right to accessing basic social services—shelter, income, employment, healthcare (including drug treatment)—is not on the U.S. political agenda (Farmer 2003). Within the inner city itself, the glaring objective horrors enveloping the community—inadequate jobs, decrepit housing, racism, inferior public infrastructure—are understood and often acted upon with self-destructive self-blame. Doc, for example, may be the primary agent for the spread of HIV in his community. We can righteously criticize his individual irresponsibility, or we can constructively address the larger political policies that limit public-health outreach and direct the police to arrest aging addicts for needle possession.

As an anthropologist I consider participant-observation ethnography to be a useful methodological tool for violating class and ethnic apartheid and documenting extreme social suffering. Immersing oneself full-time in such disorienting settings as the underground worlds of crack dealers and heroin injectors, however, is a frightening and personally draining experience that can lead to analytic confusion. On an immediate descriptive level, given the tremendous ideological polarization around poverty in the United States, a raw presentation of ethnographic data without a critical theoretical analysis risks fueling the racist stereotypes and blame-the-victim convictions that dominate U.S. popular culture. Power and historically structured forces that impose social inequality are hard to see unless one actively trains one's analytical eye onto those forces. Descriptions of interpersonal violence and drug abuse in a vacuum make individuals appear pathological. Cultural relativism, geared toward understanding the logics for actions without imposing moral judgments, is a useful first step. For example, public violence can be understood as judicious investments in "human capital" given limited alternatives. Dealers, addicts, and just plain "wanna-bees" need to engage periodically in visible displays of aggression if they are to maintain credibility on the street. Should they fail, they will be mugged, ripped off, and ridiculed (Bourgois 2001).

The underground economy and the social relations thriving therein are best understood as an oppositional reaction to social and material marginalization. This oppositional resistance to discrimination, however, is rooted in drug dealing/using and leads to the further destruction of the community. The physical violence imploding U.S. inner cities is largely self-contained: "black/(brown) on black/(brown)." It is interpreted by most people—including most inner-city residents themselves—as proof that homeless drug addicts and street-level dealers deserve their fate. The brutality of racist white police officers that periodically surfaces in the press pales before the everyday sense of fear and distrust that most inner-city residents feel when they suddenly hear loud footsteps running behind them on the street at night. People begin blaming themselves and the individuals around them rather than recognizing the political and economic forces driving a social system that destroys record numbers of its citizens.

Memoirs from the Nazi holocaust have taught us that under conditions of extreme oppression, victims can become perpetrators (Bourgois 2005, Levi 1988). Discussions of jail experiences that I have tape-recorded echo these findings. The interpersonal violence of fellow inmates, rather than the brutality of guards or the humiliation of institutional rules, becomes the primary subject of conversation. Victims often lash out at those around them, becoming ruthless administrators and agents of violence and terror (Bourgois 2001). Inmates throughout history and around the world sometimes become the enforcers and executors of the most barbaric dimensions of their own torture. This is one of the most fundamental premises of the experience of politically structured suffering, leading to what Bourdieu calls "the misrecognition" of the larger structural fault lines of power that turns people into monsters (see his theory of "symbolic violence" in Bourdieu 2000).

We need a pragmatic understanding of the material forces driving addiction on the street (Bourgois 2003b). The multibillion-dollar drug industry—the only equal-opportunity employer thriving in U.S. inner cities since at least the 1980s—offers a powerful material base for so-called "youth street culture." It would be naïve and atheoretical to think that the dramatic economic vigor of the international drug trade could be neutral ideologically or culturally. The playground where Mikey bought his heroin is located two blocks away from the neighborhood's magnet high school and on most days throughout the 1980s and 1990s, money and drugs flowed there in fistfuls. Why should we be surprised that East Harlem posted one of the highest high-school dropout rates in the country during these years? The War on Drugs has only exacerbated the problem. Government statistics confirm that heroin was cheaper and of higher quality on U.S. inner city streets during the mid-2000s than ever before. The drug economy has been outcompeting the legal, entry-level economy for the hearts and minds of too many inner-city youth for too many decades because they cannot find decent legal jobs and they are trapped in some of the most expensive cities in the world.

Heroin and crack dealers believe with a vengeance in the Great American Dream. They hope to go from rags to riches through private entrepreneurship (Bourgois 2003a). Most will be crushed in their endeavor as they fall prey to violence, drug addiction, and/or paralyzing depression. Most of the crack dealers and heroin addicts whom I have befriended over the past two decades worked at legal jobs in their childhood. In fact, many dropped out of school in order to make money to obtain the childhood "necessities"— candy, potato chips, sneakers, basketballs, baseball cards—that most pre-teenagers in the United States are able to buy with their allowance money.

The material alternative to entry-level employment that the drug industry offers could explain all by itself the powerful appeal of street culture. In the case of youth street culture, however, U.S. racism conflates with an economically generated appeal to create an even more dynamic and persuasive alternative to white middle-class suburban culture. The inner-city resident who does not faithfully imitate white middle-class society's modes of interaction at the workplace will be fired—or, worse yet, ridiculed into submission. Selling drugs on the street offers a real economic alternative to low-wage service jobs in which the cultural identities of inner-city youth are a source of humiliation rather than an asset.

The extraordinary vitality of cultural expression on the poorest, most violent streets in the United States wells forth in opposition to this conjugation of racism and marginalized employment. The appeal of the oppositional style even crosses class, ethnic, and national boundaries, as the hugely successful gangsta rap/hip-hop music industry has proved in the 2000s. Ironically, however, on the street, where this alternative cultural framework is rooted in the drugs economy and its logic for violence, the outcome destroys individuals and communities. Worse yet, this destructive dynamic leads to blaming the victim, thereby cementing in place a status quo of gross socioeconomic inequality.

Exercise

Are the drug users described in the article above responsible for their own situation in life? Discuss ways in which this might be said to be true and ways in which it is not (be sure to engage Dr. Bourgois's ideas with respect to the subject). See if the class can arrive at a consensus regarding the question.

References

Bourdieu, Pierre. 2000. *Pascalian meditations*. Stanford, CA: Stanford University Press.

Bourgois, Philippe. 2001. The power of violence in war and peace: post-cold war lessons from El Salvador. *Ethnography* 2(1): 5–37.

————. 2002. Anthropology and epidemiology on drugs: the challenges of cross-methodological and theoretical dialogue. *International Journal of drug policy* 13(4): 259–269.

————. 2003a. *In search of respect: selling crack in El Barrio*. Cambridge: Cambridge University Press.

————. 2003b. Crack and the political economy of social suffering. *Addiction Research & Theory* 11(1): 31–37.

————. 2004. U.S. inner city apartheid and the War on Drugs: crack among homeless heroin addicts. In A. Castro and M. Singer, eds., *Unhealthy health policy*. Walnut Creek, CA: Alta Mira.

————. 2005. Missing the Holocaust: my father's account of Auschwitz from August 1943 to June 1944. *Anthropological quarterly* 78(1): 89–123.

Bourgois, Philippe, and Eloise Dunlap. 1993. Exorcising sex-for-crack: an ethnographic perspective from Harlem. In M. Ratner, ed., *Crack pipe as pimp: an ethnographic investigation of sex-for-crack exchanges*, 97–132. New York: Lexington Books.

Bourgois, Philippe, and Julie Bruneau. 2000. Needle exchange, HIV infection, and the politics of science: confronting Canada's cocaine injection epidemic with participant observation. *Medical anthropology* 18(4): 325–350.

Bourgois, Philippe, Bridget Prince, and Andrew Moss. 2004. Everyday violence and the gender of hepatitis C among homeless drug-injecting youth in San Francisco. *Human organization* 63(3): 253–264.

Bourgois, Philippe, Alexis Martinez, Alex Kral, Brian Edlin, Jeff Schonberg, and Dan Ciccarone. 2006. *Reinterpreting ethnic patterns of street-based drug use among White and African American men who inject heroin: a cross-methodological social science of medicine approach.* PLoS Medicine (Public Library of Science).

Bourgois, Philippe, and Jeff Schonberg. In Press. *Righteous dopefiend.* Berkeley: University of California Press.

Ciccarone, Dan. 2003. With both eyes open: notes on a disciplinary dialogue between ethnographic and epidemiological research among injection drug users. *International journal of drug policy* 14(1): 115–118.

Ciccarone, Dan, and Philippe Bourgois. 2003. Explaining the geographic variation of HIV among injection drug users in the United States. *Substance use & misuse* 38(14): 2049–2063.

Ciccarone, Dan, Josh Bamberger, Alex Kral, Brian Edlin, Chris Hobart, A. Moon, E. L. Murphy, Philippe Bourgois, Hobart W. Harris, and D. M. Young. 2001. Soft tissue infections among injection drug users—San Francisco, California, 1996–2000. *Morbidity & Mortality Weekly Report* 50(19): 381–384.

Dávila, Arlene. 2004. *Barrio dreams: Puerto Ricans, Latinos, and the neoliberal city.* Berkeley: University of California Press.

Duster, Troy. 1987. Crime, youth unemployment, and the black urban underclass. *Crime and delinquency* 33(2): 300–315.

Farmer, Paul. 2003. *Pathologies of power: health, human rights, and the new war on the poor.* Berkeley: University of California Press.

Gans, Herbert. 1996. *The war against the poor: the underclass and anti-poverty policy.* New York: Basic Books.

Koester, S., R. Booth, and W. Wiebel. 1990. The risk of HIV transmission from sharing water, drug-mixing containers and cotton filters among intravenous drug users. *International journal of drug policy* 1(6): 28–30.

Koester, S., R. Heimer, A. E. Baron, J. Glanz, and W. Teng. 2003. Re: Risk of hepatitis C Virus among young adult injection drug users who share injection equipment. *American journal of epidemiology* 157(4): 376; author reply 376–378.

Levi, Primo. 1988. *The drowned and the saved.* R. Rosenthal, transl. New York: Summit Books.

Wacquant, Loïc. 2002. From slavery to mass incarceration: rethinking the 'race question' in the US. *New Left Review* 13: 41–60.

———. 2006. *Prisons of poverty.* Minneapolis: University of Minnesota Press.

Wilson, William Julius. 1996. *When work disappears: the world of the new urban poor.* New York: Alfred A. Knopf.

14

Mickey, Nicky, and Barbie: Kinderculture in America

Richard H. Robbins

SUNY at Plattsburgh

In the wake of the September 11 attacks on the World Trade Center and the Pentagon, President George W. Bush declared a "war on terror." However, he assured us, this would not be a war in which we would have to tighten our belts—we could still shop, and, indeed, should shop. Having ceded so much productive activity to overseas manufacturers, the American economy is nowadays largely driven via consumption. It is essential, then, not only to urge those currently consuming to continue, but to create new consumers. Hence the American child is immersed in a culture of consumption, and the power of parents to shape the enculturation of their own children is usurped by corporations like Disney and McDonald's, as Richard Robbins writes in this article.

Richard H. Robbins, a University Distinguished Teaching Professor at the State University of New York at Plattsburgh, received the 2005 American Anthropological Association/McGraw-Hill Award for Excellence in the Undergraduate Teaching of Anthropology. He has produced such teaching-oriented volumes as the popular textbook, Cultural Anthropology: A Problem-Based Approach *(Thomson/Wadsworth 2006, 4th edn) and* Global Problems and the Culture of Capitalism *(Allyn & Bacon 2004, 3rd edn). In his teaching, he has taken full advantage of new pedagogical tools, creating and maintaining websites associated with his books.*

The idea of culture is central to anthropology, culture being, among other things, the symbols, objects, and meanings that allow people to turn the chaos of shifting impressions that constitute raw experience into a seemingly ordered and coherent universe. But, in some ways, culture has become our enemy.

That may seem a strange thing for an anthropologist to say. The study of culture is, after all, the anthropologist's stock in trade; it is what anthropologists claim makes human beings unique, what distinguishes us from the rest of the animal world. It has permitted the birth of language, reason, and the building of seemingly great civilizations. I believe, however, that in the United States today, a case can be made for the possibility that culture has become our greatest threat.

In traditional, small-scale, and relatively isolated communities, there were persons—the elderly, the male and female family heads, shamans, and priests—who were assigned the task of maintaining culture and the values that supported the community. But virtually everyone was active in the maintenance of the culture and given the opportunity to introduce innovative variations.

In modern society, however, with its vast global communications technology, culture is no longer communally created and maintained; rather, it is created and maintained by those with the political and economic powers to control how the world is represented and the mechanisms through which these representations reach us. This is an awesome power, for it truly is the power to influence, even determine, the meanings we assign to our experiences. Never in the course of human history have so few been empowered to dictate how so many define the purpose of their existence and define the values that they live by.

A common word used to describe the power to define how society members define their world is *spin*. Politicians, of course, are constantly "spinning" the version of events or policies that they want people to accept. Public relations specialists earn their living by "spinning," getting people to view their clients in ways favorable to them. And advertisers, of course, use the power of spin to control the meaning that consumers attribute to everything from baby formula to sex enhancement products. "The job of a leader is to define reality and give hope," said Kenneth Chenault, chief executive of American Express, of President George Bush after 9/11, "and you are giving us a great deal of hope" (Walsh 2006). Ron Suskind wrote in *The New York Times* of boasts by officials in the Bush administration that they did in fact get to define reality. "People like you," one official told Suskind, live "in what we call the reality-based community," which he identified as people who "believe that solutions emerge from your judicious study of discernible reality." When Suskind responded with a remark about enlightenment principles and understanding the facts, the official interrupted:

> That's not the way the world really works anymore. We're an empire now, and when we act, we create our own reality. And while you're studying that reality—judiciously, as you will—we'll act again, creating other new realities, which you can study too, and that's how things will sort out. We're history's actors . . . and you, all of you, will be left to just study what we do. (2004)

Americans do not talk much about power. One of the reasons, I suspect, is that power works in such a subtle and hard-to-define manner. Ask Americans how McDonald's, or Disney, or General Motors, or George W. Bush has shaped them or constructed their consciousness, and you will likely draw blank stares. What does it mean to argue that power involves the ability to ascribe meanings to various features of our lives?

Let me illustrate. In the 1960s, Ray Kroc dedicated his organization to ensuring that people associated his company, McDonald's, with the American nation-state. In what up to that time was the most costly advertising campaign ever, he succeeded in making McDonald's into an American icon, a place where the American flag was to fly twenty-four hours a day, decorated with an eagle carrying a banner in its beak that proclaimed, "McDonald's: The American Way." Little effort or expense was spared to ensure that anyone thinking of McDonald's would think of it as American. The association is so complete that protesters in Sweden and France have tried to block the opening of McDonald's because it represents, to them, "creeping Americanism" (see Kincheloe 1997: 252ff).

McDonald's, of course, is not alone in the attempt to colonize our consciousness. Globally, businesses spend an estimated $300 billion on advertising, most of it spent by large corporations. Disney, for example, spent almost $2 billion in 2006 to define its image and persuaded us to purchase its products, while McDonald's remains the number one advertiser in TV. American corporations employ almost 200,000 public-relations specialists engaged in manipulating news, public opinion, and public policy to serve the interests of paying clients. These public relations specialists now outnumber actual news reporters by about 40,000—and the gap is growing. A 1990 study found that almost 40 percent of the news content in a typical U.S. newspaper originates from public-relations press releases, story memos, and suggestions, and there is little to suggest that the percentage has declined.

Others have certainly warned about how advertising and other forms of corporate persuasion influence our lives: Vance Packard's classic work, *The Hidden Persuaders* (1957), did that almost sixty years ago. But I don't think we are yet aware of the extent to which these efforts and the power they represent define our entire culture and consequently influence our behavior.

The Construction of Childhood

What I propose to do is to illustrate how corporations control our culture by focusing on one aspect of it—what Shirley Steinberg and Joe Kincheloe (1997) call "kinderculture." One thing that anthropology teaches us is that childhood, much like the rest of our culture, is socially created. That is, childhood, and how it is defined, varies from society to society and from era to era. Even childhood in America in the nineteenth century was very different from what it is today. Prior to the nineteenth century, the major role of children in the capitalist economy was as workers (Lasch 1977: 14ff). There were few industries that did not employ children at some level, and there were few families whose children did not contribute economically in one way or another through either their farm or factory labor. This began to change dramatically in the twentieth century, largely because of the effort of business, with the cooperation of the government, to change children from laborers into consumers. This is not to say that there was no childhood culture. Children's culture in America has always existed in playgrounds and schools, but this culture was produced by children and maintained through child-to-child contact. Today's childhood culture is created by adults and maintained largely by the mass media, especially TV, and schools for the purpose of convincing children to consume (see, e.g., Milner 2006).

The economic stakes in kinderculture are considerable, and so it should come as no surprise that children have become a main target of corporations. As one marketing specialist told the *Wall Street Journal*, "Even two-year-olds are concerned about their brand of clothes, and by the age of six are full-out consumers" (Durning 1992: 120). Almost 60 million school-age children spend well over $100 billion a year of their family's money as well as their own on sweets, food, drinks, electronic products, toys, games, clothes, and shoes. Children under twelve spend more than $12 billion of their own money and influence over $165 billion worth of family spending. One study determined that children influence $9 billion worth of car sales. As one car dealer put it, "Sometimes the child literally is our customer. I have watched the child pick out the car" (Beder 1998).

McDonald's, along with Disney, Mattel, and other corporations such as Saban Entertainment, the producer of what was once the number-one rated children's TV show the *Mighty Morphin Power Rangers* have created a kinderculture that is designed to produce consumers and to separate them from any other institution that might challenge that goal. If you have a problem conceptualizing power, you only need to examine the extent to which kinderculture works to promote childhood hedonism, produce an ethic of pleasure, and separate children from parents, teachers, and other community members who would challenge corporate authority.

This kinderculture represents a cultural pedagogy, an educational curriculum taught largely outside the school on TV, in movies, newspapers, magazines, toys, advertisements, video games, books, sports, and so on. The curriculum of kinderculture has replaced traditional classroom lectures and seatwork with

> dolls, "magic kingdoms," animated fantasies, interactive videos, virtual realities, kick-boxing TV heroes, spine-tingling horror books, and an entire array of entertainment forms produced ostensibly for adults but eagerly consumed by children. (Steinberg and Kincheloe 1997: 4)

Our most important teachers are already no longer in schools, and educational policy is no longer being constructed by elected officials. Instead, our educational curriculum is being crafted by corporate producers in the interests of generating consumption and accumulating profit. Corporate America, as Steinberg and Kincheloe put it, has revolutionized childhood by creating a "consumption theology" that in effect promises redemption and happiness via the consumptive act (1997: 11).

The Curriculum of Kinderculture

If an anthropologist, unfamiliar with American culture, were to examine the way that kinderculture represents such things as the family, gender, and ethnicity, they would find some things that even they, aware of the variety of human cultures, might find bizarre. Let us first take a look at the family curriculum in kinderculture.

The Family Curriculum in Kinderculture

While anthropologists have described hundreds of varying family structures, none with which I am familiar shares the dominant feature of the family in kinderculture—the irrelevancy of parents, in general, and the absence of mothers in particular. Think for a moment about how the family is depicted in the classic Disney releases *Aladdin, Beauty and the Beast, The Little Mermaid, Pocahontas,* and *The Hunchback of Notre Dame.* None of the major characters has mothers. Ariel has none, Belle has none, neither Aladdin nor

Jasmine has one, Pocahontas has none, Quasimodo's mother is killed by his protagonist and substitute father Frodo at the opening of the film, while Esmeralda, the gypsy dancer, I believe, has neither father nor mother. Interestingly, this has long been a feature of Disney characters. In fact, the only mothers I can recall in Disney films are the Elephant mother in *Dumbo,* the short-lived mother in *Bambi,* and the evil stepmothers in *Snow White* and *Cinderella.*

The Duck family is made up of Donald, his three nephews, his uncle Scrooge, Grandma Duck, who is Donald's aunt (but not Scrooge's wife), along with all kinds of cousins such as Gus and Moby Duck; even Daisy's family consists only of nieces. Mickey also has only his nephews Morty and Ferdy, while Goofy has Gilbert and Gyro Gearloose has Newton. The Beagle Boys have only uncles, aunts, and nephews, though their female cousins occasionally appear (see Dorfman and Mattelart 1975). Whether this absence of parenthood is a way to obliterate any suggestion of sexuality, as some have suggested, or whether it is an expression of Disney's own unhappy relations with his parents is difficult to judge. But since the same meanings about parents are present in other classic films, such as the *Home Alone* movies, in which a ten-year-old does quite well when his parents forget him, and in such movies as *Halloween* or *Friday the 13th,* in which parents are irrelevant or hostile, it is safe to say that the absent mother is a common theme in kinderculture.

We might speculate that these representations are simply based on the reality of the American family today. But my own suspicion is that, intentionally or unintentionally, the goal is to create in children a sense of their own agency that clearly isolates them from any parental authority and suggests, to borrow a phrase used by sociologist Robert Bellah and his associates (1996), that "they have given birth to themselves."

The ultimate mythic expression of children as their own creators occurs in the movie, *Back to the Future,* in which the hero, played by Michael J. Fox, is shot back into the past where he faces the task of ensuring that his mother and father fall in love lest he, and his siblings, never be born.

The practical consequence of this family form, or lack of it, is anything but benign, for it suggests to children that they live in a world in which they must act alone, a world in which collective, or at least family, action is nonexistent or futile. The result is to leave the corporation (or the state) as the only benevolent agency capable of exerting collective power, and as the major benevolent force in the lives of children. Don't worry, children, Ronald McDonald, Mickey, and Barbie will always be there to fill your needs, as long as you can pay for them. *American society has succeeded in commodifying nurturance.*

Gender: Women as Altruist-Shoppers

While women as mothers are largely absent in kinderculture, women are not absent altogether. On the contrary, they play an important role as what might be termed "Altruist-Shoppers," beings characterized first and foremost by their evident mandate to subordinate their interests to those of men and secondarily by their proclivity to buy things. Disney films are good examples of this. Ariel in *The Little Mermaid* trades her beautiful singing voice for a chance to pursue her handsome prince, while Ursula, the evil octopus, assures Ariel that men do not like women who talk anyway, a sentiment with which the prince clearly concurs since he bestows the kiss of true love on Ariel even though she has never spoken to him.

In *Beauty and the Beast*, Belle first sacrifices herself for her father, then falls in love with the Beast whom she attempts to civilize by instructing him to eat, control his temper, and dance. In the end she has become another woman whose life is valued for solving a man's problems. *The Lion King* portrays the animal kingdom as clearly ruled by males, and even the evil Scar is served by unresisting lionesses as he assumes control, defeated only by the return of the grown-up Simba. The *Pocahontas* story, of course, was just made for the woman whose major role is to sacrifice herself for a man (see Giroux 1997).

The altruistic theme is further developed with Barbie, who, like Disney's Ariel, Belle, Pocahontas, and Esmeralda, is the ultimate altruist, giving up something for the good of men or mankind. Barbie stories, in case you haven't seen them, revolve around Barbie's willingness to take in everyone and to sacrifice her own interests for theirs.

It is clear, I believe, that the gender curriculum in kinderculture instructs little girls to believe that it is more important to give up one's goal than to disappoint anyone else. It is the place of the female in our society to sacrifice for the good of others (see Steinberg 1997: 216ff). This in itself might, for some, be an appropriate goal, but only if boys were also instructed in the same value. However, it is the boys or the men who always achieve the goals that they have set for themselves. Aladdin marries the princess and rules the kingdom, the Beast fulfills his goal of achieving his past glory, and Simba becomes king of the jungle.

Of course, that is not all that girls do. The real power of Barbie is her power to consume. It is unlikely that any female has escaped unscathed from "Barbie buying," leading Shirley Steinberg (1997) to label Barbie "the bitch who has everything." Barbie has clothes galore, of course, and virtually every form of transportation—cars, dune buggies, motorcycles, speed boats, yachts, and horses—and virtually every sort of pet, appliance, and beauty aid. From a marketer's point of view, Barbie defines the cultural inventory of what every young woman should possess.

The Collective Other

Finally, while the family is devalued and women are reduced to Altruist-Shoppers, adult groups do appear in kinderculture. The problem is that these groups generally take the form of evil "others" who are often racially coded.

In Disney films racial stereotyping is apparent. For example, this is the opening song from *Aladdin*:

> Oh, I come from a land
> From a faraway place
> Where the caravan camels roam, where they cut off your ear
> If they don't like your face
> It's barbaric, but hey, it's home

Clearly Howard Ashman, who wrote the lyric, was sufficiently aware of its racism to submit an alternative verse ("Where it's flat and immense/And the heat is intense") along with the original he evidently preferred. The less offensive version replaced the original in the video release.

Nonetheless, the characters themselves remain stereotypes. As one representative of an Arab organization put it:

> All of the bad guys have beards and large bulbous noses, sinister eyes and heavy accents, and they're wielding swords constantly. Aladdin doesn't have a big nose; he has a small nose. He doesn't have a beard or turban. He doesn't have an accent. What makes him nice is they've given him this American character . . . I have a daughter who says she's ashamed to call herself an Arab, and it's because of things like this. (Giroux 1997: 61)

Worse yet is the racial stereotyping in *The Lion King*, in which the despicable hyena storm troopers speak with the voices of Whoopi Goldberg and Cheech Marin in racially coded accents that have the nuances of Black and Latino youths. These films suggest to viewers that cultural differences that do not bear the imprint of white, middle-class ethnicity are deviant, ignorant, inferior, and a collective threat to be overcome.

Particularly interesting is how Mattel, through Barbie, defines ethnicity. Mattel Toys, the creators of Barbie, sought to contribute to ethnic and racial tolerance with a series of Barbies that represent different cultures. There is the Jamaican Barbie, Polynesian Barbie, Indian Barbie, Native American Barbie, and the German Barbie whose country is known for its "breathtaking beauty and hard-working people," as if south of the equator Barbies don't work.

At first one might applaud Mattel's efforts at increasing cultural awareness. Yet, from an anthropological perspective, the message is quite different. Mattel, like Disney, defines ethnicity as anything other than white. The multi-cultural Barbies are all defined by their foods, their "dances," and their language. Since white, middle-class Barbie is the norm from which others are defined, no regular Barbie ever talks about her culture's favorite foods (hamburgers, French fries and milk shakes), the personality of "her" people, or their customs. In the words of one researcher.

> Barbie has otherized dolls into dominant and marginal cultures. Barbie's whiteness privileges her to not be questioned; she is the standard by which all others are measured. (Steinberg 1997: 214)

In brief, then, I would suggest to you that kinderculture portrays a world in which goal-oriented, white, Christian, American men and their altruistic female companions alone face the forces of ethnically coded, evil others. It is as if the only forces remaining to protect them, the only remaining sanctuaries, are Disney World and McDonald's.

The Masking of Reality

I mentioned earlier that our culture has become our enemy, partially because we have lost any semblance of control over it. It is our enemy in another sense: not only does culture portray a particular world for us, but it also has the capability to mask other realities. One of the more ironic things about kinderculture is that it subtly hides from us the real state of childhood in the United States and the world.

In Ronald Reagan's final address from the White House in 1989, he called for Americans to adopt "an informed patriotism," to return to the basics of American history, and emphasize what it means to be an American. He suggested to the children in the audience that all great change in America begins at the dinner table and that if their parents have not been teaching them what it is to be an American, to "nail 'em on it," adding that that would be the "American thing to do."

Yet only 50 percent of the children President Reagan was talking to lived with both the parents and only 12 percent even lived with their two biological parents, let alone sat down to dinner with them. Furthermore, one in five of those children lived in poverty—one in four if they were under the age of five, and seven out of ten if they happened to be African American females.

American children likely had more than patriotism on their mind. Adolescent suicide was not even a category thirty to forty years ago, yet by the 1980s it was second to accidents in accounting for teenage death. Today some 400,000 adolescents attempt suicide each year (Ferguson 1994: 60–61).

How many Americans are aware that the toys and clothing that they purchase for their children are made in sweatshop conditions, often by children, in countries such as Haiti, Thailand, Indonesia, and Guatemala. One reporter who visited a factory just outside Bangkok, where Barbies and Disney toys are made by 4500 (mostly female) workers, was greeted by women and children in a rally, carrying banners that said, "We are not slave labour!" These workers, earning U.S.$0.60 to 0.70 an hour, were astonished to hear that there are two Barbies sold somewhere in the world every second, that over a billion pairs of shoes have been made for Barbie (many in Bangkok), and that the Mattel corporation grosses from $3–4 billion a year.

But perhaps the most powerful contrast can be drawn between American 12- and 13-year-olds playing soccer with balls made in sweatshop conditions by 12- and 13-year-old children in Bangladesh. How are these things kept from us, how are they masked?

This is where Nicky—St. Nicholas, or Santa Claus—comes in. Every culture has its myths, the stories that purport to explain how things came to be. Santa Claus, and his accompanying ritual of Christmas, is perhaps the ultimate myth of kinderculture, one that idealizes consumption, production, and profit. This is a grossly simplified and idealized model of the American political economy. It depicts a world in which commodities (toys) are manufactured by happy elves, working in Santa's workshop, and distributed, free of charge, to good boys and girls by a corpulent, grandfatherly male in fur-trimmed clothes. It is perhaps ironic that when political cartoonist Thomas Nast created, in 1862, what has become the contemporary image of Santa Claus, he modeled Santa's costume after the fur-trimmed clothes worn by the fabulously wealthy Astor family (Restad 1995: 149).

Nast also created Santa's workshop, perhaps in nostalgic remembrance of pre-factory production. Writers as early as the 1870s recognized the irony of this idealized version of Christmas and toy production. One magazine editorial in 1873, commenting on a picture of Santa's elves working gaily in their workshop, noted the reality of the situation: poor immigrants working six days a week in factories and not some magical workplace, turning out dolls, boats, tops, and toy soldiers, and added that "the cost of these toys is small; and yet there is a profit in them" (Restad 1995: 149). William Waits, in his recent book *The Modern*

Christmas in America: A Cultural History of Gift-Giving, suggests that Santa's major role was to "decontaminate" Christmas gifts, removing the stigma of industrial manufacture (Waits 1992: 25).

So, What Can We Do about It?

If the above analysis is valid, a question then follows: what can parents, schools, and others do to regain a role in building the cultural reality in which our children live?

Parents

What can you do as parents? Very little, I suggest. As popular movies, such as *Home Alone* and *Halloween,* tell children, parents have become largely irrelevant. When she was five years old, my daughter Rebecca doted on her collection of Barbie dolls, spent too many hours engrossed in the Disney channel, and anxiously awaited the arrival of Santa. I did not accept this passively. I was constantly pointing out to her that Disney just wants her to buy stuff, and that nobody looks like Barbie, and I tried to convince her that "Terrible Sid," the little boy in *Toy Story* who tears the heads off his sister's Barbie dolls and replaces them with the heads of dinosaurs and is depicted as the villain, is the real hero of the movie, but to little effect. She just said dismissively, "Oh, Daddy."

Corporations, largely but not exclusively through TV and movies, have taken over the task of child-rearing, and have been allowed to do it partially because of our collective sense that what they do is trivial, that it is only entertainment, and also because of the economic realities and necessity of the multiworker household. With the absence of any meaningful national daycare program, TV and its corporate sponsors have been handed the responsibility for daycare in America, much to the relief of many parents grateful for the free time they gain through the largesse of the Disney Channel, the *Mighty Morphin Power Rangers,* Barbie, and Barney.

Schools

How about the schools? I suspect that they too are largely irrelevant in American kinderculture. Furthermore, corporations are even threatening to take over our schools, McDonald's, Disney, and Mattel, along with scores of others, have targeted the public schools for child marketing. McDonald's has its "A's for hamburgers" program along with advertising-based learning packets for science, foreign language, and other subjects; McDonald's and other fast-food firms have attempted to operate school cafeterias, and Disney is establishing a model school while it promotes its "Teacher of the Year" awards. These and other corporations freely distribute promotional material to be used in classrooms, material that financially strapped schools are only too happy to accept. Privatization of our schools, if the penchant to "downsize government" continues, will likely occur within the next decade, and along with it the emergence of dominant "education corporations" (Disney and McDonald's will probably be in the forefront) that will parallel the development of megacorporate health management organizations.

Even the so-called charter school movement, groups of concerned people empowered by the federal government to begin their own schools, will likely fall prey to the easy money of corporations only too anxious to begin building consumer loyalty at earlier and earlier ages.

Hold Corporations Responsible for What They Do

We could make more of an effort to hold corporations responsible for what they do. Certainly a possibility, but one for which I hold no great hope. Not that the potential is not there. As consumers, after all, we have, collectively, as much if not more power than the corporations. They depend on us. Yet I think that, as consumers, we are so disciplined by our possessions and convinced of the evils of collective action that any effective national consumer movement is unlikely.

Taking Back Our Culture

Anthropologist Ruth Benedict used to tell her students that "You can't beat your culture." Anthropology, she said, by bringing to bear knowledge of other cultures, can help you gain a useful perspective on your own culture, but, to quote another anthropologist, Eleanor Leacock (1993: 14), "it is folly to think one can transcend it."

In his 1991 novel, *The Sweet Hereafter,* Russell Banks describes a community plunged into grief by the deaths of its children in a school bus accident that leaves few families untouched. A lawyer, Mitchell Stephens, is hired by parents to handle their lawsuit. At one point Stephens, who has had problems with his own daughter, muses about the fate of children in America. His soliloquy is worth repeating in full:

> . . . the people of Sam Dent are not unique. We've all lost our children. It's like all the children of America are dead to us. Just look at them, for God's sake—violent on the streets, comatose in the malls, narcotized in front of the TV. In my lifetime something terrible happened that took our children away from us. I don't know if it was the Vietnam war, or the sexual colonization of kids by industry, or drugs, or TV, or divorce, or what the hell it was; I don't know which are causes and which are effects; but the children are gone, that I know. So that trying to protect them is little more than an elaborate exercise in denial. Religious fanatics and superpatriots, they try to protect their kids by turning them into schizophrenics; Episcopalians and High Church Jews gratefully abandon their kids to boarding schools and divorce one another so they can get laid with impunity; the middle class grabs what it can buy and passes it on, like poisoned candy on Halloween; and meanwhile the inner-city blacks and poor whites in the boonies sell their souls with longing for what's killing everyone else's kids and wonder why theirs are on crack. It's too late; they're gone; we're what's left.
>
> And the best we can do for them, and for ourselves, is rage against what took them. Even if we can't know what it'll be like when the smoke clears, we do know that rage, for better or worse, generates a future. (Banks 1991: 99–100)

Exercise

Be prepared to discuss the cartoons and films that influenced you most as a child. Did you accumulate the consumer goods associated with these media products? How did these cartoons and films have an impact on your development as a person, as a boy or girl, as an American?

References

Banks, Russell. 1991. *The Sweet Hereafter*. New York: Harper Perennial.

Beder, Sharon. 1998. Marketing to Children. http://homepage.mac.com/herinst/sbeder/children.html (accessed on March 26, 2007).

Bellah, Robert N., Richard Madsen, William M. Sullivan, Ann Swidler, Steven M. Tipton. 1996. *Habits of the heart: individualism and commitment in American life*. Berkeley: University of California Press.

Dorfman, Ariel, and Armand Mattelart. 1975 [1971]. *How to read Donald Duck: imperialist ideology in the Disney comic*. New York: International General.

Durning, Alan. 1992. *How much is enough: the consumer society and the future of the earth*. New York: W. W. Norton and Company.

Ferguson, S. 1994. The Comfort of Being Sad. *Utne Reader* 64(July/August): 60–61.

Fischer, P., et al. 1991. Brand log recognition by children aged 3 to 6 years. *Journal of the American Medical Association* 266(22): 3145–3148.

Giroux, Henry A. 1997. Are Disney movies good for your kids? In Shirley R. Steinberg and Joe L. Kincheloe, eds., *Kinderculture: the corporate construction of childhood*. Boulder: Westview Press.

Kincheloe, Joe L. 1997. McDonald's, power, and children: Ronald McDonald (aka Ray Kroc) does it all for you. In Shirley R. Steinberg and Joe L. Kincheloe, eds., *Kinderculture: the corporate construction of childhood*. Boulder: Westview Press.

Lasch, Chistopher. 1977. *Haven in a heartless world: the family besieged*. New York: Basic Books.

Leacock, Eleanor. 1993. Being an anthropologist. In Constance Sutton, ed., *From Labrador to Samoa: the theory and practice of Eleanor Burke Leacock*. Washington D.C.: American Anthropological Association.

Milner, Murray, Jr. 2006. *Freaks, geeks, and cool kids: American teenagers, schools, and the culture of consumption*. New York: Routledge.

Packard, Vance. 1957. *The hidden persuaders*. New York: D. McKay Co.

Restad, Penne L. 1995. *Christmas in America: a history*. Oxford: Oxford University Press.

Steinberg, Shirley R., and Joe L. Kincheloe, eds., 1997. *Kinderculture: the corporate construction of childhood*. Boulder: Westview Press.

Steinberg, Shirley R. 1997. The bitch who has everything. In Shirley R. Steinberg and Joe L. Kincheloe, eds., *Kinderculture: the corporate construction of childhood*. Boulder: Westview Press.

Steinberg, Shirley R., and Joe L. Kincheloe. 1997. Introduction: no more secrets—kinderculture, information saturation, and the postmodern childhood. In Shirley R. Steinberg and Joe L. Kincheloe, eds., *Kinderculture: the corporate construction of childhood*. Boulder: Westview Press.

Suskind, Ron. 2004. Faith, certainty and the presidency of George W. Bush. *New York Times Magazine,* October 17, 2004 http://www.nytimes.com/2004/10/17/magazine/17BUSH.html?ei=5090&en=890a96189e162076&ex=1255665600&adxnnl=1&partner=rssuserland&adxnnlx=1157297345-WE/kdbziLwV7Q0HvQZORMw (accessed March 26, 2007).

Waits, William. 1992. *The modern Christmas in America: a cultural history of gift-giving*. New York: New York University Press.

Walsh, Kenneth T. 2006. Leadership. *U.S. News and World Report*. http://www.usnews.com/usnews/9_11/articles/911bush.htm (accessed March 26, 2007).

Part IV

Language and Thought

15

Nuf *and* E-Nuf *Among The Nacirema*

Robert Myers
Alfred University

About this article, Dr. Myers writes, "One important result of living abroad for extended periods is that when you return many aspects of your home culture tend to appear strikingly different from the way they did before you left. This was the case with the thorough emphasis on nuf *in Naciremaland, which I describe in the article. Indeed, the Nacirema devote such importance to* nuf *that when one considers the variety of forms and uses it takes in daily life as well as the amount of money and time spent on it,* nuf *must be one of their most significant cultural themes."*

Robert Myers was born and raised in Naciremaland, where he received most of his formal anthropological training. To gain insights into his home culture, he spent a year studying at a German university, approximately two-and-a-half years conducting fieldwork in the Caribbean on St. Maarten, Jamaica, Dominica, and most recently, Belize, as well as briefly in the Netherlands. He taught at the University of Benin and did ethnographic research in southern Nigeria for two years, focusing on health issues and on circumcision practices among males and females. For the last several years, his interest has been in describing a wide range of cultural patterns among the Nacirema. He continues to reside in Naciremaland, in the state of Kroywen. (Current biographical information of Myers heads the next article.)

The Nacirema, members of a complex, stratified, postindustrial, highly competitive, affluent, materialist, consumer culture of North America, are well known to anthropologists. Their body rituals are among the most familiar of any cultural habits anywhere, and Miner's seminal article, "Body ritual among the Nacirema" (1956), surveying these patterns, is the most reprinted of all anthropological studies. Even before Miner, Ralph Linton described

Nacirema totemic patterns (1924) and the borrowed inventions of a patriotic everyman (1937), and Warner analyzed a Nacirema sacred ceremony (1953). Lionel Tiger proposed a quarter-century ago that Nacirema diffuse marriage patterns be called "omnigamy" (1978). Weatherford examined their federalist political culture (1981). Henry critiqued Nacirema secondary school experience (1963) and Walker reported on folk linguistic concepts of the Nacirema ti'yčir caste (1970), while Moffatt's ethnography investigated Nacirema advanced education at one location (1989) and Nathan did so recently at another (2005). LaBarre depicted behavior at a ritual gathering called a *koktel parti* (2002). Wolfenstein and Leites (1950), Powdermaker (1950, 1966), and Drummond (1996) inquired into constructions of Nacirema fantasy life, in which *nuf* appeared after World War II (Wolfenstein 1951). Sodeman reported on Nacirema healers (1979). Arens (1975) and Shore (1990) have written about Nacirema sports. Professional and student researchers have explored varied facets of Nacirema culture (Spradley and McCurdy 1972, Spradley and Rynkewich 1975, Arens and Montague 1976, Kottak 1982, Peacock 1988). Wolf analyzed the origins and deeper meanings of an important Nacirema mythical figure (1964) and Myers updated the consumer shaman's evolution (2003). At least two observers speculatively anticipated the demise of Nacirema culture due to extreme environmental conditions (Thompson 1972, Macaulay 1979). It is no longer true, as Kluckhohn once wrote, "Of this culture in the anthropological sense we know less than of Eskimo culture" (1949: 229).[1]

Despite this extensive examination of the Nacirema over decades, the pervasive role of *nuf* in Nacirema life has gone unappreciated. In fact, several famous examinations of the Nacirema neglect mention of nuf altogether (Mead 1942, Mead 1965, Lipset 1996, Montagu 1967).

Nuf, in both tangible and abstract forms a quality which permeates or is sought in nearly every aspect of life, motivates much Nacirema behavior and figures prominently in the constellation of Nacirema values. To the Nacirema, nuf is an attitude, a sentiment, a condition, a state of being, an attribute of personality, a way of behaving, or an animistic essence which can inhabit people, objects, or gatherings. Nuf has magical qualities said to diffuse contagiously in certain social situations. The Nacirema expend large amounts of hard-earned capital to acquire objects considered to radiate nuf or to facilitate its diffusion. They pay considerable sums to ritual nuf specialists who manipulate or alleviate psychological states to induce feelings of well-being. Child-rearing patterns are considered most effective and desirable if nuf is present. When its conspicuous and subtler forms are considered, nuf emerges as a significant cultural theme of the approximately 300 million Nacirema, but one taken for granted by most members of the society, as cultural themes usually are.

Prolonged residence, linguistic competence, and ongoing fieldwork among the Nacirema have convinced me that, among the "extremes to which human behavior can go" (Miner 1956: 503), nuf stands out. Even within the Nacirema language in general (a language spoken in dialectical variations by other large groups as well), a European cultural historian noted that the word "nuf" itself was distinctive, without a precise equivalent in any other modern language (Huizinga 1955: 3). This linguistic background forms the foundation on which the Nacirema have elaborated their obsession with nuf.

As will become obvious, other professional observers have noted the importance of nuf in particular circumstances in Nacirema society previously, but the pervasive nature of nuf has remained elusive and undescribed until now. When viewed holistically, in the broad spectrum of behaviors and verbal usages, the multidimensional prominence of nuf in

Nacirema life emerges. Thus, in considering the Nacirema, any effort "to grasp the native's point of view, his relation to life, to realize *his* vision of *his* world" (Malinowski 1961:25, italics in original) must include the profound role of nuf.

Nuf is present in virtually every area of Nacirema life and at every age. For reasons of space, I do not examine nuf's presence in Nacirema sports, politics, science and science museums, technology, clothing, tourist industry, or entertainment, but consider the following limited sample of examples and references to nuf, offered in partial translation.

The Nacirema refer frequently to nuf in their everyday expressions and in familiar phrases (Myers 1999a). They frame daily comings and goings with nuf in one of their most common transitional exchanges. When someone departs, whether for a casual outing or for a more important activity, they say "Have nuf!" Upon a person's return, he or she will be asked, "Did you have nuf?"

The importance Nacirema attach to nuf is heightened by the intensity with which it is said and indicated in its written form by the use of an exclamation point. No other Nacirema word in common usage is written as often with this punctuation as is "nuf!" (A close rival in this economically driven culture may be "Free!" but this descriptor has a considerably more limited range of reference.) Nacirema salesmen recognize value in highlighting the nuf element of innumerable products in this way. Thus the Nacirema call attention to nuf, advertise it, promote it, and create expectation or anticipation with nuf when it is coupled with this particular marker, whether in print or with voiced enthusiasm.

The Nacirema highlighted nuf in their popular songs throughout much of the twentieth century. The most popular song of the 1920s was "Ain't we got nuf?" (Kahn and Egan 1921). In the 1960s famous Nacirema performers sang about having "nuf, nuf, nuf" (Beach Boys 1964) and about ". . . lookin' for nuf, and feelin' groovy" (Simon and Garfunkle 1966). In the 1980s, it was "Girls just want to have nuf" (Cyndi Lauper 1984), and in the 1990s a big hit was Sheryl Crow's "All I wanna do is have some nuf" (1994). Nuf was a lyrical success over and over.

Nuf affects perceptions of time, has bulk, and takes up space. The Nacirema experience, describe, and promote their time, relationships, and many activities as "nuf-filled!" When time is nuf-filled, it is said to pass quickly. They say, "Time flies when you're having nuf," an expression so common, it is sometimes used to sell products. When the rapid passage of time is noted, a person may remark, "But it was nuf while it lasted," introducing an element of nostalgia or lament for a period which has ended. Nuf is thus a marker shaping the remembrance of times past and present, as well as an intensifier of anticipation for potentially pleasurable activity in the future (Myers 1999b).

Nuf refers to an active state, just as the Nacirema are an active rather than a contemplative people. They frequently describe themselves engaging in activities or behaviors for nuf. "Why did you do that?" they may inquire of one another. "I did it for nuf," is a common reply, as is "just for nuf," or "just for the nuf of it," meaning something was actively done for no particularly clear reason. They *do* something to *have* nuf. A well-known Nacirema sign attached to car bumpers, advertising cold sugar snacks from a pair of successful entrepreneurs, was "If it isn't nuf, why do it?"

The Nacirema do many things "in nuf" and "for nuf," jokingly, in jest. Or they may describe themselves as "looking for nuf" while searching for a way to "spend" time or while participating in diverse activities. In a culture notable for its obsession with germs and sanitation as well as with culturally approved behavior, they use the expression "good, clean nuf" to describe acceptable activity.

Nacirema quantify experience with nuf. Exaggerated modifiers are often attached to nuf to emphasize an especially pleasant time, as in, "It was great nuf," or "It was over-the-top nuf." Nevertheless, small quantities of nuf are often sought and marked as well. Individuals describe themselves as hoping to have "a little nuf" in many activities.

Yet, as with most behavior taken for granted, Nacirema are not used to trying to explain exactly what "having nuf" means. In fact, they are not always even conscious that they are acting in accordance with a nuf orientation. Despite its active status, nuf tends to remain an abstract state, even as it may be performed. Its unarticulated nature as part of the "set of assumptions so unselfconscious as to seem a natural, transparent, undeniable part of the structure of the world" (Swidler 1986: 279) was exemplified by Tommy Fox, age 19, demolition derby contestant, who explained, "Well, you know, like when you hit'em, and all that. It's nuf" (Wolfe 1966: 29). Similarly, at a large annual gathering of professional anthropologists, a Nacirema healer elected to discuss patterns of a particularly emotionally distressing, potentially mortal disease, breast cancer, because he "thought it would be nuf" (American Anthropological Association annual meeting, 12/5/1998). Nuf's utility covers an especially wide range of situations, conditions, and expectations.

Nuf has spiritual and religious qualities. Professor Conrad Kottak, a prominent Nacirema observer of his tribe, notes that since the Nacirema were unable to put nuf in their religion, they made a religion of nuf (1994: 522). Nuf's flexible, adaptable qualities enable its fit with Nacirema spirituality. In a culture known for its emphasis on individualism and self-reliance, as well as the importance of voluntary associations, nuf contributes to individual or group perceptions of inner states. A former Nacirema political chief characterized fishing as a spiritual endeavor in *Fishing for nuf—and to wash your soul* (Hoover 1963).

Anthropologists have identified the high value with which Nacirema regard pleasure, a positive state often related to, but not identical with, nuf. Without mention of nuf, Kluckhohn noted the Nacireman "conscious quest for pleasure" (1949: 232). He observed that "having a good time is an important part of life" and that "the pleasure principle attains its fullest development in American youth culture," but that this emphasis is restrained or even guilt-producing by the Puritan tradition of "work for work's sake" (1949: 238). Lionel Tiger notes the nuf and banal pleasure first-time parents experience, often to their surprise (1992: 275), as well as the ambiguity posed by pleasure in contemporary society about the workplace as an "arena of effortful nuf" (1992: 284). When he asks the more usually ironic question "Are we having nuf yet?" (283), his playful style suggests his own high value of nuf.

The contradictions posed by nuf, as an intensified form of pleasure, in a society which historically has seen hard work as a nearly sacred activity, have led to changing attitudes about both work and nuf. Without discussing nuf specifically, Rybzinski examines the dangerous role played by leisure, a potential breeding ground for nuf, as attitudes about the weekly rhythm of work have evolved (Rybczynski 1991). In their broad description of Nacirema culture, Arensberg and Niehoff opposed work with play, which is "nuf, an outlet from work, without serious purpose except possibly to make subsequent work more efficient" (1971: 217). The blurred boundary between the important categories of work and nuf was noted by a visiting Indian poet who wrote that the Nacirema "work hard at having nuf" (Peeradina 2002: 117). Indeed, occasionally scientists will describe their work as nuf (Washburn 1977: 51).

Laughter, smiles, "positive thinking," and pleasure form part of a large constellation of nuf-related behaviors and their accompanying verbal responses. "Perhaps no huge society has ever had such generalized patterns for laughter" (Kluckhohn 1949: 230). Indeed, laughter among the Nacirema has long been valued for its important medicinal and therapeutic qualities, as well as for its intimate relationship with nuf.

Chief among the dimensions of nuf is *e-nuf*, an adjectival and behavioral first-cousin. The Nacirema apply e-nuf to a wide range of settings to imply aspects of the idea of nuf. Nacirema refer to something being e-nuf as being amusing or comical. They see this as a valuable mechanism for reducing widespread tension and stress experienced by many members of the culture. An important class of Nacirema performers called *naidemoc* measure their success according to the degree to which they are perceived as e-nuf. If they attract crowds and elicit laughter, or even smiles, they are said to be e-nuf. Certain members of this specialized group have achieved such prominent status that they are known by all Nacirema and are among the highest paid of ritual specialists. Nacirema culture managers promote their entertainment vigorously as "enormously e-nuf!" "hilariously e-nuf!" "e-nuf for the whole family," or even "so e-nuf, it's scary!"

The Nacirema infuse their lifespans with nuf. From the earliest interactions with infants, to the end of life (Adams 1993), nuf appears in one form or another. One of the most popular Nacirema child enculturators, known by the pseudonym "Dr. Seuss," asserts in a book read to millions of very young Nacirema, "Did you ever milk this kind of cow? . . . If you never did, you should. These things are nuf and nuf is good" (Geisel 1960: 51). Or as widely known mythological figures Rabbit said to Winnie the Pooh in an animated entertainment for young Nacirema, "But nuf! We're supposed to be having nuf!" (*Pooh Party*, n.d.). To induce six- to ten-year-old Nacirema boys to participate in a tribal training program, another popular cartoon figure was used: "Join Cub Scouts, because too much nuf is never enough!" (Garfield the cat, 1999). Both primary and secondary education appears to have a "dominant emphasis" on nuf activities to a Swiss Nacirema observer (Drechsel 2002: 194). At even higher levels of education at a state university, Moffatt found that students "enjoyed a considerable amount of sexual nuf" (1989: 49) as well as about four hours a day of "friendly nuf," "the bread and butter of college life" (33). Students at Nacirema universities are frequently urged by administrators and faculty to "have nuf," so it is hardly surprising that students had or thought they should have equal amounts of academic work and friendly nuf (Moffatt 1989: 33).

At the senior end of life, a study of a retirement community was named "Nuf City" (Jacobs 1974). The largest association of elder Nacirema recruits more members with ads such as, "They're fit, nuf and ready for more. Why not join them?" (AARP March/April 1999: 25). A famous Nacirema healer promotes a "nuf death" (Adams 1993), meaning one in which the deceased has played an active role in planning his funeral rituals.

Among Nacirema child-rearing patterns is an effort to connect bravery with nuf. I have seen a father at a nuf-park vigorously encourage his tearful son, who was reluctant to join him on a frightening ride, "It's not scary, it's nuf!" This theme is reflected in certain popular children's readers as well as during one of the prominent annual celebrations of ritual rebellion and cultural inversion (*neewollah*), when there is great emphasis on children masquerading as frightening cultural figures, yet having nuf. Ultimately, Nacirema adults may make this same connection in their careers as, for example, at a gathering of Nacirema anthropologists, one prominent scholar described his professional need to acquire multidisciplinary skills as "the scariest thing I ever did, but it was the most nuf" (Emilio Moran, American Anthropological Association, annual meeting, 11/19/99).

Similarly, an attitude of nuf is strongly associated with adventure among the Nacirema. The first volume of a famous early twentieth-century Nacirema boys' book series was subtitled, "Nuf and Adventure on the Road" (Appleton 1910). One of the most adventurous female Nacirema personalities of the 1930s titled her autobiography *The Nuf of It* (Earhart 1932). Current advertisements encouraging Nacirema to visit sacred national outdoor regions link "nuf and adventure," as does extensive Nacirema tourist literature. Explains one catalogue for affluent Nacirema travelers, "Trip leaders should be catalysts for our primary objective: having nuf" (Cole 2003: 5). Implicit in contemporary Nacirema "extreme" sport endeavors is an attitude of adventure and nuf. An advertising campaign for one of the Nacirema political units promoted tourism with the advertisement, "Storm-tossed seas. Gut-wrenching roller coasters. Air-to-air combat. What family wouldn't have nuf?" (for Connecticut, *Country Living,* April 1999, TE3).

The Nacirema have a saying about women that "blondes have more nuf." Thus females need not seek nuf through adventure if they are already blonde. If they are not naturally blonde, they can become more nuf by simply coloring their hair, as a substantial percentage of Nacirema females do. Once again, nuf works to shape personal identity.

At the same time, other arenas of Nacirema life acknowledging the potential risks adventurous nuf may pose, associate nuf with an emphasis on safe behavior. "Nuf and Safety Go Together" asserts one National Park Service brochure. The motto printed on the membership cards of a famous clan of elders touring Naciremaland in the Honda Gold Wing Road Riders Association reads, "Friends for Nuf, Safety, & Knowledge."

In recent years the Nacirema have attracted the attention of healers for their unhealthy increases in weight and girth. Nuf may well play a role here too, as many foods and *skans* are packaged as being nuf. Indeed, food producers and fast food establishments are among the most aggressive purveyors of nuf. Varied food labels demand "Spread the nuf," "Squeeze the nuf," "Let the nuf out!" and "Put a little nuf on your bun," or encourage, "Nuf to eat, no need to heat." Other slogans include, "bursting with nuf," "succulent, all white meat, all flavor, and all nuf!" "Nuf packs," and "The nuf way to dress" for "today's nuf salads." And a major sugar drink campaign persuaded, "Be young. Have nuf. Drink Pepsi." Many candies come in a "nuf size." One expensive advertising campaign even compared automobiles to an ice cream bar: "Zero calories. 100% nuf!"

The Nacirema are famous for their commercial and marketing vigor, and here nuf appears prominently. The range of products packaged as some form of nuf is remarkable. A popular brand of camera is the "Nuf Saver." Subway day tickets are sold as "Nuf Passes" in the largest Nacirema city.

Many objects are marketed in association with nuf which would not seem to be a likely connection. Containers, clear plastic straws, adhesives, and flexible lamps are among the numerous Nacirema products packaged as nuf, as well as cars, mattresses, and pet fish. There are few products which have not either been sold in some form of nuf packaging, promoted as having inherent qualities of nuf, or as increasing the buyer's inner nuf.

The variety and range of contexts into which nuf is inserted suggests an emptiness in Nacirema life which must be filled. Nuf is used everywhere possible because it is a positive way to enliven mundane life. In many respects nuf is to the humdrum of everyday Nacirema existence as cayenne is to white rice, cornmeal, or pasta. In a culture based on individualism, self-reliance, and go-it-alone attitudes, nuf provides stimulation to individuals and an excuse or bond for group activities. It often counteracts the isolation and loneliness repeatedly noted by observers of the Nacirema (Riesman 1950, Slater 1970, Edgerton 1979, Putnam 2000).

At one time or another, the Nacirema have sought nuf in most activities. The Nacirema Federal Emergency Management Agency in a radio ad, in part, suggested "For nuf, have your children practice diving for cover." The Nacirema Postal Service encourages collecting commemorative stamps because, "They're nuf. They're history. They're Nacirema." On the thirtieth anniversary of the original Nacirema lunar landing, a reporter asked one of the astronauts, "Did you have any nuf on the moon?"

Nuf is a popular euphemism for sex. In the advertisements for sexual mates which Nacirema place in their newspapers and on electronic dating sites, as well as those comments used in face-to-face communication, they refer to "hot nuf," "nuf-loving," "romantic nuf," "intimate nuf," and "adult nuf." In a famous film, renowned Nacirema actor Woody Allen declared to his mate after they had sex the first time, "That was the most nuf I've had without laughing."

Nuf contributes to the paradoxical nature of Nacirema noted by Kluckhohn (1949: 230). "Serious nuf" describes the profound impact nuf, a quality taken as trivial and superficial by casual observers, has in Nacirema society.

While in general nuf is considered to be a positive quality, it is also commonly used to express distaste, sarcasm, and irony. The Nacirema "poke nuf at" and "make nuf of" people and situations. As Nacirema anthropologist Clyde Kluckhohn reported, "No one becomes so great that we cannot make nuf of him" (1949: 230). When they refer to "nuf and games," they usually mean that the event is neither. Occasionally, when engaged in activity they would prefer not to be doing, people will say with dismay, "this is *nuf*" or "*this* is nuf." In the late 1970s, the expression "Are we having nuf yet?" emerged and diffused through popular entertainment.[2] While "e-nuf" has the meaning of humorous, it is also used to identify someone or something as odd, strange, or different.

Thus, throughout Nacirema culture nuf works in innumerable ways in service to personal identity, framing relationships, mediating the realms of work and leisure, and as a vehicle for cargo in a hyperconsumer society. Its examples are legion.

Nuf's significance among the Nacirema has not gone entirely unnoticed or unchallenged. During the last decade of the twentieth century when nuf behaviors were at a height, one Nacirema commentator prematurely announced nuf's collapse from a sort of widespread cultural exhaustion (Atlas 1996). Excess nuf may have been a factor in the recent assault by al Qaeda terrorists on Naciremaland. A leading attacker proclaimed in the second sentence of his surviving letter, "The time of nuf and waste has gone" (Atta 2001).[3] Despite these difficulties, the Nacirema have invested so much time, energy, and capital embedding nuf deeply in their culture, and nuf continues to function in so many desirable ways for the Nacirema, that it persists as a prominent cultural theme, perhaps muted by global and economic events, but unbowed and enduring (Myers 2002).

Questions for Further Discussion

1. What is gained by adopting the descriptive framework for the Nacirema first used by Horace Miner? Is anything lost by this approach?

2. Can you identify (in their speech or behavior, in their entertainments, and in their consumer products) additional uses of nuf by the Nacirema?

3. How does the use of nuf differ between males and females, within and among ethnic groups, and among social classes?

4. How has nuf changed over time? Did the events of September 11, 2001, permanently alter Nacirema patterns of nuf?

5. If you are familiar with the use of nuf in another culture, share your experience with the class.

Notes

1. In his survey of ethnographic writing about American culture, Moffatt (1992) identifies 160 research-based monographs and some 85 other articles and writings, about half by anthropologists, most over the preceding twelve years. The Spindlers earlier described numerous studies (1983). Moffatt notes, "Anthropologists have done more research in the United States in the last dozen years than in the entire previous history of the discipline—far more, perhaps twice as much" (1992: 205).

2. Bartlett's credits cartoonist Bill Griffith in his strip "Zippy the Pinhead" with the question in 1979 (Kaplan 1992: 773). Carol Burnett popularized the expression in the 1981 film *The Four Seasons* (Nowlan and Nowlan 1994: 231). The phrase is so commonplace, it appeared in the leader of a *New York Times* op-ed article with respect to the role of the U.S. as the world's superpower (Steel 1998: WK15).

3. Nuf appears as an attribute opposed by the attackers but valued by a prominent Nacirema intellectual: "I do not question that we have a vicious, abhorrent enemy that opposes most of what I cherish—including democracy, pluralism, secularism, the equality of the sexes, beardless men, dancing (all kinds), skimpy clothing and, well, nuf" (Sontag 2002: A31). In televised comments on anti-terrorist efforts, Retired U.S. Army General Barry MacCaffrey said, "Focused intelligence has taken the nuf out of jihad" (MSNBC 6/8/2006).

References

Adams, Patch. 1993. *Gesundheit! Bringing good health to you, the medical system, and society through physician service, complementary therapies, humor, and joy.* Rochester, VT: Healing Arts Press.

Appleton, Victor. 1910. *Tom Swift and his motor-cycle, or fun and adventure on the road.* New York: Grosset & Dunlap.

Arens, William. 1975. The great American football ritual. *Natural History* 84(8): 72–80, October.

Arens, William, and Susan P. Montagu, eds. 1976. *The Nacirema: cultural myths and social realities.* Port Washington, NY: Alfred.

Arensberg, Conrad, and Arthur H. Niehoff. 1971. American cultural values. In C. M. Arensberg and A. H. Niehoff, eds., *Introducing social change: a manual for Americans overseas*, 207–231. 2nd ed. Chicago: Aldine-Atherton.

Atlas, James. 1996. The fall of fun. *The New Yorker,* 18 November: 62–71.

Atta, Mohamed. 2001. Oh God, open all doors for me. *The Washington Post*, September 28: A18.

Cole, Tom. 2001. To the ends of the earth: the GeoEx style. *Geographical expeditions*, p. 5. San Francisco: Geographical Expeditions.

Drechsel, Emanuel J. 2002. A European anthropologist's personal and ethnographic impressions of the United States. In Philip R. DeVita and James D. Armstrong, eds., *Distant mirrors: America as a foreign culture*, 177–197. 3rd edition. Belmont, CA: Wadsworth/Thomson Learning.

Drummond, Lee. 1996. *American dreamtime: a cultural analysis of popular movies, and their implications for a science of humanity.* London: Littlefield Adams.

Earhart, Amelia. 1932. *The fun of it: random records of my own flying and of women in aviation.* New York: Brewer, Waren & Putnam.

Edgerton, Robert B. 1979. *Alone together: social order on an urban beach.* Berkeley: University of California Press.

Geisel, Theodor S. [Dr. Seuss]. 1960. *One fish, two fish, red fish, blue fish.* New York: Random House.

Henry, Jules. 1963. *Culture against man.* New York: Random House.

Hoover, Herbert C. 1963. *Fishing for fun—and to wash your soul.* New York: Random House. Edited by William Nichols.

Huizinga, Johan. 1955. *Homo ludens: a study of the play-element in culture.* Boston: Beacon.

Jacobs, Jerry. 1974. *Fun city: an ethnographic study of a retirement community.* Prospect Heights, IL: Waveland.

Kaplan, Justin, general editor. 1992. *John Bartlett's familiar quotations.* 16th edition. Boston: Little, Brown.

Kluckhohn, Clyde. 1949. *Mirror for man.* New York: McGraw-Hill.

Kottak, Conrad Philip. 1982. *Researching American culture: a guide for student anthropologists.* Ann Arbor: University of Michigan.

Kottak, Conrad Philip. 1994. *Anthropology.* New York: McGraw-Hill.

LaBarre, Weston. 2002. Professor Widjojo goes to a koktel parti. In Philip R. DeVita and James D. Armstrong, eds., *Distant mirrors: America as a foreign culture,* 32–36. 3rd edition. Belmont, CA: Wadsworth/Thomson Learning.

Linton, Ralph. 1924. Totemism and the A. E. F. *American anthropologist* 26: 296–300.

Linton, Ralph. 1937. One hundred per cent American. *The American Mercury* 40: 427–429.

Lipset, Seymour Martin. 1996. *American exceptionalism: a double-edged sword.* New York: Norton.

Macaulay, David. 1979. *Motel of the mysteries.* Boston: Houghton Mifflin.

Malinowski, Bronislaw. 1961 (orig. 1922). *Argonauts of the Western Pacific.* New York: E. P. Dutton.

Mead, Margaret. 1942. *And keep your powder dry: an anthropologist looks at America.* New York: Morrow. Expanded edition. 1965. New York: Morrow.

Miner, Horace. 1956. Body ritual among the Nacirema. *American Anthropologist* 58(3): 503–507.

Moffatt, Michael. 1989. *Coming of age in New Jersey: college and American culture.* New Brunswick: Rutgers University Press.

Moffatt, Michael. 1992. Ethnographic writing about American culture. *Annual Review of Anthropology* 21: 205–229.

Montagu, Ashley. 1967. *The American way of life.* New York: Tower.

Myers, Robert. 1999a. The discourse of fun: how Americans talk about an important cultural theme. Paper presented at the annual meeting of the Popular Culture Association and the American Culture Association, April 1, San Diego, CA.

Myers, Robert. 1999b. Time, agency, and utopia: fun in American culture. Paper presented at the annual meeting of the American Anthropological Association, November 20, Chicago.

Myers, Robert. 2002. And we'll have fun, fun, fun . . . *USA Today,* March 7: 13A.

Myers, Robert. 2003. Svelte Santa still king of sales. *The Providence Sunday Journal,* December 21.

Nathan, Rebekah. 2005. *My freshman year.* Ithaca, NY: Cornell University Press.

Nowlan, Robert A., and Gwendolyn W. Nowlan. 1994. *Film quotations: 11,000 lines spoken on screen, arranged by subject, and indexed.* Jefferson, NC: McFarland & Co.

Peacock, James L. 1988. America as a cultural system. In Charles Reynolds and Ralph Norman, eds., *Community in America,* 37–46. Berkeley: University of California Press.

Peerandina, Saleem. 2002. Giving, withholding, and meeting midway: a poet's ethnography. In Philip R. DeVita and James D. Armstrong, eds., *Distant mirrors: America as a foreign culture,* 110–121. 3rd edition. Belmont, CA: Wadsworth/Thomson Learning.

Powdermaker, Hortense. 1950. *Hollywood, the dream factory.* New York: Grosset & Dunlap.

Powdermaker, Hortense. 1966. *Stranger and friend: the way of an anthropologist.* New York: Norton.

Putnam, Robert. 2000. *Bowling alone: the collapse and revival of American community.* New York: Simon & Schuster.

Riesman, David, with Nathan Glazer and Reuel Denney. 1950. *The lonely crowd: a study of the changing American character.* New Haven: Yale University Press.

Rybczynski, Witold. 1991. *Waiting for the weekend.* New York: Viking.

Shore, Bradd. 1989. How our tribe projects its own image into the national pastime. *The Sciences* 30(3): 10–18, May/June.

Slater, Philip. 1970. *The pursuit of loneliness: American culture at the breaking point*. Boston: Beacon Press.

Sodeman, William A., Jr. 1979. Return to the Nacirema. *Forum on medicine*. December: 806–807.

Sontag, Susan. 2002. War: Real battles and empty metaphors. *The New York Times,* September 10: A31.

Spindler, George, and Louise Spindler. 1982. Anthropologists view American culture. *Annual review of Anthropology* 12: 49–78.

Spradley, James P., and David W. McCurdy, eds. 1971. *The cultural experience: ethnography in complex society*. Chicago: Science Research Associates.

Spradley, James, and Michael A. Rynkiewich, eds. 1975. *The Nacirema: readings on American culture*. Boston: Little, Brown.

Steel, Ronald. 1998. Lonely at the top. *The New York Times,* March 1: WK15.

Swidler, Ann. 1986. Culture in action: Symbols and strategies. *American sociological review* 51(2): 273–286.

Thompson, Neil B. 1972. The mysterious fall of the Nacirema. *Natural History* 81(10): 11–14, 17–18, 80–82, 84, 86–87, December.

Tiger, Lionel. 1978. Omnigamy: The new kinship system. *Psychology today* 12(2): 14, 17, July.

Tiger, Lionel. 1992. *The pursuit of pleasure*. Boston: Little, Brown.

Walker, Willard. 1970. The retention of folk linguistic concepts and the ti'yčir caste in contemporary Nacireman culture. *American Anthropologist* 72(1): 102–105.

Warner, William Lloyd. 1953. *American life*. Chicago: University of Chicago Press.

Washburn, Sherwood L. 1977. The fun of human evolution! *Colloquia in anthropology* (Taos, NM) 1: 51–66.

Weatherford, J. McIver. 1981. *Tribes on the hill*. New York: Rawson Wade.

Wolf, Eric R. 1963. Santa Claus: Notes on a collective representation. In Robert A. Manners, ed., *Process and pattern in culture: essays in honor of Julian H. Steward*. Chicago: Aldine.

Wolfe, Tom. 1966. Clean fun at Riverhead. In *The kandy-kolored tangerine-flake streamline baby*, 24–30. New York: Pocket Books.

Wolfenstein, Martha. 1951. The emergence of fun morality. *Journal of social issues* 7(4): 15–24.

Wolfenstein, Martha, and Nathan Leites. 1950. *Movies: a psychological study*. Glencoe, IL: Free Press.

16

Gunspeak: The Influence of America's Gun Culture on Everyday Communication

Robert Myers

Alfred University

As illustrated repeatedly in this volume, one of the things sociocultural anthropologists do is pay special attention to the commonplace, to those patterns which are taken for granted by members of a culture. Then we examine these patterns and ask questions about their origins, their obvious and not-so-obvious functions, and just what they mean to the people who use them. Finally, we add our interpretations to what we find. One of the most important aspects of every group is its language. How are some words or expressions used instead of others, and why? This article provides an investigation of one set of words appearing frequently in all forms of communication, nonverbal as well as verbal, spoken as well as written, among English-speaking residents of the United States.

Robert Myers is Professor of Anthropology and Public Health at Alfred University in Alfred, New York, where he has taught for twenty years. He received his B.A. from Davidson College, his M.A. and Ph.D. from the University of North Carolina at Chapel Hill, and his M.P.H. from the Harvard School of Public Health. He has lived in Europe, conducted fieldwork in the Caribbean, and spent two years at the University of Benin in Nigeria on a Fulbright Fellowship. These experiences lend perspective to his primary interests: contemporary cultural patterns and the roles of language in the United States.

When I bit the bullet to work on this, I put the subject in my anthropological crosshairs, drew a bead on it, and carefully targeted the topic, although I found it hard not to take a shotgun approach. For a high-caliber analysis, I gathered my ammunition, determined to be armed with facts, in order to fire off comments, to be on target, to shoot down any arguments. I'm loaded for bear. I hope not to jump the gun, to be a loose cannon, or to go off half-cocked as a result of my hair-trigger temper, no matter how under the gun I feel to examine this. In short, I used the language of gunspeak to examine one way we speak.

This article describes the linguistic ways an aspect of United States culture, guns, gun-affection, and gun ownership, considered important by significant numbers of citizens, appear in familiar speech. In putting common linguistic elements of the world's third largest society in my sights, I am attempting a small contribution to what Marcus and Fischer call a "repatriated anthropology" in which "the most important subject for cultural criticism . . . is not these conventionally defined topics [of kinship, migrants, public rituals, and ethnic minorities, for example], but the study of mass-cultural forms, and . . . mainstream middle-class life . . . [including] the formation of public consciousness" (1986: 152). According to Traube, anthropologists have shied away from studying American popular culture, regarding it as an "impoverished object," without the "exoticism inscribed in the anthropological culture concept" (1996: 128). However, I see American popular culture as a vast, barely gleaned cultural field, whose residents are as much Exotic Others as any population anywhere. I approach U.S. culture as a native, with the advantage of long-term familiarity and fluency. The tendency in American anthropology to discount work in our own complex society where practices examined may be shared by tens of millions of people, while highly valuing ethnographic work that has been carried out among tiny distant groups, is one of the ironies of our profession. The case of gunspeak stands out as a perfect example, to use Whorf's words, "where the 'fashions of speaking' are closely integrated with the whole general culture" (1941: 93).

To frame this description in sociolinguistic terms, I use the concept of "cultural presupposition," meaning "participants in speech interaction come to encounters with an array of knowledge and understandings (models) of their culture as expressed and transmitted through language" (Bonvillain 2003: 61). The cultural presuppositions underlying gunspeak are taken for granted by its users, and as is normally the case with cultural biases, applied automatically, without conscious reflection or decision-making. As such, the pervasive presence of guns in American culture, in history as mediated by film and story, and through all forms of entertainment and boy enculturative practices, is as familiar and influential as are camels in traditional Bedouin society or cattle among the Nuer.

Gunspeak appears as a diverse semantic field, sometimes almost literally, as with "top gun," or the Gettysburg College logo the "Bullets" and a snack-bar there called "The Bullet Hole"; sometimes indirectly as with the use of "bullets" in list-making (such as the "Bullets and Numbering" option of Microsoft Word I am using), figuratively as in "firing back," or "magic bullet"; and sometimes subtly or symbolically as in applying "gun" to parts of the body or in familiar phrases from popular films. Similes abound, such as "Written words are like bullets. I'm shooting at death" (W. T. Vollmann, author of *Rising Up, Rising Down*, interview, National Public Radio, "Bookworm," November 27, 2004).

Metaphor and metonymy, types of semantic transfer, permeate gunspeak. Metaphor, for example, exists with the common attribution of someone as a "big gun," "big shot," or "hot shot," in which the entire person is identified as prominent or powerful in terms of firearms or firepower. Metonymy, "the substitution of one entity by another based on their shared occurrence in context rather than similarity of their attributes" (Bonvillain 2003: 66), is a more limited form of substitution than metaphor. For example, in two references to body parts as "guns," a gun refers only to a specific part of the person. In recent years the fitness and body-building craze has teenage males saying, "Look at my guns," or "show me your guns," meaning muscles, particularly biceps. Over the preceding century, the penis has often been referred to as a "gun." In his novel *Battle Cry,* Leon Uris describes the humiliating instruction of a marine private being taught not to call his rifle a gun: "Jones then stood there, holding his 'gun' in his right hand and his rifle in his left and recited: 'This is my rifle/This is my gun/This is for fighting/This is for fun" (1954: 53). This same usage appears in at least five other sources (Lighter 1994: 990; Wentworth and Flexner 1967: 235). In a recent popular magazine, a reader wrote to a sex question-and-answer column, "My boyfriend likes to 'get the bullets out of the chamber' (you know, masturbate before sex so he can go longer)" (Jill 2006: 94). When considered in its fullest presence and richness, gunspeak is one of our most familiar and useful ways of expressing ourselves, revealing a relationship with firearms so strong it may surprise some. Other examples of metaphor and metonymy appear below.

In their slender volume *Metaphors We Live By,* Lakoff and Johnson assert that metaphor is pervasive in everyday life, not just in language but in thought and action (2003: 3), calling attention to the "often beautiful, sometimes disturbing, but always profound, realities of everyday metaphorical thought" (243). Indeed, gunspeak provides some of those metaphors by which we live.

Gunspeak metaphors describe varied relationships with guns, firearms, and their qualities or projectiles. In some cases people speak of themselves as firearms (a loose cannon; a straight shooter; to target something; to take a shot at something; as having a hair-trigger), or describe themselves as having attributes of a gun (hair-trigger; to be out of bullets or ammunition), or feel shaped by a firearm (to be armed, to feel under the gun). Metaphors of gunspeak suggest cultural attitudes about power and hierarchy embedded in competition. Over and over the influences of firearms seen through the action-based words and images of gunspeak bespeak a contentious society based on ranking, domination, aggression, and conflict. The relationship between culture and metaphor as described by Lakoff and Johnson sounds much like the ideas expressed above by B. L. Whorf: "The most fundamental values in a culture will be coherent with the metaphorical structure of the most fundamental concepts in the culture" (Lakoff and Johnson 2003: 22).

U.S. Gun Culture

According to sociologist Gary Kleck, the United States "almost certainly has more firearms in civilian hands than any other nation in the world" (1997: 63). Exact numbers of civilian firearms are arguable and difficult to ascertain, but in 1994 they numbered between 170 million based solely on guns produced since 1954, of which 69 million are handguns, and 235 million when all U.S. civilian guns are counted, of which 80 million are handguns (Kleck 1997: 64). Data suggest that gun-owing households often own more than one. "Among households with a handgun, the average number of handguns owned is about 2.8" (69). Cross-nationally, the proportion of U.S. households with guns in "extraordinarily high," with Norway a close second at 32 percent (68). Switzerland and Israel are other industrial societies with high rates of gun ownership, yet among these four countries, only the United States has a significant problem with gun-related violence and might be described as gun-obsessed, judging by the high emotions generated by gun-control debates. The social vigor and political lobbying of the "nearly three million"-member strong National Rifle Association (www.nramembership.org/history.htm), and the fame of its recent leader Charlton Heston's "not from my cold, dead hands" speech are but two prominent examples of gun-addiction in the United States.

Although the number and rate of firearm-caused deaths in the United States has declined significantly since a high of 39,595 in 1993, the number killed by guns in 2001, the most recent year available, was still 29,573 (Centers for Disease Control and Prevention 2003), a figure not approached in any other industrial nation. In addition to those killed by guns, an estimated three to four times as many suffer nonlethal wounds, numbering perhaps as many as 200,000 (medlib.med.utah.edu), although these data are not systematically collected. As many as 2.6 million children live in 1.4 million homes where firearms are kept loaded or stored with ammunition (Schuster, Franke, Bastian, Sor, Halfon 2000). Another phenomenon of U.S. firearm deaths is that the percentage of those killed as suicides has steadily grown to 57 percent of all gun deaths in 2001. A gun provides the most common means of suicide, and the most successful. Guns as sources of identity, authority, and power, including the ultimate power to end one's life, are unrivaled in American culture. Perhaps most striking of all is the accumulation of gun deaths over time. In the last twenty-five years in the United States, a period of remarkable affluence and domestic "peace," more than 830,000 people have died in gun violence, about fourteen times the number of Americans who died in the Vietnam War.

Gunspeak

Given this background of widespread gun presence, it is unsurprising that an impressive number of words, phrases, and nonverbal gestures pertain to the culture of firearms, and provide us with familiar metaphorical grounding.

We define our honesty and trustworthiness with gunspeak when we call someone a straight-shooter, or our willingness to try something when we agree to take a shot at it. If the chances of success are low, it is a long shot, but regardless of the difficulty or obstacles, we should stick to our guns and not be gunshy. If something is definite, it is a sure shot; if unfocused, it is scattershot. If I want to try out an idea, I'll run it up the flag pole and see if it gets shot down. If we feel strongly, we'll stick to our guns. We might take verbal pot shots at someone who annoys us, and if really annoyed, give them both barrels. He shot a glance at his rival and took a parting shot before leaving the room. If someone becomes psycho, they "go postal," or "go ballistic."

Gunspeak seems to be everywhere. A recent Tom Jones's CD is "Reloaded, Greatest Hits" (National Public Radio December 1, 2003, Terry Gross interview). Perhaps I'll shoot up to Target and buy a copy. The headline "5 Young Guns Who Nearly Took Memphis" is about an international bridge tournament, not an armed assault (Truscott 2001: A21). A young musician describes his home recording studio as bulletproof because it is easy to use. "Young guns shine at Hollywood premier" (*USA Today* August 31, 2000, p. 2D). Many a corporate hot shot became a big shot by rising through the ranks faster than a speeding bullet.

Decision-making or causal activity has become pulling the trigger: "They looked at four different stores before pulling the trigger and buying" (*NPR Morning Edition* December 5, 2003, on buying patterns over the Internet). In an article about whether or not Hillary

Clinton would run for president, "I didn't get the impression that she had pulled the trigger in her mind." "Genetics load the gun; the environment pulls the trigger" (*NPR Morning Edition* July 19, 2001). "Could sour markets trigger a recession?" (*USA Today* March 16, 2001, p. 17A). ". . . the Fear Room at Kerry campaign headquarters is on a hair trigger to turn any breaking news into a personal threat" according to William Safire (2004a: A27). A golf tournament commentator said, "He's playing too fast. He's pulling the trigger very quickly" (Golf TV, August 25, 2006).

Lawyers and detectives are always searching for a "smoking gun," a phrase which became popular during the Watergate hearings (Safire 2003: 18). Court TV's www.thesmokinggun.com brings you "exclusive documents" you won't find anywhere else.

Television shows may attract viewers with their combative natures as in CNN's *Crossfire,* MSNBC's *Firing Line* or AMC's *Shootout*, and William Buckley's *Firing Line* was on for thirty-three years, but I would rather watch the sitcom, *Just Shoot Me*. The title of the letters-to-the-editor page of the *New York Times*'s Circuits section is "Incoming." Among cars currently are the Chrysler Crossfire and the 2007 Dodge Caliber.

Some gunspeak has a particular history. When Andy Sipowicz on "NYPD Blue" said, "You just be keeping your powder dry," he was encouraging his partner to act cautiously and prudently, to be on the alert. He echoed Oliver Cromwell's centuries-old advice to his troops, as well as Margaret Mead's only book on American culture, *And Keep Your Powder Dry* (1942). Moving anything completely, lock, stock, and barrel, refers to the three basic parts of a rifle, and was used by Sir Walter Scott in 1817. Surprise registered as "son of a gun!" may derive from children registered as such who were conceived or born among the cannon of a sailing ship. When the Florida Gators arrived for a basketball game "locked and loaded," as a centuries-old rifle phrase puts it, they were ready to play, not drunk.

"A magic bullet for obesity? Sorry about that," apologized a *Newsweek* ad, drawing from German bacteriologist Paul Ehrlich's phrase for a precisely targeted syphilis medicine in 1910 and now a familiar usage describing a specific cure for any problem. A silver bullet was once thought to be the only effective defense against werewolves or other magical threat (Safire 2004b: 28). Now it means a quick solution to a difficult problem, as "Condoleezza Rice testified that there was no 'silver bullet' action that would have prevented the terrorist attacks" (*USA Today* April 9, 2004, p. 1A) or the "local leader came up with what they thought would be a silver bullet for the area's problems" (September 16, 2001, p. 25). But the two expressions are sometimes used interchangeably.

Gunspeak thrives in the hypercompetitive world of U.S. sports. Michael Jordan "set a great example for what his team," the Washington Wizards, renamed from the Washington Bullets, "[was] fighting for. He strapped it on. . . . He skipped the Wizards' shootaround" (*USA Today* March 6, 2003, p. 4C). Jordan said, "I told the guys that we have 28 games left, and I'm not going down with any bullets. I'm going all out. . . . I want to have fun" (*New York Times* February 23, 2003, p. 1SP). He proceeded to shoot the lights out. Pitcher Roger Clemens is now forty-two years old, and "he's still throwing bullets out there" (*New York Times* July 5, 2001, p. C10). And "AL West reloads for 2002" (*USA Today* March 27, 2002, p. 4C). "Mets try to turn season around minus big guns" (*New York Times* July 1, 2001, p. 3SP). From a football headline and article: "Shootout. Two quarterbacks winging passes as if they were gunslingers firing bullets at each other in dusty Dodge City" "Favre shoots himself in the foot in a showdown that fizzles" (*New York Times* January 21, 2002, p. D5). "The Raiders had some of pro football's oldest gunslingers." NASCAR Winston Cup driver Joe Memechek was a "hired gun" for the race at Watkins Glen (*New York Times* July 1, 2001, p. 3SP).

Less expected is the diffusion of gunspeak to fishing. Although fishing with guns is legal in Vermont where "every spring, hunters break out their artillery—high caliber pistols, shotguns, even AK-47s—and head to the marshes to exercise their right to bear arms against fish" (Belluck 2004: A1), I never anticipated gunspeak applied to fishing when casting: "*Hold your fire*, remember, he can see that well. Get the fly right in front of his eyes when he is 30 feet out" (P. Kaminsky, *New York Times* February 23, 2003, p. 8SP, emphasis added).

Bullets are everywhere. "He asked me if I had any bullets in my tank" that is, whether I had any energy (*New York Times* October 19, 2004, p. 1SP). "PowerPoint has become a generic term for any bullet-ridden [riddled?] presentation" and "when [PowerPoint] bullets are flying, no one is safe" (Schwartz 2003: 12WK). The anti-missile defense system is described as a system to "hit a bullet with a bullet." Last winter, "the citrus crop dodged a bullet." Investors are always looking for "funds that can dodge tax bullets" (Braham 2001: 78). "This budget shoots with real bullets," asserted a Congressman on National Public Radio (April 25, 2001). But if a man is infertile or has a low sperm count, he is said to be shooting blanks.

The legacy of the imagined Wild West lives on in gunspeak. President Bush is known for his "gunslinger's stance" and portrayed as a gunslinger, especially in foreign media such as the cover of *Der Spiegel* on March 1, 2004. Gunslinger-faced Lance Armstrong won the Tour de France again on his gun-metal gray bicycle, but he had to sweat bullets to do it. Compaq computer ads echo gunfighter sentiments: "Fastest PC deployment ever. . . . Wanna see it again?" A popular lottery game is called "Quick Draw." Stagecoaches are long gone, yet we refer to sitting in the front passenger seat as riding shotgun, or as one student said, "shottie." Continental Airlines used this as, "Sit up front. Without calling 'shotgun,'" in one of its ads (*New York Times* August 2003). The gunfighters we hear about now do not shoot up Old West movie sets; they're gunning for someone in a drive-by looking to ice someone with their heat. Other bad guys shoot up drugs. "Bush and Rumsfeld may have to holster guns," according to one headline (*New York Times* June 3, 2001, p. 20). When Canon advertises "Shoot first. Edit later," it is playing on stereotypical constructions from the Old West (*New York Times* May 31, 2001, p. D5). Or it may be used in association with historic individuals. Extended StayAmerica uses Annie Oakley in its advertising series of "Famous Road Warriors" quoting her, "I only wanted a hotel room. I wasn't planning to shoot the whole budget," adding, "Aiming for a comfortable hotel at an affordable price? Bulls-eye!" (*USA Today,* September 27, 2000, p. 12A).

Gunspeak may work by implication when it draws on famous film scenes. "Go ahead, make my day," said Clint Eastwood as huge-pistol-wielding detective Dirty Harry Callahan in *Sudden Impact* (1983). This shows up in ads for Father's Day, "Go ahead, make Dad's day," and for Mother's Day as well, "Go Ahead, Make My Day" in magazine ads from FTD.com (*Time*, May 15, 2000: 101), and in a cellular phone ad, "The free phone will make your day. Make their day" (*Washington Post*, August 27, 2000, p. A3).

When President Bush tells terrorists, "You can run, but you can't hide," he implies they are being hunted like prey. Arnold Schwartzneger's killer phrase, "Hasta la vista, baby" from *Terminator 2: Judgment Day* can show up anywhere, as when I heard it said in mock imitation of the actor while three boys buried a dead bird. Many boys remember his line, "Consider that a divorce," when he shoots his wife in *Total Recall,* and recall Bruce

Willis's lines, "Thanks for the advice" and "Happy trails, Hans," while he kills terrorists in *Die Hard*. Dick Cheney after a shooting accident appeared on a *Time* cover described as "sticking to his guns" (February 27, 2006).

Top Gun, the top grossing film of 1986, amplified that title phrase so powerfully that it was applied to President Bush on a *Newsweek* cover (November 18, 2002). *Motor Trend* used the expression for a cover story about "America vs the World" (August 1993), as did *Sports Illustrated* for a story on Peyton Manning (December 20, 2004). During his 2004 campaign, President Bush used the music from *Top Gun* at his campaign rallies (*New York Times* October 25, 2004, p. 24), conspicuously continuing his association with the popular film.

The brutal political scene in 2000 provided ample gunspeak. Four years ago, Mr. Cheney took "dead aim at Gore" and on a *Newsweek* cover Bush and Cheney, "The Avengers" were "Taking Aim at the Age of Clinton" (August 07, 2000). After the election was over, it was widely reported that "Mr. Gore took a bullet for the country" (Friedman 2000: A29). It was a war out there then too.

Guns lurk in our gestures as well as our words, as parents of boys know well. The single-handed, index finger–gun gesture frequently used toward other cars while traveling and in play has become more complex. Now boys use both arms and hands, pretending to chamber a round in a rifle and aim it, often with sound effects; if they are "shooting" a finger pistol, they use both hands to steady it, as they have seen in police dramas. In 2001, two New Jersey kindergartners were suspended for pointing their finger guns at each other. Adults use the gestures too. After scoring a direct conversational hit, someone might pretend to blow smoke from the barrel of an index finger, or having made a foolish statement, might hold a finger gun to his head in mock suicide.

So embedded is gun culture that my son's keyboard offers "gunshots" as one of the instrumental modes of choice. He can play "Ode to Joy" or "Jingle Bells" completely with gunshot sounds. In the popular adolescent world of PaintBall, however, an interesting reversal has taken place. The fierce weapons used to shoot paint globules are called "markers," not pistols or guns, and they can therefore be sold over the Internet.

Conclusion

Does gunspeak matter? That is, does our abundance of gun-related and derived expressions make us more prone to act violently or less sensitively? Or said otherwise, if cultural patterns influence language, does language in turn affect behavior, or the culture itself? Is there a feedback loop? No matter how tempting or likely, I cannot demonstrate that a consistent feedback circuit exists.

At the very least, however, I would argue that not only does gunspeak reflect our societal obsession with firearms but it couples easily and unconsciously with our violent entertainments to create a world in which we remain primed to be aggressive, and combative, in which we are ready to fight, in which we can be readily mobilized to strike any perceived enemy if necessary, be it on the playing field, in the boardroom, or overseas.

Who uses gunspeak? We all do. I detect little difference between the anthropological observer and the "native." There may be a male preference for gunspeak, in the same way that violence appears occasionally in young boys' speech, but never in girls' speech

(Tannen 1994: 99), but I do not have systematic data for such a claim. Are there class differences in gunspeak? The readership (and writership) of *USA Today* and *The New York Times* may differ, but there is no difference in the frequency of gunspeak terms in these papers, nor is it less common on National Public Radio. Gunspeak exists in popular or mass culture, as well as in high(er) or "non-popular" culture (Traube 1996: 133).

Gunspeak did not emerge suddenly after 9/11. It has been here for years, decades in many cases, centuries in some. Perhaps it has increased during the twentieth century, but it has been around, priming us in subtle ways.

Gunspeak is generalized throughout the language. As such it becomes an unself-conscious complement to violent non-gunspeak language which also laces our speech, whether when we say we "bombed" a test, or in our "culture wars," political "wars of words," our wars on terror, cancer, drugs, or ideas (Friedman 2005: WK17), in the speech of adolescent boys (and college students) as they endlessly play video games, shouting, "Die. Die. I killed you," or in discussion of "battleground" states and the "voter-drive ground war" (*New York Times* October 20, 2004, p. A1) in the fall 2004 election.[1]

Gunspeak (and warspeak, at which I have fired only a volley) is reminiscent of Toni Morrison's passionate view of violent language expressed in her Nobel acceptance speech:

> The systematic looting of language can be recognized by the tendency of its users to forgo its nuanced, complex, mid-wifery properties, replacing them with menace and subjugation. Oppressive language does more than represent violence; it is violence; does more than represent the limits of knowledge; it limits knowledge. (1994: 15–16)

Gunspeak is thus a "fashion of speaking" supporting Whorf's assertion that "there are connections but not correlations or diagnostic correspondences between cultural norms and linguistic patterns" (Whorf 1941: 93). Hoijer might as well have had gunspeak in mind when he described "a functional interrelationship between socially patterned habits of speaking and thinking and other socially patterned habits" (1964: 148).

Catching up on a newspaper I had a gunspeak moment when I read the headline, "An Itchy Trigger Finger Draws Lethal Return Fire" (Byrne 2002: 41), but the article was about a chess match. Last week, a publisher's representative finished talking to me and "holstered" the stylus of her ThinkPad. In Steve Martin's appreciation of Johnny Carson, he wrote, "You enjoyed the unflappable grannies who knitted log-cabin quilts, as well as the Vegas pros who machine-gunned the audience into hysterical fits" (2005: A23). At one of my son's Little League games I snapped awake fearing the worst when I heard the coach shouting to the batter, "Pull the trigger, Sam! Pull the trigger!" But he was only urging a cautious child to swing the bat, not to shoot anyone.

Frankly, all this gunspeak just blows me away. If cartoonist Walt Kelly had been an anthropologist examining U.S. culture, he might have had Pogo say, "We have met the Exotic Other, and they are us."

Questions for Further Discussion

1. Can you identify and bring to class additional examples of "gunspeak"?

2. Argue the position that "gunspeak" is simply a reflection of something very common in U.S. society, guns, and nothing more.

3. Does "gunspeak" play any role whatsoever in the high rates of firearm violence for which Americans are internationally famous?

4. How do other aspects of modern U.S. life reinforce frequent, varied uses of "gunspeak"?

5. Describe other metaphors or styles of speaking in the United States which derive from a broad cultural pattern much as "gunspeak" does from American firearm obsession.

Note

A revision of a paper presented at the 103rd annual meeting of the American Anthropological Association, Atlanta, Georgia, December 15, 2004, as part of the panel "Beyond the Exotic Other: Popular Culture and Critical Thinking in Teaching Anthropology" organized by Paul Grebinger, chaired by Robert Myers.

It *is* a war out there. On the front page of *The New York Times* on October 22, 2004, appeared the following headlines and photograph: "In other frays, 6 battlegrounds for governors;" "Mixed results for Bush in battles over judges;" "UN aide says Iraqi elections are on target;" "For families of autistic, the fight for ordinary." And a photograph of John Kerry and two other men dressed in camouflage suits, carrying shotguns and geese just killed on a hunt appeared as well. On October 24, a writer described the "ground-force execution" necessary to bring out voters (A. Nagourney and K. Q. Seelye, *New York Times,* p. 24). Florida is "Ground Zero" and there are "armies of lawyers" waiting for the election (heard on Fox News, October 27, 2004).

Further Reading

Collins, John, and Ross Glover, eds. 2002. *Collateral language: a user's guide to America's new war.* New York: NYU Press.

Nunberg, Geoffrey. 2004. *Going nucular: language, politics, and culture in controversial times.* New York: PublicAffairs.

References

Belluck, Pam. 2004. How to catch fish in Vermont: no bait, no tackle, just bullets. *The New York Times,* May 11: A1, A20.

Bonvillain, Nancy. 2003. *Language, culture, and communication: the meaning of messages.* 4th ed. Upper Saddle River, NJ: Prentice Hall.

Braham, Lewis. 2001. Funds that can dodge tax bullets. *Business Week January* 29: 78.

Byrne, Robert. 2002. An itchy trigger finger draws lethal return fire. *The New York Times,* April 14: 41.

Centers for Disease Control and Prevention. 2003. Firearm-related deaths in 2001. http/ /:www.cdc.gov/ncipc/dvp/dvp.htm. Accessed October 8, 2004.

Friedman, Thomas. 2000. Medal of honor. *The New York Times,* December 15: A29.

Friedman, Thomas. 2005. Divided we stand. *The New York Times,* January 23: WK17.

Hoijer, Harry. 1964. Cultural implications of some Navaho linguistic categories. In D. Hymes, ed., *Language in culture and society,* 142–153. New York: Harper & Row.

"Jill." 2006. Is this normal? *Jane* August: 94.

Kleck, Gary. 1997. *Targeting guns: firearms and their control.* New York: Aldine.

Lakoff, George, and Mark Johnson. 2003. *Metaphors we live by.* 2nd ed. Chicago: University of Chicago Press.

Lighter, J. E., ed. 1994. *Gun. Random House dictionary of American slang,* vol. 1, 990–993. New York: Random House.

Marcus, George, and Fischer, Michael M. J. 1986. *Anthropology as cultural critique: an experimental moment in the human sciences.* Chicago: University of Chicago Press.

Martin, Steve. 2005. The man in front of the curtain. *The New York Times,* January 25: A23.

Mead, Margaret. 1942. *And keep your powder dry*. New York: Morrow.

Morrison, Toni. 1994. *Lecture and speech of acceptance upon the award of the Nobel Prize for Literature, delivered in Stockholm on the seventh of December, Nineteen Hundred and Ninety-Three*. New York: Knopf.

Safire, William. 2003. Smoking gun. *New York Times Magazine,* January 26: 18.

Safire, William. 2004a. The year of fear. *The New York Times,* October 20: A27.

Safire, William. 2004b. Silver bullet. *The New York Times,* April 25: 28.

Schuster, M. A., T. M. Franke, A. M. Bastian, S. Sor, and N. Halfon. 2000. Firearm storage patterns in U.S. homes with children. *American journal of public health* 90: 588–594.

Schwartz, John. 2003. The level of discourse continues to slide. *The New York Times,* September 28: 12WK.

Spier, Leslie, A. Irving Hallowell, and Stanley S. Newman, eds. 1941. *Language, culture, and personality: essays in memory of Edward Sapir*. Menasha, WI: Sapir Memorial Publication Fund.

Tannen, Deborah. 1994. *Gender and discourse*. New York: Oxford University Press.

Traube, Elizabeth. 1996. 'The popular' in American culture. *Annual Reviews in Anthropology,* 25: 127–151.

Truscott, Alan. 2001. 5 young guns who nearly took Memphis. *The New York Times,* January 6: A21.

Uris, Leon. 1954. *Battle cry*. New York: Bantam.

Wentworth, H., and S. B. Flexner, eds. 1967. Gun, and shoot. *Dictionary of American slang*, 235, 469–470. New York: Crowell.

Whorf, B. L. 1941. The relation of habitual thought and behavior to language. In L. Spier, A. L. Hallowell, and S. S. Newman, eds., *Language, culture, and personality: essays in memory of Edward Sapir,* 75–93. Menasha, WI: Sapir Memorial Publication Fund.

17

American Cultural Denial: The CATs' Compass

E. L. Cerroni-Long

Eastern Michigan University

As has been pointed out elsewhere in this anthology, Americans have no compunction about applying the word "culture" to Others, but can react with surprise or even anger at the idea of American culture. Americans tend to have the same sort of reaction to the word "ethnicity"—are not ethnic, after all, despite surnames, favorite recipes, family traditions, and so on, that link them to other parts of the world. Liza Cerroni-Long found the conceptual tools that had served her in good stead in her studies of Europe and Asia were rejected by her nonminority American students. Their final essays, however, were remarkably similar, and from these she has distilled a working model for American culture despite—or because of?—the better efforts of the students to deny its existence.

Early in her childhood in Italy, E.L. Cerroni-Long developed an interest in Asia. After earning a doctorate in Oriental Studies at the University of Venice, Italy, she studied at the University of Kyoto, Japan, where the actual experience with a "foreignness" she had previously understood only from books was sufficiently unsettling to inspire her to study anthropology in the United States, a country whose people still intrigue her. She continues her work on ethnicity and has also edited an anthology, Anthropological Theory in North America *(Bergin & Garvey 1999). Currently she teaches at Eastern Michigan University in Ypsilanti, Michigan.*

And Keep Your Powder Dry, subtitled "An Anthropologist Looks at America," is a book written by one of the most influential anthropologists of her times as part of an attempt "to develop a series of systematic understandings of the great contemporary cultures so that the special values of each may be orchestrated in a world built new" (Mead 1965 [1942]: viii). That such an objective now sounds not only unrealistic but also quaintly obsolete clearly indicates how far American cultural anthropology has moved away from its foundational disciplinary commitment to the scientific study of culture. Also, any basic review of the social-science literature on the Americans (e.g., Wilkinson 1992) clearly reveals the striking scarcity of anthropological contributions. I believe that these two facts are connected, in the sense that the disciplinary path taken by American anthropologists since the mid-1970s has been at least partially defined by their inability—or unwillingness—to apply the theoretical and research approaches of their discipline to "complex" societies, and especially to their own. I also believe that this phenomenon has been at least partially catalyzed by cultural reasons, to the extent that denying the existence of American culture is a very culture-specific American tendency.

The Cultural Context of American Anthropology

Franz Boas is considered the father of modern cultural anthropology precisely because he zeroed in on the species-specific adaptive aspect of culture and saw cultures, in the plural, as the product of this process. This was a breakthrough conceptual development, because it provided a more useful lens than the one offered by the concept of society for studying and understanding human behavior. The Boasian concept of culture called attention to the interaction between a population and its environment on the one hand, and its history on the other, and it emphasized how all aspects of behavior both emerge from and affect the adaptive social processes underlying such interactions. Boas was a German Jew who emigrated to the United States, and while he was very successful in establishing cultural anthropology as an academic discipline in this country, he also saw many of his students and disciples moving steadily away from his own theoretical position and embracing, instead, psychological models of culture.

This, in my view, is a consequence of the Americanization of cultural anthropology, and it was triggered by the profound interest Americans have in the "mental premises" of human behavior. Psychology is such an extraordinarily successful and influential discipline in the United States because it encompasses the modern version of the theological preoccupations characterizing the religious dissidents that so crucially contributed to the ideological foundations of American culture. The great attention Americans give to exploring the boundaries of the self, and the constant tension perceived to exist between the individual and the community, the need for affiliation and autonomy, the corrupting drives of the body and the redeeming influence of morality are all emerging from an intellectual tradition that made the data collected by cultural anthropologists the "mirror for humanity" through which such preoccupations could be more effectively expressed and social amelioration attempted.

And then, in the last quarter of the twentieth century, postmodernism could easily be grafted onto such an ideological tradition. While postmodernism—as the epistemological translation of the Zeitgeist catalyzed by consumer capitalism (Jameson 1991)—has affected the entire Western (and Westernized) intellectual world, its impact on anthropology has been particularly acute in the United States (Cerroni-Long 1999). My contention is that postmodernist notions fit particularly well certain characteristics of American culture, and this is what has made them particularly influential.

The postmodern emphasis on narcissistic self-reference and interpretive autonomy, its implicit denial of structural constraints (even the constraint of facts versus the freedom of fiction), and its alluring play on the potential for personal self-invention and reinvention were bound to resonate very strongly with American competitive individualism. In the postmodern world, as famously stated by the British Prime Minister Margaret Thatcher, "societies do not exist, only individuals do." Translated into disciplinary terms, this means that culture, as a behavioral framework, is denied, and the *jouissance* of individual choice is celebrated and documented. Thus, a recent print advertisement for the Center for the Ethnography of Everyday Life at the University of Michigan (*Anthropology News,* October 2003, p. 59) is headed by a banner that proclaims: "Everyday? Yes. Ordinary? No." and continues by declaring: "Before the abstractions of social science, there are people's stories, the emotional worlds of disappointment and uncertainty, and the brave coping of everyday life." One can almost hear the crescendo of Hollywood music introducing a movie on "the American dream"!

This is as should be expected. Academic practices are as affected by culture as any other form of human expression, and that is why there are national, culture-specific schools of anthropology (see Barth et al. 2005). Indeed, it would be foolish to expect that because anthropology focuses on the study of culture, it is somehow exempt from the influence of culture. But because of their training, anthropologists should be particularly sensitive to the cultural embeddedness of their theory-building and research approaches. Cultural reflexivity and cross-cultural analysis should be the tools brought to bear on the cultural specificity of their perspectives. As Mary Douglas pointed out: "the pressing agenda for anthropologists [is] not how to escape from our own cultural bias, but how to generate theoretical questions from a systematic comparison of different cultural biases" (1995: 93). There seem to be two prerequisites for this. First, we have to model culture in a way that permits us to truly operationalize ethnographic research. Second, we have to engage in cross-cultural, comparative analyses in a more effective and dedicated way than has been done in the last fifty years.

Unfortunately, the application of the comparative method in anthropology still suffers from association with social evolutionism. Indeed, in the chapter "The Comparative Method and Its Application," Robert Carneiro highlights such correlation (2003: 250–261) and argues that the method came under specific attack by Boas and the Boasians. Certainly, wariness about the pitfalls of social evolutionism has contributed to marginalizing comparativism in anthropology and has obscured the fact that such a method can be used very effectively (as, for example, it continues to be used in area studies) outside the evolutionist paradigm.

Methodological resistance to comparativism and current theoretical contestation of the culture concept both have led to little ethnology being done in the American context over the last twenty years. As one of the grand old men of anthropology wrote recently: "To compare and contrast cultures, the task of ethnology, we must have dependable pictures of other cultures" (Werner 2003: 7). Such comparable units of analysis have become increasingly unavailable as ethnographic research has abandoned its holocultural focus, and even fragmentary analyses of American culture remain especially scarce. What anthropologists have typically contributed, instead, are either social assessment studies (e.g., Baker 2003, Forman 1995, Naylor 1998, Spindler and Spindler 1990, Tannen 1998) or ethnographic thumbnail sketches (e.g., Moffatt 1989, Perin 1988). On the other hand, ethnographic-type research and writing are now used by sociologists, psychologists, other assorted social scientists, and even journalists and travel writers. Consequently, some valuable recent attempts at anthropological analyses of American culture (e.g., Carroll 1988, Hall and Hall 1990) have been given very little attention, being dismissed as "trivially anecdotal" and theoretically irrelevant (Greer 1989).

This is unfortunate, because a holistic understanding of American culture could also provide a useful framework for analyzing ethnicity and, especially, the thorny issue of continuing inter-racial conflict in American life. I discovered this backwards, having come to the United States to study ethnicity and realizing that both ethnic and subcultural groups can only be studied with reference to the characteristics of the culture in which they emerge. Thus, a robust theory of culture can also provide a unique handle on how to distinguish a culture from an ethnic group, and each of them from a subculture.

Behavior is the Key

I was first exposed to ethnicity in Hawaii. By that time I had spent almost a decade studying the culture of Japan, a country that happens to be just as ethnically homogeneous as my native Italy, where I was raised and trained as an Asian Studies scholar. What particularly struck me in Hawaii was the behavior of the Japanese-Americans, which seemed to differ in consistent and interesting ways both from that of mainstream Americans and from that of the Japanese. This discovery triggered both my interest in becoming an anthropologist and my formulation of a theory of culture that would provide a useful framework for the study of both subcultural and ethnic variation (see Cerroni-Long 1993a).

In line with the theoretical founders of cultural anthropology, I came to believe that "we *are* our culture" (Mead 1965 [1942]: 21), but I also distanced myself from the typically American attempts at searching for the mental causes of culture. Certainly, culture must impact cognitive and emotional processes (and that is why it influences intellectual endeavors, such as anthropological research) but culture neither emerges nor gets transmitted, and certainly cannot be studied on the basis of some mental blueprint, be it "modal personality," "values orientation," or "collective unconscious." Rather, I became convinced that culture is an open system of behavioral constraints, constituted by environmental, historical, and social factors, shaping the behavior of people born and raised in a particular society. A society, in turn, can be defined as an enduring human group, recognized as distinct from all others and in which all the functions necessary for the continuation of communal life are performed by in-members. In line with this, an ethnic group is any community viewing itself as culturally distinct from others to which it is fundamentally related at the sociopolitical level. In other words, at a minimum, ethnicity differs from culture to the extent that an ethnic group has no political sovereignty, and a sovereign political structure is an extremely important component of the system of behavioral constraints constituting a culture (Cerroni-Long 2001). Consequently, in broad general terms, many cultures coincide with nation-states (as, indeed, in the case of "the culture of Japan"), and many ethnic groups (such as, for example, the Maori or the Basques) could be defined as "nations without states" (Cerroni-Long 2001).

A culture, then, is not a "thing," but nonetheless it profoundly affects and characterizes human behavior—more than factors such as age, sex, personality, socio-economic status, or ideology—simply because of the pervasiveness of the behavioral constraints it encompasses. In a similar way, a disease is not a thing either, but it may mold behavior, frame lifestyle choices, define one's sense and presentation of self, and affect everyday activities. Just as diseases can only be studied through the patients' symptoms, cultures can be detected only by observing and documenting the behavior of their "carriers"—that is, people whose behavior is recognizably different from the behavior of members of different cultures. Without human carriers, human diseases would not exist, so it must be understood that one's culture enables behavior just as it constrains it. Like a traffic jam, which is both caused by and affecting the behavior of drivers caught in it, each individual shapes the culture just as they are shaped by it.

However, being born and raised in a particular culture leads to a form of blindness; we consider our behavior "natural" and take it so completely for granted that we are not consciously aware of its cultural specificity. That is why, typically, anthropologists study—at least in the early phases of their training—cultures different from their own. Engaging in "native anthropology" is fraught with difficulties, especially since it removes the comparative frame of reference through which we easily identify the characteristics of foreign behavior (Cerroni-Long 1995). But cultural analysis is important and necessary precisely because cultures differ. "As soon as there is contact with another culture (and this has always been the case), there is potential for conflict" (Carroll 1988: 3). I would add that intercultural encounters can also lead to interest, excitement, and pleasure (the international tourist industry and the travel-writing literature are built on this). Documenting cultural differences proves that there are many ways to be human, which deepens our understanding of human behavior, and can provide tremendous examples of different approaches to social organization and of the culture-wide consequences of particular institutional choices, be they polygamy, theocracy, or economic reciprocity.

The most dangerous type of reaction to intercultural encounters, however, comes from the unwillingness to recognize the legitimacy of cultural differences, leading to the ethnocentric denial of the common humanity of the culturally "others" and to concocting all sorts of ideological justifications—such as supposed "racial" inferiority or "innate" evil tendencies—for their exploitation or victimization. Unfortunately, ethnocentrism is a tendency found in most cultures, and when combined with military power, it can lead to the most aberrant phenomena, ranging from slavery to colonialism. The blindness leading to ethnocentrism, though, has nothing to do with cultural denial. Confronted with specific questions about the characteristics of their culture most people will recognize their cultural membership, correlating it perhaps to attachment to particular customs or to the recognition of a specific cultural heritage with which they identify. In fact, a strong sense of cultural identity—and superiority—is often behind strong ethnocentrism. Not so with Americans. Even those who claim to "love their country" and "to be proud to be American" will generally discount that a distinctive American culture exists (Cerroni-Long 2004, Naylor 1998: 42–45).

I suspect that this has partly to do with the extreme competitive individualism that seems to be such a deep-rooted social norm in American culture, but I also think that it may be connected with the confused, conflicted ways ethnicity is seen in the American context.

Ethnogenesis and the CATs

When I started studying ethnicity in the United States, in the late 1970s, I encountered an interesting phenomenon. Whenever I mentioned my research interests to "the natives" in informal social situations, the most common reaction I got was mild embarrassment.

People would smile uncomfortably and often tried to change the topic of conversation. Intrigued, I started pressing on with clarification questions, and it emerged that people thought I was planning to study either "racial" groups or majority–minority relations—topics they felt constituted a negative aspect of American society, certainly not appropriate for inspection by a foreigner. And when I argued that, in a country like the United States, *everybody* had an ethnic background, they would stare at me in sincere amazement and shake their head smiling sadly, as if I had made a rather poor joke.

So, on top of denying that an American culture exists, mainstream Americans also tend to deny their ethnic roots. The fact is that most mainstream Americans feel, as Margaret Mead acutely pointed out, that "however many generations we may boast of in this country, however real our lack of ties in the old world may be, we are all third-generation, our European ancestry tucked away and half forgotten, the recent steps in our wanderings over America immortalized and over-emphasized" (1965 [1942]: 31). In spite of the ever-increasing relevance of ethnic identity for American minority groups, and in spite of the demographic changes brought about by the mounting growth of immigration into the United States since the mid-1960s, mainstream Americans still identify much more readily on the basis of coming from the same town, living in the same neighborhood, having gone to the same school, working for the same company, or even liking the same rock band, than sharing common ethnic roots.

Partly, of course, this has to do precisely with the negative connotation ethnicity has acquired in the United States because of its colonial and immigrant history. Ethnicity (often mislabeled as "race") has traditionally defined the colonized and enslaved, the "fresh-off-the-boat," the social outsiders. Ethnicity is what must be erased in the process of becoming an American—a process that typically takes place over three generations. Thus, American culture gets defined in terms of absence; it is what remains after all traces of ethnicity are erased. No wonder so many Americans deny its reality!

Furthermore, the "melting pot" ideology, together with a long record of intergroup marriage, has convinced members of the American mainstream that their ethnic roots simply cannot be traced. Thus, the closest they can come to a cultural definition is to think of themselves as WASP—or White, Anglo-Saxon, and Protestant—a term highlighting their preoccupation with "racial," historical, and religious categories (Robertiello and Hoguet 1987).

These are also typically abstract categories. By not recognizing that culture is expressed through behavior, Americans are often sincerely puzzled by the ease with which they are identified as Americans when traveling abroad. Also, by not being able to identify the ethnic origin of their patterns of behavior, they are unable to trace their roots. And the critique of "culturalist essentialism" mounted by so many American anthropologists (e.g., Goode 2001) both feeds and fits into these views. As a consequence, I have come to see what I do in some of my classes as "teaching ethnicity" rather than teaching about ethnicity (Cerroni-Long 1993b).

When I introduce my students to the concept of ethnogenesis—the process by which a new set of "people" emerges from particular historical circumstances favoring either intense cultural intermixing or subcultural isolation—they initially take notes dutifully but with little interest. But when I go on to illustrate this process by describing the emergence of American culture from the amalgamation of three distinct European populations—of Celtic, Anglo, and Teutonic background—which through intermarriage and other forms of close contact merged their cultural characteristics into a new system of behavioral constraints, they sit up and pay real attention. For many of them this analysis is a revelation of enormous proportions. For the first time in their lives they feel that they have a recognizable, documented, legitimate ethnic heritage. As I describe the American cultural patterns that can be traced back to Irish, English, or Germanic ancestry, they seem to delight in relating their own behavior to its ethnic roots. And they seem to think that being designated by the acronym CAT—for Celtic, Anglo, Teutonic—is so much cooler than being a WASP! Also, it gives members of the mainstream a way out of being defined simply as American, and, implicitly, as part of the socially dominant and culturally hegemonic group in the United States—a characterization they seem to abhor.

The enthusiasm for these discoveries, however, and for the new perspective from which behavior can be analyzed and identity defined is often short-lived. In the class in which I teach about American culture and intracultural diversity, the final assignment requires students to engage in reflexive cultural analysis by writing a paper titled "What is it like to be ———?" in which the blank should be filled in with the national, ethnic, or subcultural group with which each of the student identifies. This comes at the end of a semester dedicated to the analysis of American culture—as expressed in the behavioral patterns of the mainstream population—and of the major ethnic and subcultural groups found within it. We do a lot of documentary readings, we see illustrative films, and we have lengthy analytical discussions. Also, students are given detailed guidelines on what aspects of their own behavior to reflect on, describe, and analyze in order to answer the assignment question. But to no avail. While members of minority groups generally breeze through the assignment and turn in very well-documented descriptions of their ethnic-specific patterns of behavior, the greatest majority of students who are members of the mainstream write about "What is it like to be an American" in the most abstract, mentalistic way.

Having conducted this exercise once or twice a year for more than twenty years, and in several universities, I have accumulated an imposing array of student papers, documenting in no uncertain terms the way they perceive what it is like to be an American. "Americanness," they all agree, resides in a set of mental attitudes, acquired early on from parents and role-models, and serving as guidelines for daily behavior. Indeed even those students who reject the premises of the assignment and, against my specific request, fill in the blank of the paper title with their own name—proclaiming their unique individuality and denying any form of sociocultural membership—even these "paladins of exceptionalism" submit papers strikingly similar to those written by their more docile cultural brethrens. In their remarkable uniformity, all of these papers not only reveal how Americans conceive of what motivates their behavior—the set of mental guidelines they claim to follow in their daily lives—but also, and to me more interestingly, provide a set of *words* which seem to operate as the master tropes of the American experience. I have come to call this set of terms "the CATs' compass" and I believe that they provide some important insights into American culture.

The CATs' Compass

Cognitive scientists have been giving increasing attention to the "metaphors we live by" (Lakoff and Johnson 1980) in order to document the experiential basis of human thought

(Johnson 1990). Such an approach strongly supports cultural relativism since it highlights the embeddedness of thought in experience—which is inescapably culture-specific—and the concomitant interpretation of experience through metaphorical elaborations that are, again inescapably, derived from "cultural knowledge." The case of proverbs is the clearest illustration of the "directive force" of behavioral prescriptions that have the ring of timeless universality precisely because they express culture-specific themes (White 1987). Psychological anthropologists have long attempted to relate cultural specificity to differences in "world views" or in "cultural themes," but these approaches have "typically failed to specify the range of domains in which a given theme, alleged to be central to a culture, applies" (Quinn and Holland 1987: 35). The theory of culture I adopt in my research bypasses such preoccupations, which derive from a search for the prime causes of culture, and aims instead at describing culturally characteristic patterns of behavior, relating them to some of the specific factors that may have influenced their emergence but also placing them in the systemic context which has stabilized and perpetuates them. Still, native views on what guides behavior, whether or not empirically confirmed through participant observation, reveal a lot about culture-specific ideals. I would argue that the recurrent words used in expressing these ideals may provide even better insights into the building blocks of cultural themes.

In the case of my students' papers, there are seven words that recur with striking regularity: *challenge, control, comfort, competition, community, change,* and *choice.* Because they all begin with the letter "c," I have labeled them the "7Cs" of American culture. Also, I arranged these terms around a seven-point star—representing a compass (Figure 1)—and tried to superimpose it on the "social-factors wheel" (Figure 2) for the system model of culture I have adopted. In the process, I discovered that *each* of these seven ideas could be seen as central to one of the social factors listed. For example, "competition" is certainly at the core of the American economic structure, but it could be argued that it also shapes American social and political structures, and it is a core norm, value, and belief. Similarly, Americans definitely value "choice"—which they often define as "freedom"—but they also believe in it, and use it as a social norm, incorporating it into their social, economic, and political structure. In other words, these seven words, and the concepts they represent, pervade American culture at all levels and seem to constitute the metaphorical filters through which people give meaning to their behavior and in the process reinforce it.

Do these concepts *determine* behavior? I do not think so. The behavior is shaped by culture-specific systemic constraints, which certainly include mental constructs such as

FIGURE 1   The CATs' Compass.

CULTURE
System-Model Chart

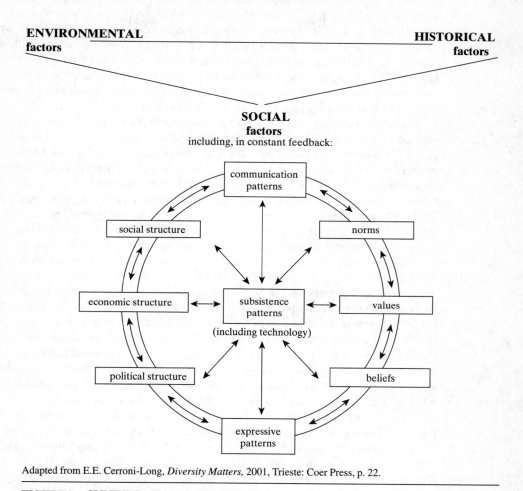

ENVIRONMENTAL
factors

HISTORICAL
factors

SOCIAL
factors
including, in constant feedback:

communication
patterns

social structure

norms

economic structure

subsistence
patterns
(including technology)

values

political structure

beliefs

expressive
patterns

Adapted from E.E. Cerroni-Long, *Diversity Matters,* 2001, Trieste: Coer Press, p. 22.

FIGURE 2   CULTURE—System-Model Chart.

norms and values, but also very material ones such as climatic conditions or availability of natural resources (see Figure 2). Nevertheless, psychological anthropologists argue that cultural knowledge "is typically acquired to the accompaniment of intermittent advice and occasional correction rather than explicit, detailed instructions; but it is learned from others, in large part from their *talk*" (emphasis added, D'Andrade 1981, cited in Quinn and Holland 1987: 22). If "cultural knowledge" is defined as the webs of signification giving meaning to behavior, then I would agree that any holistic ethnography should attempt to dissect it and analyze it. From its foundations, cultural anthropology aimed at balancing etic and emic perspectives, and the natives' point of view certainly helps understand representational, if not operational, knowledge. In attempting to sort out the three levels of behavioral analyses available to researchers—what people do, what people think they do, and what people say they do—anthropologists like me tend to be more interested in documenting the first level, but the way the natives interpret their behavior or describe what they consider their behavioral guidelines—like my American students inevitably do in their papers—needs to be acknowledged and taken into account in sorting out the cultural "package." More usefully, the actual words being used recurrently in the process of describing one's perception of behavioral guidelines may reveal the often unrecognized linguistic signification structure being applied in giving order to experience.

In a way, then, the "7Cs" of American culture could be seen as the canons for American expressive style; the "idée fixe" array filtering the American experience and giving it shape. There is nothing mystical, or amenable to psychoanalytic treatment, in this. Expressive style is certainly not "national character," but it may serve as a useful framework for discussing cultural characteristics from a behavioral perspective. Style accommodates a rich repertoire of behavioral patterns, encompassing communication, inclinations, and identification. Above all, describing a culture through the expressive style of its members takes into account the core research methodology of cultural anthropology, which continues to be focused on the observation of, and interaction with, individuals and small groups in natural settings.

In her discussion of the "cultural misunderstandings" between the French and the Americans, Raymonde Carroll (1988) attempts just such a description, and in spite of facilitating its understanding by presenting it through the lenses of cross-cultural comparison, the way the ethnography is organized—around topics such as "home," "friendship," or "the telephone"—seems so haphazard to partly justify her critics' theoretical discomfort. The Halls (1990) do somewhat better, systematically addressing American use of time and space, educational and work attitudes, communication style, and psychological framework, but their theory of culture as shaped by the way information is organized, transmitted, and perceived leads to descriptions which constantly shift from expressive style to institutional structures, often mixing representational and operational aspects of cultural knowledge.

On the other hand, organizing the description of American expressive style along the lines of traditional holistic ethnographies—that is, the topics listed in the "social factors" wheel in Figure 2—leads on the one hand to the difficulty of relating behavior to its institutionalized expressions and, on the other, to the pitfall of belaboring the trivial and the trite (Holmes and Holmes 2002). By the time Alexis de Tocqueville published the two volumes of *Democracy in America* in 1835 and 1840 the view of Americans as "isolated by self-reliance" was already well established (Wilkinson 1992: 11); what is interesting from an anthropological point of view is to look at how individualism gets expressed in American behavior, and how to trace the impact of the self-reliance social norm at the level of the cultural system as a whole.

Unfortunately, current trends in cultural anthropology have taken us increasingly away from any attempt at holistic descriptions of American culture. The rare exceptions come from anthropologists so steeped in psychological theories of culture that the ethnographic material they present seems incidental, being chiefly geared toward supporting a particular view of the human mind (e.g., Nuckolls 1998, Stein 2003). What remains are anthologies collecting the reflections of various social scientists on different aspects of

American culture (e.g., DeVita and Armstrong 2002, Jorgensen and Truzzi 1974, Plotnicov 1990, Spradley and Rynkiewich 1975).

The collection edited by Spradley and Rynkiewich (1975) takes its title from the leading article, "Body Ritual among the Nacirema"—a piece by Horace Miner, originally published in 1956, which has become a bit of a classic in the literature on American culture. In this short article, the author describes bodily preoccupations as being central to the culture of a group he calls the Nacirema and whose rituals he describes using full-fledged anthropological jargon. When the reader understands that *Nacirema* is *American* spelled backwards, amusement is derived both from the unusual perspective the article gives on common American patterns of behavior and from the gentle irony the author bestows on the anthropological approach itself. Re-reading this piece half a century after its publication, though, also highlights how unexplored the Nacirema have unfortunately remained. In spite of its strong economic and political influence on the rest of the world, American culture is still not well understood, least of all by its own members, who deny its reality and are puzzled by foreign recognition of its characteristics, and even more so by the real distaste these trigger across many national boundaries. International relations are, first and foremost, intercultural relations, and cultural reflexivity—the ability to recognize the cultural matrix of our behavior rather than considering it the universal norm—seems a crucial first step on the path toward peaceful coexistence. The characteristics of the CATs' compass offer an introductory glimpse into the culture of a people which is still awaiting a comprehensive ethnography.

Exercise

Gather information on your ethnic background by looking into documents on your family history and/or interviewing older relatives. Be prepared to discuss the results of this research in class. Is this ethnic background still somehow in evidence in your family? Were you or any of your relatives treated differently because of this background? How is this background related to "being American"?

References

Baker, Lee, ed. 2003. *Life in America.* Williston, VT: Blackwell.

Barth, Fredrik, et al. 2005. *One discipline, four ways.* Chicago: University of Chicago Press.

Carneiro, Robert L. 2003. *Evolutionism in cultural anthropology.* Boulder, CO: Westview Press.

Carroll, Raymonde. 1988. *Cultural misunderstandings.* Chicago: University of Chicago Press.

Cerroni-Long, E. L. 1993a. Life and cultures. In P. R. DeVita and J. D. Armstrong, eds., *Distant mirrors: America as a foreign culture,* 148–161. 3rd edition. Belmont, CA: Wadsworth.

———. 1993b. Teaching ethnicity in the USA: an anthropological model. *Journal of Ethno-development* 2(1): 106–111.

———. 1995. *Insider anthropology.* Arlington, VA: American Anthropological Association/NAPA Publications.

———. 1999. Anthropology at century's end. In E. L. Cerroni-Long, ed., *Anthropological theory in North America,* 1–18. Westport, CT: Bergin & Garvey.

———. 2001. *Diversity matters.* Trieste (Italy): COER Press.

———. 2004. Comparing US. *FOSAP Newsletter* 11(2): 2–4.

DeVita, P. R. and J. D. Armstrong, eds. 2002. *Distant mirrors: America as a foreign culture*. 3rd edition. Belmont, CA: Wadsworth.

Douglas, Mary. 1995. The Cloud God and the shadow self. *Social Anthropology* 3(2): 83–94.

Forman, Shepard, ed. 1995. *Diagnosing America*. Ann Arbor: University of Michigan Press.

Goode, Judith. 2001. Teaching against culturalist essentialism. In I. Susser and T. C. Patterson, eds., *Cultural diversity in the United States,* 434–456. Oxford: Blackwell.

Greer, Herb. 1989. Not so very alike. *Times Literary Supplement* July 13: 372.

Hall, Edward T. and M. R. Hall. 1990. *Understanding cultural differences*. Yarmouth, ME: Intercultural Press.

Holmes, Lowell D. and E. R. Holmes. 2002. The American cultural configuration. In P. R. DeVita and J. D. Armstrong, eds., *Distant mirrors: America as a foreign culture,* 4–26. 3rd edition. Belmont, CA: Wadsworth.

Jameson, Fredric. 1991. *Postmodernism, or the cultural logic of late capitalism*. Durham, NC: Duke University Press.

Johnson, Mark. 1990. *The body in the mind*. Chicago: University of Chicago Press.

Jorgensen, J. G. and M. Truzzi, eds. 1974. *Anthropology and American life*. Englewood Cliffs, NJ: Prentice-Hall.

Lakoff, G. and M. Johnson. 1980. *Metaphors we live by*. Chicago: University of Chicago Press.

Mead, Margaret. 1965 [1942]. *And keep your powder dry*. New York: William Morrow.

Moffatt, Michael. 1989. *Coming of age in New Jersey*. Brunswick, NJ: Rutgers University Press.

Naylor, Larry L. 1998. *American culture*. Westport, CT: Bergin & Garvey.

Nuckolls, Charles W. 1998. *Culture: a problem that cannot be solved*. Madison: University of Wisconsin Press.

Perin, Constance. 1988. *Belonging in America*. Madison: University of Wisconsin Press.

Plotnicov, Leonard, ed. 1990. *American culture*. Pittsburgh, PA: University of Pittsburgh Press.

Quinn, Naomi and D. Holland. 1987. Culture and cognition. In D. Holland and N. Quinn, eds., *Cultural models of language and thought,* 3–40. Cambridge: Cambridge University Press.

Robertiello, Richard C. and D. Hoguet. 1987. *The WASP mystique*. New York: Donald Fine.

Spindler, George and L. Spindler. 1990. *The American cultural dialogue and its transmission*. Bristol, PA: Falmer Press.

Spradley, James P. and M. A. Rynkiewich, eds. 1975. *The Nacirema*. Boston: Little, Brown.

Stein, Howard. 2003. *Beneath the crust of culture*. Amsterdam (The Netherlands): Rodopi.

Tannen, Deborah. 1998. *The argument culture*. New York: Ballantine Books.

Werner, Oswald. 2003. Ethnographers, language skills and translation. *Anthropology News* March: 7.

White, Geoffrey M. 1987. Proverbs and cultural models. In D. Holland and N. Quinn, eds., *Cultural models of language and thought,* 151–172. Cambridge: Cambridge University Press.

Wilkinson, Rupert, ed. 1992. *American social character*. New York: HarperCollins.

18

Dangerous Assumptions of American Culture

Mark Nathan Cohen
SUNY at Plattsburgh

"Dangerous Assumptions of American Culture" derives from Mark Cohen's experiences in American culture and in many other cultures, as well as his training in anthropology and his training in introspection. It deals with ways in which Americans' misunderstanding and intolerance of other cultures, and their blind faith in the "obvious truth" of their own cultural assumptions, are rooted in their limited understanding of the meaning of "culture," their lack of self-perception, and their failure to examine their own culture from the point of view of cultural outsiders.

> *Mark Nathan Cohen is University Distinguished Professor of Anthropology of the State University of New York, at the Plattsburgh Campus. He is the author of* Culture of Intolerance *(Yale 1998), from which this chapter, in modified form, is excerpted. He has written several articles and chapters describing how IQ tests, as well as SATs, GREs, and particularly Miller Analogy Tests, are drawn from a narrow concept of intelligence that fails to recognize potential differences in knowledge, perception and thought among cultures outside of the American mainstream.*

All people around the world are members of cultures, by which I mean not just art and dance, but "grammar" rules (rather like the rules of language grammar) that set up the mostly unspoken (and often unconscious) limits to their behavior. For example, culture defines the values people hold, their goals and motivations, the permitted means to achieving those goals, the roles people play and how they play them, their form of leadership and government, the styles people accept, their modes of exchange, their cosmology (how they believe their world works), the form of their supernatural beliefs, how they train their members in their culture, and even what they see and hear from the enormous amount of noise and information with which we are all bombarded (people from different cultures actually register different sights

From Cohen, Mark Nathan, *Culture of Intolerance,* New Haven, CT: Yale University Press, 1998, pp. 134–203.

and sounds). Perhaps most important, culture also defines the unspoken assumptions that must precede unconscious, rational, and irrational decisions and actions.

All of these things must be provided by every culture. They are needs that must be met in any culture to keep that culture and society intact. Behaviors and beliefs address these rules and needs often through manifest, conscious, recognized designs. But often, perhaps most often, the ways people fulfill these needs are unspoken or even unconscious, through what we call "latent" or hidden functions of a behavior of which people may not even be aware. Because these behaviors are unconscious they are the hardest parts of a culture to analyze or change.

Like the grammar of language, people's conscious and unconscious choices are learned from birth and, like language, they become so deeply ingrained that, in effect, they take people prisoner, just as people are made prisoners of the language(s) they learned as children. People are like horses with blinders, prevented by their culture from seeing and reacting to anything outside their narrow view of the world.

Cultural rules are also arbitrary. Although all cultures must provide something in each area defined above, they often provide different things, just as all people must use a language, but any of the myriad of human languages will suffice. This creates a serious problem. The blinders prevent people from seeing, evaluating, and respecting the arbitrary culture systems of others, and they convince people that their system is not only the best, but also the only real one. People cannot conceive of alternatives, so they cannot recognize how arbitrary their own choices are.

American culture is no different. Americans, too, are caught in an arbitrary system of assumptions, beliefs and action, much of it never scrutinized or questioned. We often don't comprehend what other people are doing (although we note, in line with the human propensity for ethnocentrism, that whatever they are doing is inherently inferior). Without significant training, we are unable to look at our own culture from the outside, seeing its arbitrary assumptions and its flaws. We seem totally unable to recognize that members of other cultures (e.g., those of the Middle East) may not want what we want, or believe what we believe, or see the world as we do. Anthropologists try to teach cultural relativism, meaning simply the willingness to look at other cultures fairly and to respect and understand them, even if there are pieces of those cultures we don't like. Trained anthropologists knew what would happen in Iraq if we went in. Our untrained leaders did not, and they conduct their negotiations and then their war with neither knowledge of, nor respect for, the people with whom they are dealing—but with the arrogance that comes from complete failure to value anything outside our own system. Cultural relativism also means the ability to look at our culture from outside (i.e., the way others perceive us) and examine our assumptions critically. Our leaders cannot do that either.

I wish to focus on a few major assumptions of American culture that are certainly arbitrary, often wrong, and occasionally even dangerous for ourselves and for other people: "freedom," property, profit, "efficiency," "progress," "manifest destiny," and dominance of nature.

"Freedom"

Freedom doesn't exist (unless you are a slave). A promise of "freedom" means nothing. What count are specific freedom*s* (plural): freedoms to do or say certain things; to hold certain beliefs; to go to certain places; to be different in specific ways; and many more. Different cultures permit or prevent certain things: none allows all. Our freedoms differ from those of other cultures, but are not necessarily better, nor are they necessarily more numerous. We are not legally free to practice polygamy, but despite the fact that polygamy has been standard in many cultures around the world and throughout history, we do not even question this constraint. Limits on our behavior are so ingrained, so "obvious," that we often tune them out. We can therefore, somewhat irrationally, refer to ourselves as a "free country" and to assume that other people envy our "freedom."

The Real Limits to Freedoms

Our freedoms are dramatically limited by our cultural rules and our limited knowledge and perception. We are free only within certain sets of cultural constraints. We are "free," but our blinders keep us looking straight ahead and we think and act within the limits of that view. Freedoms are limited because we cannot see alternatives. That is, our blinders limit our freedoms. This, not government, is by far our freedom's biggest constraint. The only remedy is education in alternatives through awareness of other cultures. Without such knowledge, we can't share their ecological and medical knowledge, their morality, their definitions, and their aspirations, which in many cases may be superior to our own.

We are slaves to fad, fashion, and social pressures, not only in clothing design but also in our thoughts and beliefs, and the conduct of large areas of our lives. We insist on conformity in areas where none need exist. (Do captains of industry really have to wear almost exactly the same suit? Does it matter? But they do.) Because of political and social pressures, we are not free to explore alternative economic or political systems other than within very narrow specified limits. More important, we are not free to explore alternative solutions to our problems "outside the box," if they are outside our cultural "box."

Government restrictions on our freedom are widely discussed. But government can increase freedoms for some by restricting those of others. A contemporary example is the constitutional separation of church and state that seems onerous to some, but grants others freedom to worship and make decisions as we choose and to pursue rational solutions to large-scale issues, like the uses of science, free from the dictates of particular religious beliefs. Unfortunately, that very important protection of freedoms is now being lost.

Government can also increase our freedom (and our well-being) by offering options and solutions to problems on a scale that no other institutions can match—or that have no immediate dollar profit associated with them, such as universal health care, education, and protection of the environment. Universal health care would provide freedom to move, change jobs, widen job choices, and to pause between jobs. It would widen economic choices by freeing households from fear of the costs of catastrophic illness.

Government's support of schools widens people's knowledge and the freedoms that accompany it—although it can also narrow perceptions by insisting on certain curricula, as it does when it insists on teaching uncritical patriotism or mandating the content of science classes. It can provide a range of choices of media (a particular freedom) that are not necessarily the most profitable or popular. Controls on pollution would free us from limits on our behaviors (and from health problems) related to pollution. We could, for example, again be free to swim in lakes, to smell and drink clean water, and to eat fish. Government's limits on the behavior of corporations could free us from limits to freedoms that corporate behaviors impose. "Getting governments off our backs" will not enhance freedoms for most of us. It would just permit the powerful to limit the freedoms of the rest of us. Unfortunately, our present government has decided not to impose controls on corporations.

The Perception of Unlimited Freedom

A second major problem is that "freedom" is such an overwhelming American icon that we can't imagine compromises or limits. We value freedom, but also health, prosperity, peace, family, community, and human life. These values demand some balance; freedom can't just be unlimited. All societies require the freedom of individuals to be constrained by the rules of the group and the needs of others.

Freedoms are reciprocal. Every freedom you have restricts one of mine so your freedoms must be limited by mine, and both of us must restrain our exercise of freedoms in the name of the community.

We typically fail to distinguish between "freedom *to*" and "freedom *from*," and we undervalue the latter. But again they are reciprocal: If I am free to do certain things, you are not free from their consequences. If you are free to make noise as you like, I am not free to enjoy the quiet, hear my own music, or focus on my own activities (such as sleep or studying). I think that "freedom from" should be given greater weight than it is, but in certain areas of our lives, we are aware only of "freedom to." The American concept of freedom tilts sharply toward the freedoms of the aggressor, but merely raising the battle cry of freedom, "It's a free country," trumps all further discussion.

Freedom is seen as an inflexible principle, a non-negotiable absolute rather than what it really is—a set of rights granted by a particular culture in a particular social contract, whose precise boundaries are negotiable and need careful evaluation. Freedoms must always be combined with equal doses of responsibility and civility.

Selective Application

Freedoms too often are selectively applied (like the "freedom" to own slaves, combined with force constraining the freedom of slaves to object). The freedoms of the rich are more valued (and less constrained) than those of the poor, those of whites more than nonwhites, those of men more than women, and those of husbands more than wives.

We recognize the "freedom" of the rich to take the money of the poor in various ways, many of which are ethically dubious and should be illegal: monopoly, price gouging, deceptive advertising and labeling, shoddy goods, legal sleight of hand, withholding information about the known dangers of a product, and a host of others. Some are clearly illegal—price-fixing, sweatshops, embezzlement, bribery, graft, insider trading, tax fraud. Few get serious surveillance. At the same time, government constraints protect the rich from the poor people who try to get money back using the only means available: trespass, petty theft, panhandling, and labor strikes (though strikes are nowadays far less effective in light of the latest "freedoms" granted to corporations). We focus heavily on tax compliance by the poor and effectively ignore it among the rich and the corporations. We pay a great deal of attention to welfare cheats. We even invent some, as President Ronald Reagan once did with impunity, to make the point. But cheating is a fact on the fringe of any system. We threaten to end welfare partly for this reason, we don't threaten to end banking because of its enormous frauds. We don't even threaten to cut far more costly "welfare" (subsidies) paid to already profitable corporations, despite the clear evidence of (apparently fairly rampant) major corporate cheating.

This selectivity is built into our system so deeply that many people can't see it, and therefore many people, rich and poor, come to support the image of laissez-faire freedom and equality that Americans like to project. But no one with any property actually wants a real (as opposed to selective) laissez-faire system because it would permit others to expropriate shares of all wealth.

We apply the concept of freedom selectively in international affairs. How "free" is the "free market" if it is distorted by power? Are others free *not* to participate in our "free market," to withhold land and resources from that market, to grow what they like? We do not permit them to assign resources or choose a government as they see fit. We have used force and economic power to convert land or other resources to our desired uses and to prevent them from being reclaimed. We have forcibly "opened" other countries to participation in our trade networks as exporters and consumers. We have prevented other people from using their own systems of land ownership and their often-superior understanding of the natural world. We have hunted indigenous people to extermination to claim their resources. Many times we have used military might (when "necessary") to restrict those freedoms or to insure the supply of "our" oil. We have used force, the threat of force, or "covert action" to prevent many other countries from redistributing land or revenues from resources to their people more equitably.

We seem to want freedom only from government, only for ourselves, and only in selected ways. We assume our pattern is "natural" and don't even question it. In fact the pattern is conventional and badly out of balance.

A social contract involves reciprocal obligation. The price we pay for government protections (i.e., limits to the excessive freedom of others) ought to be government protections for others as well. The balance demands more careful and constant re-evaluation.

Property

In our culture, private property is too often seen as an absolute and inalienable right. Most Americans agree that there should be individual rights to private property. But private property is a social convention, not a God-given right. The rules about what can be owned and what rights ownership conveys are arbitrary, maintained by power or group agreement.

Private property is and should be limited by the need or desire of the larger society. The principle of limited ownership is essential to our social organization, but we argue about specific applications of that principle. There is a good deal of room to think about the boundaries of ownership without denigrating the idea of private property itself, yet our blinders prevent us from thinking clearly.

No matter what a person may accomplish, success is grounded in institutional supports as basic as roads and infrastructure, and as sophisticated as cultural knowledge stored and made available from public sources. Invention builds on invention. But Americans embrace the myth that whatever success and resulting private property a person has was gained entirely by the person's own behavior and the individual alone should reap the benefits. Americans erroneously attribute both success and failure much more to individual effort and personal qualities than most cultures would—or than is justified. (For example, if members of minority groups don't succeed, we assume that it reflects their personal limits, not the limits on their freedoms or on their exposure to the support of the community or the culture that we maintain.)

We agree that the right to private property takes precedence over most other rights and needs—including the human need (people from many other cultures would say, "right") to eat; and we will defend that private property by force, if needed. For private property to become so important in our cultural system, our society must not only honor it but actively develop systems to perpetuate, transfer, consolidate, store, and move it. This requires social, legal, and economic institutions that society itself must maintain. These things are expensive. Society also cleans up the physical wastes, the pollutants, and human "waste" of discarded workers. Those favors are built on community sharing, so the society that provides it has a right to demand a share of the wealth.

Why doesn't American society (which provides so much support for any private venture and invests so much in the generation and perpetuation of private property) demand a reasonable share? Why do we count what society contributes to the poor so heavily (when they actually get relatively little) but perpetuate the myth that the rich do it all themselves and deserve to keep it all? The government provides far more services to the rich than the poor. Our services give us the right to demand a share.

Few private corporations would knowingly allow someone they had trained, nurtured, and equipped (or even just employed) to leave, taking private possession of a valuable product that the employee had developed while working at the company. In fact, many companies demand a large share, if not all, of any such product when an employee leaves. Yet our society, which could claim sponsorship, inspiration, and nurturing as far more important, regularly gives away its share of such wealth. Why doesn't our society protect its interest in developed wealth in the same manner that any corporation would?

The Profit Motive

Our focus on profit is one of our arbitrary cultural values. We allow economic profits to motivate us above all else. Such a pattern is not inevitable; it is defined by our culture. The profit motive has been an important engine for economic growth in recent Western history. There is no question of its value, at least if "growth" and "progress" (whatever they mean and if they are actually good) are the goals. Not everything that we ought—or might even want—to do is profitable, and profitability should not be the only measure. But as things like medical care and now even water are put in corporate hands, we are moving ever more in that direction. Even if we accept the profit motive, why do we accept the premise that unlimited profit needs to be offered as the only possible incentive to production? Economic profit is not the only possible motivation, and it is not sufficient for all purposes. What is profitable is not necessarily good for society or the people, although that is what we assume and teach. We could place a higher value on respect, family unity and honor, tradition, pride in craftsmanship, good works, creation of beauty, responsibility, and concern for others. We could reward such behavior with honor, respect, love, and approval of peers—mechanisms that could provide motivation for meeting many of our goals.

The national obsession with the profit motive distorts our perception of our fellows and ourselves. Why should those who are more interested in art, literature, beauty, family, friends, nature, knowledge, the environment, the education and health of our children and our neighbors' children, and the care of other people simply allow those with no ambition other than profit to take everything and destroy what we value in the process? Why should we participate in the myth that profit and wealth reflect superior "intelligence" or ability, hard work, or thrift, when it often reflects only narrow-minded ambition, greed, ruthlessness, disregard for morality or law—and, for all that, most often just reflects inheritance? In fact, profit exists largely because society picks up the associated costs in such forms as injury and incapacity, costs to health, displacement of people, pollution, waste disposal and so forth.

We have to be willing to ask ourselves whether economic profit should be the only basis for exchange and interaction, whether the pursuit of profit should continue unfettered by other concerns, whether we should continue to recognize the profit motive but limit or tax profits at a higher rate or demand accountability for the real (e.g., human and environmental) costs before the profit can be measured, and whether we should try harder to teach some other values, or to define the areas in which profit is not an appropriate incentive.

What are we to make of the recent race to profit by patenting the genes of other people? The patent, and therefore the profit, will go not to the people who have the gene but to whoever identifies it to the satisfaction of an American (or Australian, etc.) court. The profit will go to people who know how to do the paperwork, not the people who produce the needed goods. Aren't there some things that belong to people by nature and, if shared, should be shared for human good, not patented for profit?

Is there a reason why, in wartime, when society calls on its sons and daughters to sacrifice much of their youth and risk their health and lives, we cannot demand that corporations and their stockholders sacrifice their profits to the same cause? (In fact, wars tend to be highly profitable for the contractors involved, and this may be one reason why we fight so many.)

In addition to contexts where profit is inappropriate, we can recognize situations in which making a profit ought to be illegal—or is illegal but goes unpunished—as, for example, when an individual in government service profits from his or her own activities. We never seriously question the mixture of the profit motive with pronouncements of patriotism and public service in our politicians, yet these motives are potentially in conflict. Should we let our Congressional representatives profit from their association with corporate lobbyists and then make decisions affecting those lobbyists? Politicians do such things, of course—in fact, the practice is rampant—and that is what lobbying is all about. Why isn't it illegal? Elsewhere it is considered bribery.

We can regulate and harness profit-seeking more effectively. It is not radical to suggest that we need to rethink our rules and limits. What is radical and dangerous is to insist that profit should continue to dominate all other human considerations.

"Efficiency"

We Americans pride ourselves on our "efficiency," but our definition of "efficiency" is very narrow. We tend to refer to efficiency as an absolute measure that is inherently desirable. However, efficiency, like freedom (singular), does not exist. Rather, it is specific efficien*cies* (plural) that count. Efficiency is a ratio between any of various measurements of input and output. Our assessment of efficiency depends on what things are being compared, how they are measured, and what (unspoken as well as spoken) supporting assumptions are made. Different efficiencies are often in competition with one another. Something that makes the most efficient use of time, for example, does not necessarily make the most efficient use of such other resources as space, energy, or scarce resources. Driving fast to make efficient use of one's time is an inefficient use of gasoline. In agriculture, historically, the efficient use of land was often in opposition to the efficient use of labor, and even now, the most efficient use of human labor is very wasteful of other sources of energy. "Efficient" American farmers can produce many times more food for each hour of work than do Third World peasants working by hand, but they are in fact extremely wasteful of energy. Moreover, we have to decide what each value includes. Do we measure the efficiency of the farmer's own work, or include all of the other human labor that went into providing the farmer what he needs. Does the measure of a factory's efficiency include the costs of the social cleanup? We have to be careful to specify what we want to maximize and to consider the alternative forms of efficiency and the various ways to measure it before we choose our methods.

Feeding people, giving them the opportunity to participate and support themselves, and maintaining their human dignity ought to count when we assess efficiencies, as should preserving the safety and beauty of the environment, the quality and safety of the product itself, and a host of other considerations. Historically, making farming more "efficient" has typically forced people off the land, perhaps into unemployment, to become the urban poor. It typically decreases the nutrient value and safety of the food grown (because crops have to be specially bred and then fed and protected with chemical fertilizers and insecticides), so it has far larger environmental costs than farming in more traditional ways. Addressing those needs would almost certainly be more efficient for the society in many ways, if not for the farm itself. It would almost certainly increase our "efficiency" with reference to public needs and public costs.

And, even if we agree to confine ourselves to thinking about labor efficiency and dollar profits, we have an odd way of measuring productivity and costs when we estimate efficiency. We measure the output of factories and the size of private profits without evaluating the background costs in dollars (let alone in quality of lives) to the society as a whole. *Of course* a factory can be "efficient"—that is, profitable to its owners—if the rest of us absorb the costs of its pollution, transportation, discarded labor, and so forth in our taxes or in the reduced quality of our lives. Its "efficiency" results from the fact that we don't count those costs.

Examples abound in the public sector as well. Crime is terribly costly to our society but so is punishment. Putting people in prison appears to be the most efficient short-term solution to crime, but it is remarkably inefficient because it encourages future criminal activity and is very expensive (and of course we don't punish the crimes of the rich nearly so often or so severely as those of the poor). It is far more costly to keep someone in prison than in college, and four years in college clearly has a more positive effect (on earning power, not to mention breadth of vision and understanding, and therefore a range of freedoms). Moreover, the need for so many prisons is almost certainly related to our narrow definition of economic efficiency, which excludes many people from the work force. (Surely the best way to make most people obey the law is to make them feel that they, too, have a decent stake in the "system" and in the protection of the same laws.) Neither prisons nor universities will do much good, of course, if the economy is restructured, as is now occurring, so that jobs that once paid reasonably well no longer exist. Our definition of "efficiency" seems extraordinarily narrow and shortsighted.

Economic Growth and "Progress"

There is abundant evidence that, throughout history, "growth" has not always improved people's lives. We can't simply assume it will, despite assurances from government and corporations. In fact, in recent decades economic growth or improvement for corporate interests have been accompanied by declining standards of living for most people. Contrary to popular American belief, we don't all gain from "growth." We don't all share, even if the whole pie gets bigger. Can we reevaluate our cultural obsession with growth in ways that permit us to separate the useful parts from the dangerous parts? If growth doesn't improve the lives of more people, what good is it? What else are we trying to accomplish? Shouldn't those who gain from economic growth, and the effort growth takes on the part of the society as a whole, have some responsibility to those who lose as a consequence of the process?

Part of our faith in "growth" comes from a false sense of how humankind has "progressed." We have a profound belief in "progress," and we are willing to put our faith in it, even though we don't actually pay much attention to how we measure it. Our faith results partly from the fact that we usually recite only the history of privileged classes and technological advances rather than exploring the realities of life faced by the common people.

Changes in the structure of cultures and societies through historic and prehistoric time have led, through competition, toward bigger political units and the accumulation of material goods. But bigger political units and more goods have not always been successful in improving human lives, at least prior to the twentieth century (when they were somewhat beneficial, primarily for the privileged). And again in the twenty-first century, "progress" and human welfare are being separated.

Data from scientific and historical sources call into question our sense of "progress," at least if progress is about people's health, nutrition, and quality of life. (What else is it about?) For most people, the quality and quantity of nutrition have clearly declined through history; only for the affluent populations of the twentieth century have they improved. Most of the world's surviving "primitive" hunter-gatherers, measured earlier in this century, had diets that were better balanced and richer in protein, vitamins, minerals, and often calories, than those of all but the most affluent citizens of the modern world. And the hunter-gatherers' caloric intake was at or above modern Third World standards, even though those hunter-gatherers remaining to be measured had been pushed into the world's poorest environments. This comparison applies not just to the Third World, but also to the working classes of the world's most affluent nations. The nutrition of the working classes of eighteenth- and nineteenth-century urban Britain (when Britain dominated the world) was far worse than that of most "primitive" groups. Worldwide, the trend in human stature, although irregular, was more down than up until the twentieth century, when the trend was reversed for some of the affluent.

But civilization and "progress" also create the risk of disease by providing the context in which diseases can spread. Those conditions still exist, and as we "grow" and "develop" we create more diseases.

"Progress" and "civilized" lifestyles have generated or intensified most of the health problems that most people can think of, even if some diseases and health problems have existed throughout human history and some have been eliminated. Germ diseases have become more common and more widespread as human group size and overall population density increased. Malaria and schistosomiasis became more common when people began to farm and to irrigate their fields. The great epidemic diseases, like measles, smallpox, typhoid, typhus, bubonic plague, influenza, syphilis, mumps, and cholera, spread widely primarily under "civilized" conditions once large groups of people were connected by trade. It is also civilization and its trade patterns that generate the risk of AIDS, Ebola, drug-resistant tuberculosis, and a string of other once-localized infections, such as West Nile virus, that can now be spread by people traveling by airplane and in urban interactions such that it has now arrived in New York State.

With the exception of AIDS, we are now enjoying a hiatus between major epidemics. But there is good reason to assume that there will be others because natural, not to say political and military, conditions are perfect. Consider how long it is taking us to develop techniques to fight AIDS, which actually spreads very slowly. Some killer infections like SARS, which are airborne rather than sexually transmitted, and influenza may spread very quickly. We think of modern civilized science as curing or eliminating diseases, and it does, but it is barely keeping up. Tuberculosis, a disease of cities, now exists in strains that *no* antibiotic can treat.

Historically, the transmission of epidemic diseases, not cultural superiority, was a major weapon of European expansion, particularly in the Americas, where populations previously unexposed were destroyed more by diseases brought from Europe (which most Europeans had as children) than by the superiority of European technology. The conquest certainly didn't reflect superior overall European health, nutrition, or hygiene.

The major noninfectious scourges of the twentieth century—diabetes, hypertension, atherosclerosis, multiple sclerosis, coronary heart disease, and some common cancers—seem to be generated or at least exacerbated by modern dietary habits (super-refined food) and modern pollutants. Despite what most of us were taught, the increasing incidence of these diseases does not result simply or primarily from the fact that people live longer. In fact, these diseases are strongly linked to the very features of food-processing technology that make our food industry so "efficient" and profitable. These diseases rarely occur in "uncivilized" populations. When we "civilize" such people we introduce all of these health risks to them—and when we further "advance" our own society it is likely that we will add additional risks to our own lives. "Primitive" people (as opposed to the modern poor of civilization) must be doing something right, and it would be well worth our while to look at their diets and lifestyles, although our sense of superiority prevents that.

Life expectancy (approximately the *average* number of years the individuals in a population live) reflects not so much how long individual people live as how many people reach advanced ages. Life expectancy has not shown the progressive improvement through history that most people assume. Most Europeans had life expectancies indistinguishable from those of the Stone Age well into the nineteenth century, and life expectancies of working class people, especially those in many European cities, were well below any reasonable Stone Age estimate as late as about 1850. In India, despite a history of British rule, the life expectancy was at or below Stone Age levels as late as about 1920. Infant mortality in major cities generally fell below Stone Age levels only in the twentieth century; many major cities around 1900 had infant mortality rates well above the average for "primitive" tribes. The orphanages of seventeenth- to nineteenth-century Europe were commonly the places where polite society let children die, away from public scrutiny. Well-documented patterns of infant and child mortality in many of these institutions would have shocked almost any primitive population. Every act of "progress" or "modernization" threatens the well being of many people. They also call our morality in question.

Civilization is not inherently good for people or their health. The only way civilization benefits people is by sharing its wealth and knowledge and investing in public health and well-being. Civilization without investment in human welfare can be the worst environment in which people have ever lived. We need to study potential "advances" or profitable schemes more carefully. We need to look much more carefully at the costs and benefits of "progress": who pays the costs, who reaps the benefits? How do we combat the problems "civilization" has created when we are enculturated not to see them?

In addition, we should not confuse political dominance with progress. The modern dietary privilege of Americans does not rest only or even mainly on "progress" or our ingenuity as farmers. Increasingly, it rests also on our economic and political power to take the food of others or force them to grow what we want (as when relatively nutritious subsistence farming in other parts of the world is replaced by specialized cash crops that we desire). The ability of Europeans and Americans to move wealth and military power rapidly over great distances has done untold damage to people in other parts of the world, contributing significantly to our prosperity but to their poverty. It may well be that a higher percentage of the human populations is hungry than at any prior time in the history of our species.

But we assume that our "free" market and our mechanism to move wealth (backed by military might) give us the right to own property and dominate the market, even where people did not want to play by our rules. Many Maya in Belize own no land because when the Spaniards came in as conquerors (followed by the British who displaced them) they abrogated the Maya land tenure system and gave or sold the land to one another. The modern owners use the land to grow cash crops or beef that they sell to American fast-food chains, while the Maya are malnourished for want of usable land. A political stroke of expropriation, not just a miracle of indigenous European economic growth, accounts for much of the vast disparities of wealth that now exist. So people in Central America who are hungry export their beef, and people in Africa with vitamin A deficiency export the oils that they need to consume in order to absorb the vitamin. We continue to direct the economies of other nations for our own benefit.

The Iraq war in the early twenty-first century isn't about overthrowing a dictator— we have set up far more than we have toppled—or about fighting terrorism; it is, among other things, about who controls "our" oil wells. It is also about American hubris, the desire of some to destroy Islam, and the need of a presidential administration to bolster itself at home at whatever cost to others.

All this demands of Americans a bit more humility about our history, our superiority, and ourselves. It also demands a bit more caution about our future. We can't assume that improvements in our lives are guaranteed by technological advances (which are often very costly to health).

The improvements in health that we have seen in the twentieth century, such as the unquestioned dramatic increase in life expectancy, come primarily not from new discoveries, but from social investments in people's environments, their education, their nutrition, and their personal and public health. The great discovery of the germ that causes cholera would have been meaningless without massive investment in restructuring water supplies and sewage systems, particularly in cities. But we are often far behind our own medical and technological sophistication in implementing solutions. We can't simultaneously take pride in our "progress" in health while denigrating and cutting off government investment in such solutions. The idea that disease control is one of the government interventions or frills we can cut back on (apparently on the theory that we have eliminated disease) is even more dangerous than it is absurd. Yet we are cutting that part of big government in the name of economic "efficiency" while preserving defense spending, although the threat of attack by disease is far more real than the threat of military attack.

The point is that we should give more thoughtful consideration to the nature and meaning of the progress that we cherish. The health benefits of progress come only from the wealth that society diverts and invests to deal with health problems—ours and those of the countries whose economies we have dominated and which, like our own cities, are likely to share their health problems with us. Civilized structures, not dirt or individual poor hygiene or ignorance, are responsible for most modern health problems around the world, and so civilization has an obligation to make the investment. And, because our wealth, health, and well-being have been achieved partly at the expense of Third World people, we have an obligation to divert more resources to solve problems that we have helped to generate.

"Manifest Destiny"

The idea of manifest destiny is America's version of the universal "Chosen People" myth. (People everywhere consider themselves the first or best.) Our vision suggests that it is human nature and the human mandate to charge ahead toward some goal (whatever it is), like an Olympic runner, and that we are the ones selected to bear the torch. In the nineteenth and early twentieth centuries, we used the ideas as an excuse for replacing, destroying or exterminating others. Now we are a bit subtler, and don't use the term, but the feeling persists, and we still act on it. We still assume that all others must conform to our expectations.

People everywhere have a perception of world history that is distorted by their biases. Our vision nonetheless serves our chauvinism, intolerance, and racism. Ignorant of history, we can't learn from its lessons.

In our version, other people don't count. We can celebrate the birth of "freedom" and "equality" as if they were universal achievements without paying attention to the fate of Africans or Native Americans or even their descendants who became American citizens. Our children are taught a version of history that makes racism and intolerance easy to maintain. The American version of world history appropriates all the great events in human progress, reinforcing our cultural pride. Then, in a bizarre twist, we denigrate the descendants of the very groups responsible for those events, refusing to offer them full participation in our society because they are inferior. The Old Testament is "ours," but Jews have often been excluded.

The United States refused much Jewish immigration even in the midst of the Nazi holocaust. The classical Greeks and Romans or the Italians of the Renaissance are in "our" tradition, but their descendants were often denied entry into the United States when they first tried to immigrate on the grounds they were inherently inferior, not up to "our" standards. African American athletes contribute to "our" Olympic glory and our art and music and are often innovators of fashion, all while they are denied the right to full participation.

Our textbooks conveniently appropriate non-European civilizations that predate and contributed heavily to our "progress," including the Egyptians, Persians (i.e., Iranians), Indus Valley populations, and Chinese. The "cradle of civilization" in the Fertile Crescent (taken up, today, largely by Iraq) is part of "our" history, but people of the Middle East are demeaned.

We conveniently forget that the European Renaissance itself derived not directly from Greek and Roman inspiration but, in an enriched form, from Islamic Middle Eastern and North African (often dark-skinned) Moors and Arabs who dominated learning in western Eurasia between the decline of Rome and the European Renaissance, a period far longer than that of European domination.

It is conveniently forgotten that Northern Europeans were a comparatively backward people who contributed little and did not assume any form of world leadership until about four hundred years ago. Besides, many of the ancestors of Anglo-Americans were not the intellectual elite of their mother countries but the poor, riffraff, malcontents, and convicts, who are the very people dismissed as unfit today.

One obvious lesson is that no region holds cultural and political "leadership" for long. A second is that cross-fertilization of different groups of people with different traditions promotes the flowering of culture. A third is that our own "lead" is surely temporary.

Isaac Newton once said that if he could see a great distance, it was because he was standing on the shoulders of giants, and he may or should have known that many of those giants were not European. Why do twentieth-century Americans, lacking Newton's stature, so often pat themselves on the back for their "natural superiority" and their "vision" without realizing that we, too, are standing on the shoulders of others?

We have to get beyond treating our country's history as a cultural icon or a creation myth. This approach to history feeds our patriotism but stifles thought, self-perception, analysis, and tolerance toward others.

Consider, for example, what the word "colonial" means. It refers to societies created when one group dominates or takes over another in a different area and often sends settlers to live in the new land and develop it in the interests of the dominant country. Several sets of people—the various indigenous inhabitants of the colony, the various new settlers, and the people of the mother country—have to interact but share neither common interests nor common culture. Misunderstanding combines with aggression. Sounds familiar?

But most American schoolchildren never get the slightest inkling why our own early history is called "colonial." They assume that the word simply refers to a time period before the American Revolution, with buckled shoes and three-cornered hats. Or, the idea of colonies conjures images of a unified and peace-loving population of Europeans throwing off tyranny by moving into largely unoccupied space, in which Native Americans were a nuisance, not defenders of their land against aggression. At worst it conveys the mythical image of wily Europeans like Peter Minuit buying land from Native Americans who were too foolish to know the relative value of land and beads.

But our colonial history was not a morality play peopled by saints. The period was marked by ethnic and cultural disagreements, class struggles, racism, and brute force, much like other colonial situations. There were shifting alliances between varying British, American, and Native American interests and the struggle for power between the British and American colonial elites (our "Founding Fathers") over who would rule and who would profit, struggles in which common people often had relatively little at stake. (They were, however, pushed by propaganda about patriotism to do the actual fighting, as is occurring now in Iraq.) The Founding Fathers ran a revolution for the sake of their own social-class interests and then wrote a Constitution designed primarily to preserve property and privilege rather than human rights. The supreme colonial American hero, George Washington, hardly a modest farmer who "heeded his country's call," was probably the richest man in the colonies. Washington was fighting British restrictions on his own vast property claims. Like Benjamin Franklin, Washington was a large-scale land speculator. He wanted to invest in land on the western frontier that the British government had recognized by treaty as Native American land. The British tended to see the various Native American groups as sovereign neighbors. Washington had an enormous amount of personal wealth to gain by the colonies declaring independence from British rule.

My point is not to vilify Washington but to emphasize the complexity of his motivations, to better understand our modern leaders. The danger in allowing Washington and others to be sanctified is that it prevents us from thinking critically about leaders or our political system. Schoolchildren, and in fact all citizens, are taught that historic political leaders are faultless people impossibly far above them. Washington's mantle of seeming perfection and superiority reinforces uncritical approval of modern leaders who do not deserve it. It reassures people that our system is the best, even if we are not getting great leadership now or within memory. We have to expose our children to complexity if they are to be free to ponder alternatives. We have to teach children that they always have the freedom, right, and duty to be informed, to question, and to expect sensible answers. If we don't teach children to evaluate the mixed motives of our historical figures, and leaders, how can they be free to make good judgments about modern leaders or understand our country's objectives? How will they overcome their intolerance?

Understanding our history would also help explain the failures of others. Colonized people (and slaves) are forced to deny their own identity in order to survive—and, if they are to share the values of the ruling group, they must despise people like themselves. They have to learn the self-hatred that is so evident in involuntarily encapsulated ethnic groups. They have to be like the conquering group (which is, of course, impossible). And, while demanding compliance with its values as well as its actions, the larger society often does not allow members of oppressed groups who complied full membership. Should it surprise us that our society comes up with mechanisms, like IQ tests, meant to exclude—or that minorities meant to be excluded refuse to take the tests and standards seriously?

Despite our image of a great melting pot, American history is replete with examples of African Americans, Hispanic Americans, and Native Americans (like Cherokees in Georgia) who *did* assimilate and become successful, only to be threatened, exiled, ruined, burned out, or even lynched by a ruling society determined that they not succeed according to the very standards it had set. African Americans, of course, faced such pressures for more than half of the twentieth century and still often face them in the form of burned churches or in subtler forms. And they are still forced to accept white standards, even when there is no logical reason for the standards. The idea that all such people needed to do was join the "melting pot" is manifestly untrue in the face of such history. It is hardly surprising that members of "captive" or colonized minorities are ambivalent about entering the mainstream or that they lose interest in trying.

Control of Nature

At the moment there is one other aspect of manifest destiny that must be discussed. Members of the Judeo-Christian tradition are taught to believe that have a mandate to rule and exploit the natural world. They have "dominion" over it. That is in fact a very unusual and clearly dangerous perspective, since most other religions describe people as participants in nature who must obey its rules and fit into its natural cycles.

In a world in which human activities are clearly causing global warming and we are driving other organisms and resources to extinction, it becomes extremely important for us to understand how unusual and arbitrary and dangerous this vision of nature is. We cannot deal effectively with contemporary environmental problems if we think this way.

This is particularly problematic since more and more people in the United States and elsewhere, including President Bush, actively seek to undermine scientific reasoning in the name of faith and the banner of Creationism. We should perhaps ask whether they would like to fly in airplanes or use medical technology designed on faith rather than science. Worse, members of groups that have apocalyptic visions of the end of the world are actually seeking to promote it by allowing or even encouraging activities to destroy nature. That worldview, incomprehensible outside our tradition, poses a very serious threat as it spreads.

Americans have a lot to learn, but we need to get past our cultural assumptions and blinders to learn it.

Exercise

In an in-depth interview, ask a foreign student to compare his/her culture with that of the United States. Beyond the obvious differences, use the ideas discussed in this article to explore differences in values, methods of achieving goals, and perception of the world.